PROFITS, GROWTH, AND PLANNING

Techniques of Modern Financial Management

PROFITS, GROWTH, AND PLANNING
Techniques of Modern Financial Management

EDWARD L. SUMMERS

1974
DOW JONES-IRWIN, INC.
Homewood, Illinois 60430

This publication is designed to provide accurate and
authoritative information in regard to the subject matter
covered. It is sold with the understanding that the
publisher is not engaged in rendering legal, accounting, or
other professional service. If legal advice or other expert
assistance is required, the services of a competent
professional person should be sought.
*From a Declaration of Principles jointly adopted by a Committee
of the American Bar Association and a Committee of Publishers.*

First Printing, September 1974

Printed in the United States of America

Library of Congress Cataloging in Publication Data
Summers, Edward L
    Profits, growth and planning.

    1. Corporations—Finance. 2. Corporations—
Accounting. I. Title.
HG4026.S78   658.1'5   74–82927
ISBN 0-87094-085-6

I dedicate this book
to my beloved wife, Kathy,
and to our children,
Michael and Pamela

Preface

OVER THE YEARS, critics have identified shortcomings of our system of resource allocation. Yet most of us who have studied this system and its shortcomings are agreed that it is at least as efficient and equitable as any other in the world today, and that the major effort must be toward realizing the efficiencies possible within it, rather than replacing it with some other.

There are never enough resources to go around in any society, regardless of that society's underlying principles of organization or values. In the United States, the majority of resources are still allocated through market processes—according to the demand for them for various uses by individuals.

This book was written to help you learn how to use accounting information for decision making and control in situations that require utilization of scarce resources.

Accounting contributes information a market system must have to operate. Much of this information concerns the coordination and evaluation of activities of the large organizations dominating modern markets. Additional information consists of forecasts and other data required by specific decision-making situations. And still other information helps identify the public interests which responsible decision making must consider.

After reading this book, you will be able to identify the information necessary for use in planning and measuring the profitable growth of your firm.

August 1974   EDWARD L. SUMMERS

Contents

How much activity should an economic entity carry on? What products or services should it offer? What prices should it charge?

Cost and Revenue Classifications. Economic Theory and Cost-Volume Behavior: *Marginal Cost. Average Cost. The Accounting Approximation to Actual Costs. Revenue. Accounting Profit Estimation. Numerical Examples. Long- and Short-Run Decisions.* Applications of the Accounting Model: *Product Profitability. Profit Point. Cost and Price Changes. Two or More Products. Activity Analysis Using Percentages.* Maximizing Profit: *Condition for a Profit Maximum. Numerical Example. A Strange Fallacy.*

The basic business budget, the budgeting process, organizing to plan, installing a new budget, and examples of budget schedules and reports.

Budget Process Organization: *Initial Budget Policies. The First Draft Budget.* Budget Components: *Period of Time. Function or Responsibility.* Preparation of an Operating Budget. Budget Installation: *Motivation. Systems Study.* Appendix 2A: An Example of Budget Forms and Process.

How to identify information that is relevant to a specific decision, then produce and use it in the decision.

What a Decision Model Is: *Decision Models Compared to Real Decision Processes. Significance to Accountants of Decision Model Analysis.* Accounting Information and Other Information Used in Economic Decisions. Contribution Analysis Illustrated: Make or Buy. Time Dimension of Contribution Analysis: Sunk Costs. Decisions Involving Joint Products: *Joint Products Illustrated. Costing Joint Products. Continuing a Joint Product.* Further Processing of Products. At What Level Should Joint Production Be Set? When Cost Allocation Can't Be Avoided.

Using flexible budgets for control, preparing performance reports, effect of accounting information on individual behavior.

Flexible Budgeting and Planning: *Questions to Ask.* Flexible Budgeting and Control: *Sales Variances. Recomputing an Expense Budget. Performance Analysis.* Presenting and Explaining Budget Variances. Planning Fixed Costs: *A Business Pitfall. Reduce Capacity, Increase Income.* Behavioral Dimension of Accounting Reports: *The Pressure Model. A General Model.*

The net present value method of selecting capital investments and where accounting information makes this method work better.

The Time Value of Money: *Determination of Investor's Target Rate of Return. Investor's Target Rate of Return Illustrated.* Information to Consider in Planning Capital Investment Decisions: *Net Cash Revenue or Cost Savings. Acquisition Lifetime. Depreciation and Tax Effects. Initial Cost of Acquisition. Risk of Acquisition. Mildew's Target Rate of Return.* Making the Decision. Other Factors in Investment Decisions.

How to use EOQ inventory management models; some illustrative examples of the value of accounting information in setting order quantity and replenishment point.

Inventory Management and Policy: *Inventory Models Lead to Inventory Policy.* Parameters Affecting Inventory Policy: *Typical Inventory Management Method.* Simple Economic Order Quantity Models: *Influence of Inventory Parameters on Inventory Management. Cost of Inventory Policy. Economic Order Quantity Models for $Q*$ and $S*$. Applying the Models to Compute Inventory Policy. When the Shortage Cost Is Very High. Generality of Cost Formulas. Cost Savings. Delay in Restocking after Ordering. Safety Stock.* Sensitivity Analysis. Inventory Management Systems. Appendix 6A: *How the Optimal Economic Order Quantity Policy Was Computed When Con-*

come. To Beat Inflation. Accounting Statements and Price Changes: *Balance Sheet. The Income Statement. Monetary Gains and Losses.*

1

Activity Level Effect on Economic Performance

WHY ARE SOME businesses able to earn an accounting profit and others, apparently very similar, are not?

In this chapter we show you how managerial accounting information can be used to explain the actual or potential profit performance of a business when the management has provided answers to the following important planning questions:

1. What activity level should the firm *be able* to sustain? (How much capacity to have.)
2. What activity level should the firm *actually* sustain? (How much capacity to use.)
3. What products and/or services, and how much of each, should the firm offer?
4. What prices should the firm charge?

You use the record-keeping and control functions of accounting to help you understand *why* a business is or isn't profitable. In this introduction you regard a business as engaging in only one revenue-and-cost-producing activity; however, the methods of analysis you will learn are useful regardless of the size of the business, number of activities, or choice of numbers to use as dollar equivalents to physical resources and assets.

The calculation for income is: Income = Revenue — Expenses. Activity analysis draws upon concepts of economics (the study of resource

1

allocation) applied to the dollar-equivalents, revenue and expense, which accounting uses to measure benefits and sacrifices. For example, an increase in accounting profit that would result from certain operating changes is a *cost* of *not* making the changes. The only way a manager will know about such a cost is to *plan ahead,* anticipating his alternatives and the related accounting profit each is expected to produce.

A decision whether to implement changes would depend on accounting profit forecasts with and without the changes. The success of economic theory applied in business administration depends on the ability of the executive to recognize prospective benefits, sacrifices, and risks— *from accounting data.* And if accounting projections indicate that profits may be increased by certain actions, one expects that real income will actually receive an increment.

COST AND REVENUE CLASSIFICATIONS

Much of the value of accounting derives from its classification of costs and revenues according to their causes, behavior, or effects. These classifications are a bridge between the activities which produce costs and revenues and their overall effect on accounting profits. Classification lets you estimate the effect on future accounting profit of a decision in terms of the decision-related transactions and exchanges.

Here, you consider one particular base for classification—the extent to which revenues and costs are influenced by the level of business activity. Costs and revenues are related to the existence and level of business activity (be that production, research, data processing, auto repairs, or whatever).

Costs can be classified as fixed or variable. A *fixed* cost is or will be a result of the existence of ability to engage in business activity (capacity). A fixed cost is incurred at a constant rate per time period, or not at all. If there is no capability to have business activity, capacity is zero and fixed cost is zero. But if the level of activity can be greater than zero (even if there is no activity now), the fixed cost is set by the maximum capacity available. A *variable* cost is not a function of time but of the actual level of business activity. In the manufacture of fishing reels, the cost of steel and plastic fabrication materials would be a variable cost, whereas the annual salary of the foreman would be a fixed cost.

Revenues would nearly always be variable, expressed at $XX per unit of product or service sold.

Most of activity analysis describes the behavior of costs and revenues as a function of the existence and level of activity during a given interval of time—*cost-volume behavior*.

ECONOMIC THEORY AND COST-VOLUME BEHAVIOR

Assume a firm which measures its level of activity accurately in terms of a single factor: say, direct labor hours, which are the hours its employees spend working directly on products and services. Other resources are required by its production process, but *capacity* is measured by the maximum number of direct labor hours which *can* be worked, and its level of activity in any period is measured by the actual number of direct labor hours which *are* worked. This firm has no inventories and always pays the same prices for the resources which sustain its activities. Figure 1–1 shows how total inputs vary with the level of activity.

As level of activity increases, total inputs also increase. Figure 1–1 shows that even when there is no activity, there are still inputs (mea-

FIGURE 1–1
Inputs as a Function of Activity Level

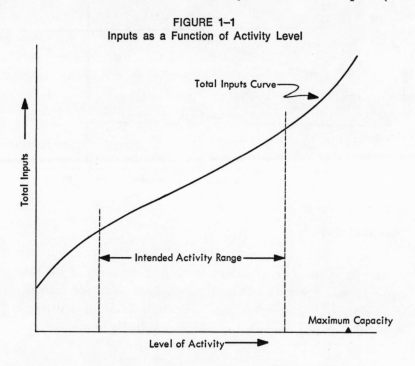

sured by fixed costs). Then, as a little activity occurs, inputs rise rapidly. This is because the manufacuring process is inefficient when operating at low levels. As activity picks up, total inputs increase at a steady rate that is lower than the initial rate. At last, as activity level approaches its maximum value, the rate of increase in total costs picks up again, for near maximum capacity the process again becomes less efficient. The middle region between the vertical dotted lines in which total inputs rise flatly and moderately is the intended activity range for the process. Within that region, inputs increase at virtually a constant rate per unit of additional activity, and the process is most efficient. If costs are used to measure inputs, the "total cost curve" will have the same shape as the total inputs curve in Figure 1–1.

The total cost curve is easily resolved into fixed (at zero activity level) and variable components. These two curves are plotted on the same coordinates in Figure 1–2.

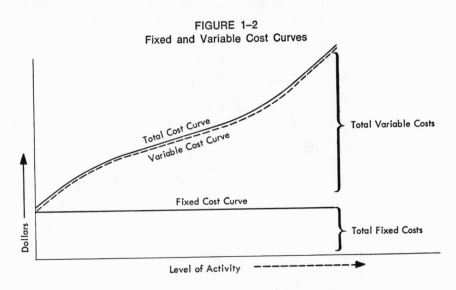

FIGURE 1–2
Fixed and Variable Cost Curves

Marginal Cost

Marginal cost is the total additional cost for one additional unit of activity at any specific activity level. It is the slope of the total cost curve at that activity level. In Figure 1–2, you can see that marginal cost is greatest at very low and very high levels of activity. In the intended operating range, marginal cost is virtually constant.

Average Cost

Generally speaking, average cost is not the same as marginal cost. Average cost per unit is equal to total costs divided by number of units of activity at a specific activity level. Thus, average cost always includes some fixed costs.

Here is a numerical example: Let fixed costs be $12,000; units of activity, 1,000; variable cost of the 1,001th unit, $5; total variable costs, $6,000. Then marginal cost is $5. Average cost per unit is ($12,000 + $6,000) ÷ 1,000 = $18. Average *variable* cost per unit is $6,000 ÷ 1,000 = $6. Average *fixed* cost per unit is $12,000 ÷ 1,000 = $12. Note that average fixed cost plus average variable cost add up to average (total) cost.

The Accounting Approximation to Actual Costs

Accounting assumes that the majority of calculations and decisions will be made in the intended operating range, where marginal costs are virtually constant. In this range, the total cost curve is almost a straight line. The accounting approximation is a straight line that extends in to the vertical axis and outward to the right. Normally, very few errors result from this approximation, and these are made up for by the simplification that also occurs in data analysis. Figure 1–3 shows the true total cost curve and the accounting approximation.

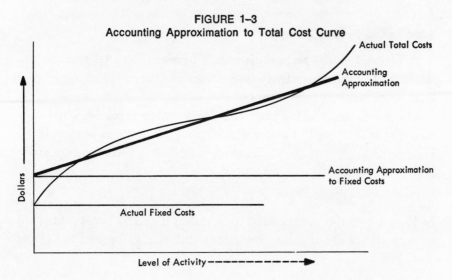

FIGURE 1–3
Accounting Approximation to Total Cost Curve

Later, we shall explain how you would obtain the linear accounting approximation to actual costs. At this point, you should accept the notion that the approximation can be made without significant loss of accuracy or of information useful in decisions.

Revenue

Most firms have some control over the prices they charge for their output. If the price set is relatively high, fewer units will be sold than if the price set is relatively low. Normally, all units will be sold at the same price during a sales period (at the end or beginning of a period, a small number of units may be sold at a discount to stimulate buyer interest in the product; we disregard these). Thus, the number of units sold and the total revenue will be determined by the price per unit charged. The revenue curve will be a straight line. If the price charged is relatively higher, the line will be steeper; if the price charged is lower, the line will be less steep.

Marginal Revenue and Average Revenue. Since the price charged is the same for each unit, unit price is equal to both marginal revenue and average revenue.

Figure 1–4 shows a total revenue curve superimposed on a linear total cost curve. No accounting approximation is needed for the revenue curve since it is already linear.

Accounting Profit Estimation

In Figure 1–4, the vertical distance Y between the total revenue and total cost lines at any activity level represents the *profit* at the level—total revenue minus total costs.

Revenue is computed as price (P) times activity level, N. Total variable cost is computed as unit variable cost (UVC) times activity level. Let period fixed costs be FC. Then the calculation of accounting profit is

$$\text{Profit } (Y) = P \times N - FC - UVC \times N$$

In Figure 1–4, the linear relationship makes it appear that profit could be increased without limit. Remember that this graph and the linear

FIGURE 1–4
Revenue and Cost Curves Together

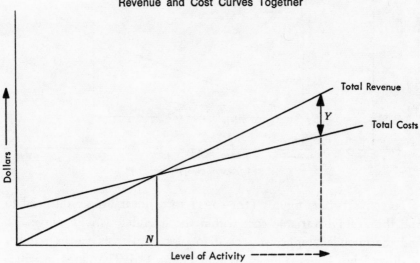

relationships it embodies are intended to be used only inside the intended operating range of the process described.

Numerical Examples

The Blewit Corporation has a particular shoe factory in which stylish boots are made. Fixed costs are a predictable and steady $30,000 per week. Figure 1–5 is the budget committee's best estimates of other costs, revenues, and activity levels, all on a per-week basis.

FIGURE 1–5
Activity Analysis Data for Blewit Corporation

Line No. (i)	Number of Direct Labor Hours N	Total Variable Costs	Total Costs	Total Revenue	Accounting Profit
1	0	$ 0	$30,000	$ 0	$(30,000)
2	1,000	10,000	40,000	30,000	(10,000)
3	2,000	18,000	48,000	60,000	12,000
4	3,000	26,000	56,000	90,000	34,000
5 . . . . :	4,000	34,000	64,000	120,000	56,000
6	5,000	46,000	76,000	150,000	74,000

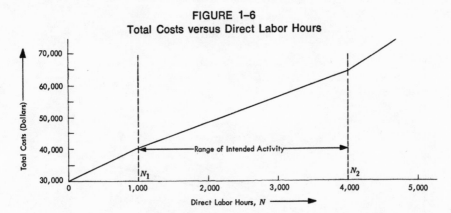

FIGURE 1–6
Total Costs versus Direct Labor Hours

To convert these figures (for costs) to a linear basis, you need to find the average variable cost within the intended activity range. To find the intended range, you need to plot total costs versus number of direct labor hours. This is done in Figure 1–6. The range in which total costs form a straight line is the intended activity range.

The intended activity range, within which the total cost line is relatively straight, is from 1,000 to 4,000 direct labor hours per week. In a real situation, you would choose activity levels slightly within these outer limits for the calculation which follows. Here, we use the limits themselves because there are so few data points (deliberately, to retain a simple illustration).

$$\text{Average variable cost per unit} = \frac{\left(\begin{array}{c}\text{Total cost} \\ @\ N_2 \text{ direct} \\ \text{labor hours}\end{array} - \begin{array}{c}\text{Total cost} \\ @\ N_1 \text{ direct} \\ \text{labor hours}\end{array}\right)}{(N_2 - N_1)} \quad (1\text{--}1)$$

$$= \frac{(\$64{,}000 - \$40{,}000)}{(4{,}000 - 1{,}000)}$$

$$= \frac{\$24{,}000}{3{,}000} = \$8 \text{ per unit}$$

At any point, then, if N = the activity level in direct labor hours,

$$\begin{array}{c}\text{Estimated} \\ \text{total} \\ \text{cost}\end{array} = \begin{array}{c}\text{Estimated} \\ \text{fixed} \\ \text{cost}\end{array} + \begin{array}{c}\text{Estimated average} \\ \text{variable cost} \\ \text{per unit}\end{array} \times N \quad (1\text{--}2)$$

Formula (1–2) has an important peculiarity: the "fixed cost" in the formula is the accounting approximation to fixed cost; it is usually higher than the actual fixed cost. Look at Figure 1–3 and see why. To check, let's rearrange (1–2) and compute "fixed costs" from it at the level of 4,000 direct labor hours:

$$\begin{matrix} \text{Estimated} \\ \text{"fixed} \\ \text{cost"} \end{matrix} = \begin{matrix} \text{Total} \\ \text{cost} \end{matrix} - \begin{matrix} \text{Variable} \\ \text{costs} \end{matrix} \qquad (1\text{–}3)$$

$$= \$64,000 - 4,000 \times \$8$$
$$= \$64,000 - \$32,000$$
$$= \$32,000 \; per \; week$$

$32,000 per week is the proper fixed cost figure to use when operating the accounting linear dynamic model. So long as you stay inside the intended activity range, you will get accurate, usable results.

What is average cost per unit at, say, 2,000 and 3,000 direct labor hours? The formula for average cost per unit is:

$$\begin{matrix} \text{Average} \\ \text{total cost} \\ \text{per unit} \end{matrix} = \frac{\text{Total cost}}{\text{Units of activity}} \qquad (1\text{–}4)$$

$$ATC \; @ \; 2,000 \; \text{hours} = \frac{\$32,000 + \$8 \times 2,000}{2,000}$$

$$= \frac{\$48,000}{2,000} = \$24 \; per \; unit$$

$$ATC \; @ \; 3,000 \; \text{hours} = \frac{\$32,000 + \$8 \times 3,000}{3,000}$$

$$= \frac{\$56,000}{3,000} = \$18.67 \; per \; unit$$

Observe that as activity level *increases,* average total cost per unit of activity *decreases*. This is because the same quantity of fixed costs are being divided over more units of activity. Estimated variable costs remain constant at $8 per unit.

Since price per unit is constant, average revenue is constant. If price per unit is greater than average variable cost per unit, the firm will show a constant accounting excess of revenue over cost on each unit of activity, regardless of the level of activity:

$$
\begin{array}{lll}
\text{Contribution} & \text{Price} & \text{Estimated average} \\
\text{per unit of} \quad = \text{per} & - & \text{variable cost} \qquad\qquad (1\text{--}5) \\
\text{activity} & \text{unit} & \text{per unit}
\end{array}
$$

Long- and Short-Run Decisions

Economic theory indicates that so long as contribution per unit of activity is greater than zero, the process should be operated *in the short run*. The short run is a period of time so short that if the process were shut down, the time-related costs associated with it (fixed costs) could not be avoided during that period. Thus, any contribution per unit (excess of revenue over variable costs) will help the business meet its period fixed costs.

In the long run, the process should not be operated unless total revenue exceeds total costs. This point occurs in Figure 1–4 at the level of activity N^*, where total revenue and cost lines cross. N^* is called the *break-even point*.

APPLICATIONS OF THE ACCOUNTING MODEL

While linear relationships provide only approximations to a firm's dynamic behavior, they are used whenever available information is insufficient to compute nonlinear relationships. In practice, the slight loss of accuracy is unimportant compared to the information gained from being able to perform the analysis.

Product Profitability

The Blewit Corporation presently only makes one boot type in the plant we used for the preceding numerical example. Direct labor hours are used to make these boots, which are sold. In order to do the activity analysis in terms of the product (rather than the process inputs), convert direct labor hours to boots by dividing them by the number of labor hours required to make one pair of boots. Let 3.2 labor hours be required per pair of boots. Thus, 1,000 direct labor hours convert to 1,000/3.2 or *312* pairs of boots. At the activity level of 1,000 direct labor hours, each of these pairs are expected to cost

$$3.2 \times \begin{pmatrix} \text{Average variable} \\ \text{cost per direct} \\ \text{labor hour} \end{pmatrix} = \begin{array}{l} \text{Average variable} \\ \text{cost per pair} \end{array}$$

$$3.2 \times \$8.00 \qquad\qquad = \$25.60$$

Each of these 312 pairs is expected to sell for

$$\left(\frac{\$30,000}{1,000}\right) \times \quad 3.2 \quad = \$96$$

| Revenue per direct labor hour | No. of direct labor hours per boot pair |

The contribution per pair of boots is, of course,

$$\$96 - \$25.60 = \$70.40$$

This unit contribution will be the same throughout the intended activity range. To determine the value of N^* in terms of boot pairs, use this formula:

$$N^* \text{ (break-even point)} = \frac{\begin{array}{c}\text{Estimated fixed} \\ \text{costs per period}\end{array}}{\begin{array}{c}\text{Contribution per} \\ \text{unit of product}\end{array}} \qquad (1\text{-}6)$$

$$N^* \qquad = \frac{\$32,000 \text{ per week}}{\$70.40} = \textit{455 boot pairs}$$

If Blewit Corporation manufactures 455 or more pairs of boots per week, it will either break even or earn a profit. In the later case, the boot-manufacturing process will produce a *contribution to company profit* in excess of its own fixed costs.

Profit Point

The boot production that will produce a specific desired profit is given by (1–7):

$$YP = \frac{\text{Estimated fixed costs} + \text{Desired profit}}{\text{Contribution per product unit}} \qquad (1\text{–}7)$$

If Blewit wishes to earn a $40,000 contribution in excess of fixed costs from this process, it can find YP, the number of boot pairs it must manufacture, by substituting into (1–7):

$$YP = \frac{\$32,000 + \$40,000}{\$70.40} = 1,023 \text{ boot pairs}$$

By multiplying by 3.2, you easily convert this back into the number of direct labor hours to be worked: $1,023 \times 3.2 = 3,273$.

Cost and Price Changes

Activity analysis can be used to study effects of changes in fixed and variable costs, units expected to be sold, and product price.

Fixed Cost Change. Fixed cost changes are not common, but suppose Blewit's rise by $10,000. What is the new break-even point N^*? Use equation (1–6).

$$N^* = \frac{\$32,000 + \$10,000}{\$70.40} = 597 \text{ boot pairs}$$

The $10,000 increase in fixed costs caused an increase in the break-even point of $597 - 455 = 142$ *boot pairs*. This means that if fixed costs or desired profit rise by $10,000, the company must then sell 142 more boot pairs to keep the same profit or to earn the new desired profit.

Variable Cost Change.   Variable costs rise from $8 per direct labor hour to $8.80 per direct labor hour, a 10 percent increase. How does this affect the break-even point?

The variable costs per pair of boots will also be 10 percent higher:

$$3.2 \text{ hours per boot pair} \times \$8.80 \text{ per hour} = \$28.16 \text{ per pair}$$

The new contribution per boot pair is $96 − $28.16 = *$67.84 per pair*

The new break-even point is:

$$N^* = \frac{\$32,000}{\$67.84} = 472 \text{ boot pairs}$$

An increase in variable costs increases the level of activity required to break even or earn a specified profit. A decrease in variable cost per unit decreases the level of activity required to break even or earn a specified profit.

Selling Price and Selling Quantity Changes.   A change in quantity sold does not affect the break-even point but does affect profit. Let the quantity of boots being sold be 500 pairs. Then the profit is computed as—

$$
\begin{aligned}
Y(500) = \text{Revenue} &- \text{Estimated} - \text{Total vari-} \qquad (1\text{--}8)\\
& \text{fixed costs} \quad \text{able costs}\\
= \$96 &\times 500 - \$32,000 - \$28.16 \times 500\\
= \$1,920&
\end{aligned}
$$

Now, let 550 pair of boots be sold. The profit here is:

$$
\begin{aligned}
Y(550) &= \$96 \times 550 - \$32,000 - \$28.16 \times 550\\
&= \$5,312
\end{aligned}
$$

Profit increased substantially on the 10 percent volume increase. The increase was more than 10 percent because profit is the difference between total contribution margin, which is proportional to the volume of activity, and fixed costs, which do not change. Thus a small change in volume (or in fixed costs, unit variable costs, or unit selling price) may produce a large change in profit. This effect is sometimes called "leverage" and occurs most often when fixed costs are several times greater in magnitude than profit. Dramatic profit changes may also occur if price and unit variable cost are nearly the same, and one or both change by even a small amount.

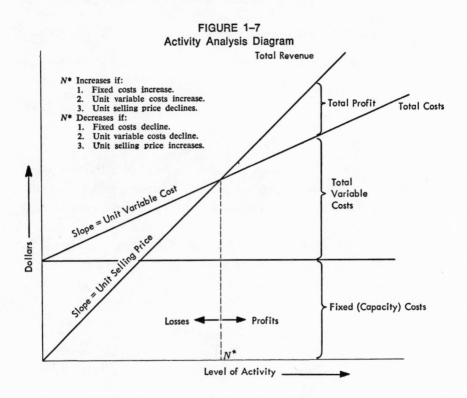

FIGURE 1–7
Activity Analysis Diagram

The effect of a change in selling price would be opposite to the effect of a change in variable cost. Let the selling price per boot pair drop to $90 per pair. The break-even point rises:

$$N^* = \frac{\$32,000}{\$90 - \$25.60} = 497 \; boot \; pairs,$$

which is an increase of 42 pairs over the 455 pairs break-even point at the original price of $96.

Figure 1–7 shows the full activity analysis diagram with all the changes described above drawn in.

Two or More Products

Let the Blewit Corporation make two types of boot—called "Clompers" and "Stompers." Up until now we have been discussing Clompers. Now let us also discuss Stompers. Figure 1–8 gives the direct labor hours required to make each boot.

FIGURE 1–8
Labor Hours in Clompers and Stompers

	Direct Labor Hour Content	Current Period Unit Production
Clompers.	3.2	400
Stompers.	1.6	1,000

Clompers, we know, sell for $96; and Stompers sell for $24 per pair. What will be the profit earned by the schedule in Figure 1–8?

```
Revenue:
  Clompers 400 pair × $96 per pair . . . . . . . .   $ 38,400
  Stompers 1,000 pair × $24 per pair . . . . . . .     24,000
      Total. . . . . . . . . . . . . . . . . . . . .   $ 62,000
Less variable costs:
  Clompers 3.2 hours per pair × $8 per
    hour × 400 pair . . . . . . . . . . . . . . . .    (10,240)
  Stompers 1.6 hours per pair × $8 per
    hour × 1,000 pair . . . . . . . . . . . . . . .    (12,800)
      Total Contribution. . . . . . . . . . . . . .   $ 38,960
  Less estimated fixed costs . . . . . . . . . . . .   (32,000)
  Net Total Profit. . . . . . . . . . . . . . . . .   $  6,960
```

Let sales of both Clompers and Stompers decline by 10 percent. What would be the new profit?

Since sales of both styles decline by the same percent, their respective total contributions also decline by a similar percent. The new total contribution will be 10 percent less than the old one, or $38,960 − $3,896 = $35,064. Now, profit is

```
Total contribution . . . . . . . . . . . . .   $ 35,064
Less estimated fixed costs . . . . . . . . .    (32,000)
Profit. . . . . . . . . . . . . . . . . . . .   $  3,064
```

Activity Analysis Using Percentages

Occasionally you will find variable costs expressed as a percentage of revenue. A retail store may report that "our variable costs are 45 percent of our sales revenues." In this case, the proper formula to use for profit is:

$$Y = \begin{matrix} \text{Total} \\ \text{sales} \\ \text{revenue} \end{matrix} \times \left(1 - \begin{matrix} \text{Fraction of} \\ \text{each \$ that is} \\ \text{variable cost} \end{matrix}\right) - \begin{matrix} \text{Estimated} \\ \text{fixed} \\ \text{costs} \end{matrix} \qquad (1\text{-}9)$$

To illustrate, let Stonehenge Rent-A-Car have variable costs of 60 percent of revenue. Last year, the firm made $50,000 on sales of $300,000. What are the estimated fixed costs of Stonehenge?

You rearrange (1–9) so that "estimated fixed cost" is on the left-hand side:

$$\begin{matrix} \text{Estimated} \\ \text{fixed} \\ \text{costs} \end{matrix} = \begin{matrix} \text{Total} \\ \text{sales} \\ \text{revenue} \end{matrix} \times \left(1 - \begin{matrix} \text{Fraction of} \\ \text{each \$ that is} \\ \text{variable cost} \end{matrix}\right) - Y$$

Substituting known information gives

$$\begin{matrix} \text{Estimated} \\ \text{fixed} \\ \text{costs} \end{matrix} = \$300,000 \times (1 - 0.60) - \$50,000$$

$$= \$70,000 \text{ per year}$$

Many other calculations of this sort, including the break-even point and volume required to earn a desired profit, can be made using percentages.

MAXIMIZING PROFIT

The accounting linear approximations are easy to use but are limited to the expected activity range; and within this range, they literally indicate that the largest profit is earned by producing and selling at the highest volume. Every businessman knows that this is not always true. To understand why, return to the nonlinear total cost curve of Figure 1–2, this time with a linear total revenue curve such as that in Figure 1–6 drawn over it. The result appears as Figure 1–9.

FIGURE 1-9
Nonlinear Dynamic Analysis

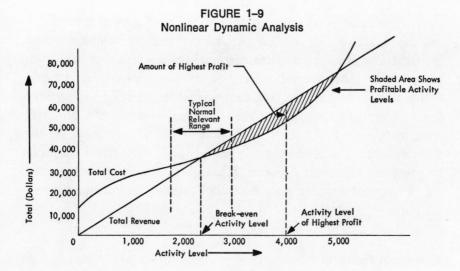

In Figure 1-9, which does not correspond to any previous examples, the normal break-even point is at an activity level of 2,400 units. There is another point, at very high activity levels, at which inefficiency and waste would cause total costs to rise above total revenue. Find this point.

The striking feature of Figure 1-9, however, is the shape of the area below the total revenue curve and above the total cost curve. Any vertical distance between these two curves represents the profit at the corresponding activity level below on the horizontal axis. For example, at an activity level of 3,000 the profit is about $7,500. Although at first, as activity level surges past 2,400 units, the profit increases, *it eventually reaches a maximum* at 4,000 units, *then begins to decline.* This business would want to produce, if possible, no more or less than 4,000 units per period.

Condition for a Profit Maximum

Briefly stated, the major condition for a profit maximum is:

Marginal cost = Marginal revenue (price)

There are other conditions which are important and are discussed in economics and advanced accounting texts. The condition that marginal cost be equal to marginal revenue is the most important condition and the easiest to discuss in an introductory text. Its rationale is this: If marginal cost is greater than marginal revenue, the firm will want to operate at a lower level, since it is losing money on the last unit it is producing and selling, and can increase its profit by cutting back some. If marginal cost is less than marginal revenue, the firm will want to operate at a higher level, since it is making money on the last few units it is producing and selling, and can increase its profit by going to a higher activity level. If marginal revenue equals marginal cost, it can neither increase nor decrease its activity level without lowering profit.

Numerical Example

An example using Figure 1–8 will make this clear. Recall that marginal cost is the slope of the total cost curve, and marginal revenue is the slope of the total revenue line (i.e., unit price). Marginal revenue is constant in Figure 1–8 and equal to $15. We computed $15 from the graph by choosing an activity level, finding the corresponding total revenue, and dividing. Thus,

$$\$15 = \frac{\$36,000}{2,400}$$

Any other level would do as well. The slope of the total cost line fluctuates along its length. We compute its slope anywhere along its length using an approximation formula:

$$\frac{\text{Marginal}}{\substack{\text{cost @ } N \\ \text{activity} \\ \text{units}}} = \frac{\substack{\text{Total costs @ } N + \Delta \\ \text{units of activity}} - \substack{\text{Total costs @ } N - \Delta \\ \text{units of activity}}}{(N + \Delta) - (N - \Delta)} \quad (1\text{–}10)$$

The value $N - \Delta$ is less than N; the value $N + \Delta$ is greater than N. The difference "Δ" is as small as can be conveniently read from a graph. For this example, let Δ be equal to 200 activity units.

Now, compute the slope of the cost curve at three points: 3,600; 4,000; and 4,400 activity units.

Values of N	Total Costs at:		
	(N − Δ)	(N)	(N + Δ)
N = 3,600	3,400	3,600	3,800
	$46,000	$48,000	$50,000
N = 4,000	3,800	4,000	4,200
	$50,000	$53,000	$56,000
N = 4,400	4,200	4,400	4,600
	$56,000	$60,000	$64,000

We may insert these data into (1–10) to obtain the approximate slopes and marginal costs.

$$\frac{\text{Marginal cost}}{@\ 3,600\ \text{units}} = \frac{\$50,000 - \$46,000}{3,800 - 3,400} = \frac{\$4,000}{400} = \$10\ per\ unit$$

$$\frac{\text{Marginal cost}}{@\ 4,000\ \text{units}} = \frac{\$56,000 - \$50,000}{4,200 - 3,800} = \frac{\$6,000}{400} = \$15\ per\ unit$$

$$\frac{\text{Marginal cost}}{@\ 4,400\ \text{units}} = \frac{\$64,000 - \$56,000}{4,600 - 4,200} = \frac{\$8,000}{400} = \$20\ per\ unit$$

At the 4,000 activity unit level, marginal cost equals marginal revenue, so this must be the maximum-profit activity level. Figure 1–10 shows how marginal cost increases and finally exceeds constant marginal revenue. The actual maximum profit itself is either measured from the graph in Figure 1–10 or computed. It is $60,000 — $53,000 = $7,000.

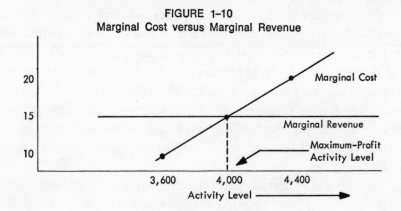

FIGURE 1–10
Marginal Cost versus Marginal Revenue

A Strange Fallacy

When nonlinear activity analysis is appropriate, some businessmen insist that the best activity level is one at which average costs are a minimum. This activity level will not be the same as the one at which profit is a maximum, so it is impossible to accept their reasoning. To produce at the lowest average cost per unit will always result in a lower activity level and lower profits than producing where marginal cost equals marginal revenue.

Let us compute average cost at several points in the interval from 3,400 to 4,600 activity units in the current example:

Activity Level	Total Costs	Average Cost
3,400	$46,000	$13.53
3,600	48,000	13.33
3,800	50,000	13.16 *lowest av. cost*
4,000 (max. profit)	53,000	13.25
4,200	56,000	13.33
4,400	60,000	13.64
4,600	64,000	13.91

Average costs are of little interest in business planning; you will use marginal costs and revenues and other cost classifications there. Average costs and revenues, however, are of interest in financial reporting.

SUMMARY

This chapter presented the basic elements of activity analysis. You first learned how costs change with activity level. As activity increases, the cost to make one additional unit (marginal cost) typically declines, remains almost constant, then rises again. The range of expected activity includes the interval in which marginal cost is constant. The accounting analysis is made by approximating the entire total cost curve by a straight line with constant marginal cost along its entire length. Estimated fixed costs (intersection of this line with zero activity level) will be a little higher than real fixed costs when this approximation is used. The total revenue line is straight, implying all units are sold at the same price.

The accounting analysis permits computation of break-even activity level and activity level required to earn a target profit. It also permits one to calculate the effect on these two activity levels of changes in unit variable cost, estimated fixed cost, quantity sold, and unit selling price.

However, accounting analysis (which is linear) does not permit computation of the activity level corresponding to maximum profit. The maximum profit point occurs when marginal cost and marginal revenue are equal. The nonlinear activity model will, if sufficient data are available, permit you to find the largest profit and the activity level at which it occurs.

An understanding of activity analysis is basic to an understanding of how resource allocation is planned in a firm. In the next chapter, we show you details of cost flow and classification as they must be understood in order to plan for resource-using processes, a common application area for activity analysis.

BIBLIOGRAPHY

Books

Bierman, Jr., Harold, and Dyckman, Thomas R. *Managerial Cost Accounting.* New York: The Macmillan Co., 1971.

Leftwich, Richard H. *The Price System and Resource Allocation.* New York: Holt, Rinehart & Winston, Inc., 1961.

Articles

Bhada, Yezdi. "Dynamic Cost Analysis," *Management Accounting,* July 1970.

Black, Thomas N., and Modenbach, Donald J. "Profit Planning for Action and Results," *Management Accounting,* January 1971.

Jaedicke, Robert K., and Robichek, Alexander A. "Cost-Volume-Profit Analysis under Conditions of Uncertainty," *The Accounting Review,* October 1964.

Jenkins, David O. "Cost-Volume-Profit Analysis," *Management Services,* March–April 1970.

2

Fundamental Planning
Using Accounting Information

As COMMERCE has developed, the size of economic units participating in commerce has increased. With the increases in size has come emergence of specialized functions within the firm. These specialized functions exist better to perform their limited set of operations, or make their limited number of decisions. By and large specialization succeeds in increasing the economic efficiency of a firm by reducing the uncertainty of operations. However, it is achieved at the cost of a reduced natural ability to communicate and coordinate intrafirm activities. Consequently one of the first responsibilities of a firm's top management is to provide formal channels, processes, and incentives for communication and cooperation within the firm between specialized functions.

In most firms the accounting information system is used as the vehicle to encourage communication and cooperation, and as you might expect it has developed a specialization especially for this purpose. This specialized function is called *budgeting* or *profit planning*. The budgeting process continues year-round. Its nominal output is a set of pro forma (looking forward) financial statements which describe the financial position and results of operations of the company during the next operating interval. The real product, however, is a detailed set of supporting performance statements showing the activities expected of each responsibility center within the business. These performance statements can be compared later with actual performance statements; the results, condensed through variance analysis, enable pinpointing problems while at the same time promoting management efficiency.

In this chapter we shall explain the budgeting process and the planning decisions which it incorporates. Budget preparation is a fundamental activity of the managerial accountant; nothing else he does can be so intimately involved with fundamental business processes or have such a profound influence on the operating profitability of the firm.

BUDGET PROCESS ORGANIZATION

Responsibility for the budgeting process is divided among the components of an organization structure:

—The budget committee of the board of directors is responsible for financial and planning policy for the firm.

—The president's budget committee oversees the budgeting process and makes certain that there is high-level support and enthusiasm for the budgeting process.

—The chief budget officer or budget director must execute budget policies through his administrative services and coordination of the budgeting process.

—The budget advisers are scattered through the profit centers and functional areas and provide staff services to operating vice presidents, enabling them to prepare their parts of the overall budget.

Figure 2–1 shows the general relationships between these various segments of a firm.

Within a firm, budget preparation proceeds continuously throughout each operating period. Each segment of the firm must prepare detailed proposed operating plans. In a small business, the process is the same except that many steps are simpler and functions combined.

Initial Budget Policies

These policies will be based upon initial assumptions which are formulated by the board of directors, the board of directors' budget

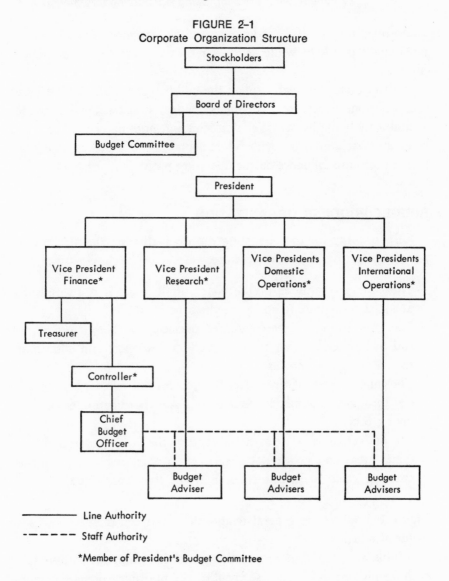

FIGURE 2–1
Corporate Organization Structure

Line Authority

- - - - - Staff Authority

*Member of President's Budget Committee

committee, and the president's budget committee. These policies should deal with:

1. *Major economic trends* that will be assumed to operate in the firm's environment during the forthcoming budget period.
2. *Major goals* of the firm during the coming period (rate of return on investment, sales volume, profit level, equity readjustment, em-

ployment level, pricing policies, share of the market, emphasis on exports, environmental protection, and other goals).

3.   *Mechanics and sequence* of the budgeting process.

Major economic trends should be developed through *long-range planning*. Such planning would be assisted by an economic analysis staff advising the president and other top-level executives. To forecast trends, you would call in expert statisticians and economists, as prediction must be carried out with some precision to be reliable. The predictions of the economists and statisticians would be compared with the intuitive predictions of operating management. For example, the chief marketing officer of each of the profit centers may be asked his opinion of marketing trends and developments. His opinion will serve both as a check on the statistical predictions and as input to the ongoing process of revising such predictions.

Major goals would be part of budget policy so that the plans prepared by the various profit and cost centers have in common some fundamental assumptions about the firm. The budget committees, in formulating these general goals, do not take the initiative for proposing change in operations from lower responsibility levels. One purpose of the budget process is to encourage a flow of such ideas upwards through the administrative structure to higher levels of management.

Mechanics and sequence may be delegated to the chief budget officer. This person should be sure that common forms are supplied and consistent documentation required whenever budgeting takes place. Because budgeting may not be a familiar process to many new employees, the CBO operates several training schools or management development programs during the year to explain the budgeting process in his company. A few managers (and especially the CBO himself) will attend outside seminars and programs to trade budgeting experiences with other managers in other companies. The CBO will also consult with operating executives and set a schedule for completion of the various steps of the budgeting process.

The First Draft Budget

The result of the first round of steps will be a complete "first draft" budget. This budget will be assembled and scrutinized for inconsistencies or projected results which are obviously not acceptable to higher management. (For example, one department may have exceeded a tentative ceiling on its projected expenditures.) When such are found, the CBO informs the responsible departmental executives and offers his services in helping prepare an improved budget. The CBO can never order revision of a proposed budget. If an impasse develops between himself and a department executive, it must be passed up the line of responsibility to the executive's superior for resolution.

The "first draft" budget will receive close examination from the president's budget committee. It is probable they will suggest revisions to produce a more acceptable plan. The board of directors budget committee, and finally the board of directors,[1] would examine the revised budget. All parties recognized that budgeting is an iterative process; that is, that it should not be expected to produce an acceptable result right away; several trials will be necessary. The result of each trial will be an improvement on the result of the previous trial. Finally a trial will produce pro forma financial statements which appear satisfactory to the board of directors; this trial will be adopted as the formal budget and the processes and policies leading to those pro forma statements will become the *expected operations* of the business, and the benchmark against which actual operations are compared.

BUDGET COMPONENTS

The components of a total budget may be viewed in two ways: (1) with regard to the period of time covered and (2) with regard to the function or responsibility covered.

Period of Time

There will be two or possibly three distinct budget periods. The first has already been mentioned—the *long-range budget*. The long-range budget covers a period of time running from the present forward to a point in time perhaps 7 to 15 years distant. The purpose of this

---

[1] Usually the board looks at only the "final" budget.

budget is to anticipate long-range needs or opportunities which require specific steps to be taken now or in the near future. The company should not be taken by surprise by any developments which occur gradually over an extended period of time. Prospective restrictions on the sales of cigarettes or leaded gasoline are examples of events which have cast long shadows before them, which were (or could have been) foreseen, and for which preparation could be made. Long-range planning should be more than trend projection; trends rarely project to the extremes. Consequently long-range planning and budgeting must involve operating executives in the firm, possibly through retreats or regularly scheduled conferences. But because operating executives are not fundamentally planners, a staff of trained planners—statisticians, mathematicians, economists, and accountants—attends such meetings and interprets their results as input into a process of defining long-run problems, opportunities, environmental conditions, and company weaknesses which can be fed back to operating managers for further reaction at another meeting. The level of detail in long-range budgets is not high. There are pro forma financial statements, but they are condensed statements. Functional areas may be combined for these planning purposes, and much of the budget will consist of economic reports, scenarios, analysis, and narrative.

The *intermediate range budget* covers a period of time from the present forward perhaps three to six years. Its purpose is to schedule the continuance of programs already underway and the startup of programs necessary to achieve long-range objectives. The construction of a larger plant or systematic introduction of a new product line might be shown in such a budget.

The *operating budget* covers a relatively short time interval—normally equal to one year (or to one financial reporting period). It is prepared in considerable detail—as much detail as is necessary to compare the major operations of the firm with the plans made for them.

All of these budgets articulate together very closely. In fact, the intermediate range budget is simply the first few years of the long-range budget, and the operating budget may be the first year of both of these. This is possible because as the point in time budgeted for becomes closer, progressively more information is collected and included in the budget. Figure 2–2 illustrates these relationships.

FIGURE 2–2
Budgeting through Time

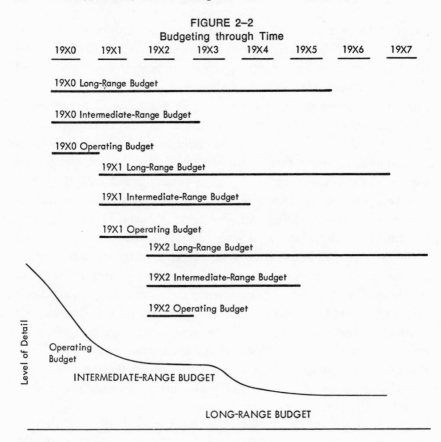

| 19X0 | 19X1 | 19X2 | 19X3 | 19X4 | 19X5 | 19X6 | 19X7 |

19X0 Long-Range Budget

19X0 Intermediate-Range Budget

19X0 Operating Budget

19X1 Long-Range Budget

19X1 Intermediate-Range Budget

19X1 Operating Budget

19X2 Long-Range Budget

19X2 Intermediate-Range Budget

19X2 Operating Budget

Operating Budget

INTERMEDIATE-RANGE BUDGET

LONG-RANGE BUDGET

Level of Detail

Function or Responsibility

The components of an operating budget will include (but may not be limited to):

Sales forecast and plan	Administrative budget
Sales budget	Capital budget
Inventory policy	Research and development budget
Purchases budget	Cash flow schedule
Manufacturing budget	Pro forma financial statements

In all cases, the budgets follow a form that will permit later comparison with operating results of the responsibility center involved. These comparisons lead to control over operations.

Let us discuss each component in turn.

Sales Forecast and Plan. It is most difficult to look ahead and develop reliable predictions of sales during a future interval because of the large numbers of variables involved. This task will fall upon the economic planning group and the marketing specialization, with the former acting as staff to the latter. Two methodologies will be used together to develop forecasts: statistical analysis and intuitive methods. Statistical techniques may include plotting on graph paper all sales in previous periods and extending the trend thereby revealed. More exact statistical methods such as regression analysis, moving averages, and exponential smoothing are employed by many businesses. When a business management does not itself possess these skills, it is as a rule able to engage outside consultants to provide statistical sales forecasts. Intuitive methods may include the judgments of individuals whose hunches have proven reliable on previous occasions, telephoning a few major customers to determine their buying plans, or exchanging views with marketing executives in other firms. If the two methodologies produce radically different pictures of future sales, the budget staff must try to bring them closer together. Usually one methodology confirms the other and most businesses will accept the redundancy to obtain the additional assurance of reliability in the sales forecasts. The sales *plan* is based on the most reliable sales forecast. Sales plans are prepared by month, by quarter, or other useful subperiod within the overall operating budget interval. In addition, the plan should be broken down into sales by products (or, where there are many products, by product groups) and by selling regions, if there is more than one region. Sales should be expressed in physical units and also in dollars.

Sales Budget. The sales budget is the marketing function's proposed expenditures and activities in support of the sales plan. It may include an advertising budget, a sales administration budget, a direct selling expenses budget, and other subbudgets which detail each activity in this function. A sales budget is always related to a particular sales plan; it should be understood that if either the sales plan or budget is materially changed (to reduce by half the number of calls by salesmen on purchasing agents, for example), the other should be scrutinized for possible revision.

Inventory Policy. The inventories policy will be largely the work of the manufacturing function, which will share responsibility with the marketing and finance functions for determining inventories of finished goods. The purpose of inventories is to provide service—quick deliveries of orders to customers, few or no delays in intraplant transfers, raw materials available as needed. The purpose of the inventories policy is to specify the levels of service inventories will provide. The level of service has to be balanced against the cost involved—and inventories maintenance represents capital which might be better invested elsewhere in a firm. In Chapter 6 you will learn ways of developing sensible inventory policies; here you only need to know that the inventory policy will specify *inventory levels* at the beginning, interim points, and end of the operating budget interval.

Purchases Budget. The purpose of the purchases budget is to schedule materials and supplies acquisition during the year to support the inventory policy and sales forecasts as well as manufacturing schedules. It is easy to compute purchases:

Purchases = Desired ending inventory + Withdrawals

by production − Expected beginning inventory   (2–1)

Since inventories are specified at several interior points during the budgeting period, we can show at what times materials and supplies have to be delivered to the firm (and, if there is more than one plant, at what locations). If there is a delay period between the time an order is placed and the time the goods arrive at the plant, this period can be subtracted from the desired delivery time, an additional safety factor subtracted, and the necessary order date determined. If suppliers have been tentatively picked, now is the time to alert them and to inquire whether they are able to meet the firm's anticipated needs. The expected costs of purchases are used to prepare dollar estimates of purchases also.

Manufacturing Budget. The manufacturing budget may be the most complex of all the budgets in the firm. It will show the quantities of finished products to be manufactured, the quantities of in-process materials, and the units to be started. From the latter information the purchases budget takes its starting point. The manufacturing budget can be extremely complex when there are many plants and outputs of some of these are inputs for the others. However, many firms have relatively simple manufacturing operations for which there is little difficulty in preparing budgets.

A manufacturing plant should budget at each of its responsibility centers, measuring activity in terms of a major key resource input such as direct labor hours or machine-hours. Other variable costs may be keyed to these major resource inputs. If production responsibility centers are budgeted first, service responsibility centers may be budgeted based on the services they would provide production centers operating at those budgeted levels. When manufacturing activity cannot be forecast very far ahead, the "flexible budget" described in Chapter 4 will be used.

Administrative Budget. The administrative budget sets out the activity levels and expenditures of the major nonmanufacturing, non-sales activities of the firm. Some of these are:

Accounting and finance	Purchasing
Public relations	Merger and acquisition staff
President's staff	Legal counsel and litigation
Economic planning	

These responsibility centers submit budgets in which are detailed—

Number of employees, rank of employees, salaries
Supplies expenses
Travel and entertainment (if any)
Indirect costs and departmental fixed costs

The budgets should cover the programs to which administrative centers are committed. Although program budgeting is most widely accepted in the public sector, it is also appropriate wherever there is no clear-cut criterion of efficiency (such as standard costs provide in the factory and profit margins provide in marketing) by which to judge scarce factor input utilization. Thus, finance may have to report its operations research, computer software development, debt management, and budgeting *programs* and show how each responsibility center in finance contributes to these programs. Program budgeting lets management judge the effect on all responsibility centers of changing the pace of a specific program.

Capital Budget. Capital budgeting decision making is intended to provide the firm with long-lived assets to deploy in future situations with profit potential. Long-lived (capital) assets require a relatively long lead time for getting into place and use (they cannot be ordered up or replenished as can inventory, for example); at any given moment the business must use the long-lived assets it has on hand. Consequently a major consideration in capital budgeting is to plan the acquisition of assets which have enough flexibility in use to meet all of the future profit opportunities that are likely to occur.

The business pays a price in achieving such flexibility. Multipurpose assets are unlikely to be as profitable in any specific use as assets designed especially to be profitable in that particular use alone, and the more uses an asset is designed to have, the less efficient it will be in any one of them.

The capital budgeting process begins at several levels. Efficiency improvements that require capital expenditures will originate at operating responsibility centers. Proposals for new plants, major capacity expansion, or replacement of one production process by another may originate in the manufacturing function at the highest staff levels or in the economic planning staff. Proposals for capital expenditures in support of marketing, distribution, or research and development will originate within those respective functions—usually at a high level. Proposals for mergers and acquisitions will originate in the finance function, the president's office, or even with the board of directors.

As capital expenditure proposals accumulate, their disposition cannot wait for the budgeting process to be completed. Decisions on proposals are made as they arise. (The selection processes themselves are reviewed in Chapter 5.) The budgeting process attempts to anticipate major categories of capital spending and the functional or profit areas which will receive the benefit of the expenditures. Each area vice president may be asked to make a capital expenditures forecast for his area; these forecasts will be reviewed in the CBO's office. Any revisions or changes will be cleared with the vice presidents involved.

Research and Development Budget. This may be a difficult area to budget since much R&D cannot be directly related to profits earned or to be earned. Fortunately, much research is of the applied variety and may be related to a forthcoming product line, adaptation of equipment to new purposes, and other programs which can be accounted for and controlled. The R&D budget measures the resources going into R&D and the consistency of their use by R&D responsibility centers with planned use. Although there is no logical justification for doing so, some businesses tie their overall R&D expenditure to total revenue, total profit, return on investment, or some other measure of business activity. This attempt to limit R&D costs may be reasonable if it is applied with regard for the programs underway in R&D; it would make little sense to cut back programs with strong promise of increasing future revenue simply because current revenues were falling.

Cash Flow Schedule. From all the budgets prepared, the treasurer identifies cash receipts and disbursements within the budget period. The receipts and disbursements should be identified as to source and sub period so that cash position during the budget period is anticipated.

For example, 94 percent of sales may be on credit; of this percentage, 80 percent is collected in the month following sale, 10 percent is collected in the second month following sale, and 4 percent is uncollectible or paid out in returns and allowances. The 6 percent noncredit sales are for cash, which of course is collected immediately.

Once a sales forecast is developed, cash receipts from sales can be scheduled. The purchases and manufacturing budgets will show the timing and amounts of accounts payable and wages payable liabilities; from these are computed the amount and timing of cash disbursements. To operating disbursements add disbursements for dividends, interest, and capital expenditures. Naturally, the firm may discover a substantial excess of receipts over disbursements (or disbursements over receipts) at times which may be invested in short-term securities to earn extra interest income for the firm. A cash shortage projection is the signal to reduce or defer some activities which lead to cash expenditures, increase activities which lead to cash receipts, or seek additional sources of cash through issue of stock or credit equities.

Pro Forma Financial Statements. These statements are the final rigorous test of the budget process's success in producing an acceptable plan of operations. The pro forma statements present the picture of the business that investors will see at the end of the budgeting period, after the budget has been transformed into history by the firm's operations. If this picture is favorable to the firm, in the opinion of investors, the business will continue to receive capital and support from the financial community. If it is not favorable, capital may be withheld or withdrawn, and the firm will fall upon difficult days.

You have already seen that financial statements present a precise but not always complete description of a firm, and it is quite possible that the firm's operations will be sound, yet this will not be reflected by the financial statements. The firm which realizes this knows that its choices are *limited to those productive activities which will "look good" in the financial statements.*

If the financial statements projected by the budgeting process do not present a picture of the firm which in the opinion of the board of directors will be attractive to outside capital sources (stockholders and creditors), a new budget may have to be prepared which does produce such statements. Thus financial reporting rules and principles do influence the planning and activities of management by channeling them away from business processes which do not look good in financial statements. Examples of such processes might be (until recently) environmental preservation, labor skill upgrading, and waste material recycling.

Activities which may be contrary to the public interest but are encouraged by the rules of financial reporting may include business combinations (certain types), stock options, and market monopolization (restraint of trade).

Accountants are aware of potential for abuse in financial reporting and have established authoritative bodies to minimize it. The foremost of these is the Financial Accounting Standards Board, which attempts to spot abusive financial reporting and eliminate it before it becomes an embarrassment to the accounting profession. Through such activity the quality of financial reporting is being steadily improved; it is approaching the goal of being an objective channel of information to permit efficient capital allocation between firms.

PREPARATION OF AN OPERATING BUDGET

The budgets and schedules you have just read about are best prepared in a recognized sequence, which is illustrated in Figure 2–3.

FIGURE| 2–3
Budget Preparation Sequence

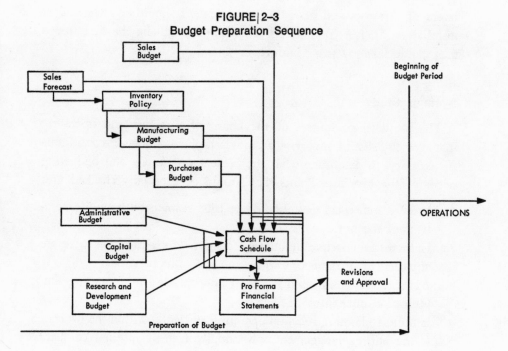

Figure 2–3 could be more detailed since there are many unshown connections and feedback loops between individual budgets. For example, the capital acquisitions budget may be revised based on the results of preparing the cash flow schedule; the manufacturing budget may be revised if a supportive purchases budget cannot be developed. Not shown is the "financial budget" which will be the treasurer's schedule of proposed investments and borrowings to maintain a smooth and adequate cash flow.

BUDGET INSTALLATION

Surprisingly, many businesses large and small do not have budget systems in operation. This section will give you some idea of what such a business must do to develop a useful budget.

Motivation

Some managers will view a budget as a potential threat to their security rather than as a way for them to be rewarded for their efficiency. To encourage their cooperation, a top-level committee of the board of directors and operating management should oversee budget installation. Such a committee's establishment will be the first step a firm should take towards a budget.

Systems Study

The top-level committee of the board of directors and operating management should supervise a study, employing outside consultants if necessary, to determine what the present operations and budgeting needs of the firm are. Points that should be especially checked are:

1. Is there a clear-cut definition of decision responsibility in all operations of the firm?
2. Is there an effective accounting system which produces accurate and timely management information system reports?
3. Are standard costs used wherever appropriate for accounting simplification and control of operations?
4. Is there a planning function operating efficiently within the firm?
5. Is the entire management substantially free of internal conflict?

If these questions can be affirmatively answered, the process of budget installation may proceed.

First Steps. Perhaps one first step is to prepare an annual profit plan. As this plan is in process, the business ought to be preparing sales forecasts, cash flow schedules, capital budgeting procedures, and inventory policies.

Additional Steps. If a standard cost system is appropriate for the business and doesn't yet exist, this would be the time to install it. Using standard costs and production scheduling techniques, a manufacturing budget should be developed. Administrative and research and development budgets can be begun.

Finally. From there, budget installation is a matter of refinement and improvement. Continuously throughout the installation stage, the budget committee must maintain the interest and enthusiasm of all managers for the budget. They should especially understand that the budget is not imposed on them from above but is prepared from the lowest decision-making levels of the firm and travels upward in the organization. It is a formal communication process in which these levels tell top management what can be done, and top management evaluates whether this is acceptable—and if it isn't, provides operating management with the tools to do better.

SUMMARY

A business is organized in a systematic manner, with logical separation of specialized functions such as research, finance, production, and sales. Responsibilities within these functions are clear-cut. Accounting reports permit descriptions of the ways responsibilities are discharged by executives.

Budgeting provides a planning benchmark for comparison with accounting reports to determine how well a responsibility center is performing. Budgets are complex representations of business plans for future operations. The preparation of a budget is not simple. Budget preparation is supported at the highest levels within a business, but the budget itself must be prepared by all levels of responsibility across all functional areas. The budget staff, which is usually responsible to the controller, provides advisory services in assisting executives prepare their budgets.

The first part of the operating budget to be prepared is usually the sales forecast, followed by the sales, inventories, manufacturing, purchasing, research, capital additions, and administrative budgets. These budgets result in many performance schedules, a cash budget, and pro forma financial statements. Such financial statements and budget summaries are forwarded to the board of directors for their study and approval or criticism. It is not uncommon for a budget to be revised or even rejected by the directors if they feel that it doesn't represent an effective operating plan for the business.

The operating budget, described above, is not the only part of the budgeting process that is important. In fact, budgeting can be regarded as going on for a period of time extending into the future as much as 15 to 20 years, with the detail becoming more and more involved and explicit as the plan approaches the present moment—until the budget for the next period is in fact the operating budget.

It is still common to find firms without budgets; however many of these are moving over to some sort of budgeting process to facilitate planning. Computers in many firms simplify and speed up preparation of budget schedules.

APPENDIX 2A: AN EXAMPLE OF BUDGET FORMS AND PROCESS

This section shows you one way different budget components are prepared and assembled. The Gowingplaces Company sells two products, A and B. These products are made in a single plant and sold in the northern and southern sales regions. Budgeting is by quarters

TABLE 2A–1

Schedule S-1
Ref: Sales forecasting
    support folder

GOWINGPLACES COMPANY
Budget for Year Ending 12-31-74
Sales Plan

	Quarter 1	*Quarter 2*	*Quarter 3*	*Quarter 4*	*Year*
PART 1–UNITS					
Northern region:					
Product A	1,000	1,200	1,600	1,200	5,000
Product B	2,000	2,000	2,000	2,000	8,000
Southern region:					
Product A	1,000	1,000	1,000	1,000	4,000
Product B	1,500	1,200	1,200	1,600	5,500
Quarterly unit totals:					
Product A	2,000	2,200	2,600	2,200	9,000
Product B	3,500	3,200	3,200	3,600	13,500
PART 2–UNIT SELLING PRICES					
Northern region:					
Product A	$ 100	$ 120	$ 120	$ 125	
Product B	200	200	200	200	
Southern region:					
Product A	90	90	100	100	
Product B	200	200	200	200	
PART 3–DOLLARS					
Northern region:					
Product A	$100,000	$144,000	$192,000	$150,000	$ 586,000
Product B	400,000	400,000	400,000	400,000	1,600,000
Subtotal.	$500,000	$544,000	$592,000	$550,000	$2,186,000
Southern region:					
Product A	$ 90,000	$ 90,000	$100,000	$100,000	$ 380,000
Product B	300,000	240,000	240,000	320,000	1,100,000
Subtotal	$390,000	$330,000	$340,000	$420,000	$1,480,000
Total sales	$890,000	$874,000	$932,000	$970,000	$3,666,000
Product A both regions . . .	$190,000	$234,000	$292,000	$250,000	$ 966,000
Product B both regions . . .	700,000	640,000	640,000	720,000	2,700,000

for a one-year budget period. Sales forecasting for the next budget period begins in June preceding beginning of the next year in January. Final forecasts are prepared by September.

Standard cost assumptions are finalized in November preceding the January 1 effective date of the new budget. During November, contacts are made with suppliers and Gowingplaces' bankers and auditors are briefed on the budget. The board of directors acts informally on the budget in draft in late November and formally on the official version sometime before Christmas.

The *sales plan* is prepared with primary reliance on the sales estimates of salesmen in the two sales regions. Selective contacts with major customers and forecasts using two computer programs developed by the economic planning staff are used to validate the data from salesmen. The sales plan which was produced is shown as Schedule S–1 in Table 2A–1. The *sales budget* supporting this plan is shown as Schedule S–2 in Table 2A–2. The assumptions underlying the sales budget are these:

Direct selling cost per
  sales dollar:
    Northern region. $0.03
    Southern region. 0.02
Indirect fixed selling costs:
    Northern region. $45,000
    Southern region.   60,000

TABLE 2A–2

Schedule S–2 Ref: S–1 and other support	GOWINGPLACES COMPANY Budget for Year Ending 12-31-74 Sales Budget				
	Quarter 1	*Quarter 2*	*Quarter 3*	*Quarter 4*	*Whole Year*
PART 1–DIRECT SELLING EXPENSES					
Northern region.	$15,000	$16,320	$17,760	$16,500	$ 65,580
Southern region.	7,800	6,600	6,800	8,400	29,600
Total.	$22,800	$22,920	$24,560	$24,900	$ 95,180
PART 2–FIXED SELLING EXPENSES					
Northern region.	$11,250	$11,250	$11,250	$11,250	$ 45,000
Southern region.	15,000	15,000	15,000	15,000	60,000
Total.	$26,250	$26,250	$26,250	$26,250	$105,000
Grand total costs	$49,050	$49,170	$50,810	$51,150	$200,180

The *inventory policy* is, roughly speaking, to hold at the end of any quarter an inventory equal to 30 percent of the expected transfers out of that inventory during the next quarter. This policy applies to both finished goods and raw materials. The Gowingplaces Company manufacturing process is very rapid and produces virtually no "work in process"; the latter will therefore be ignored in the budgeting schedules. The next budget, shown in Table 2A–3 as Schedule M–1, is the production schedule, which is prepared only in terms of physical units and shows the requirement for production in each quarter as a function of the inventory policy and expected demand for finished goods.

TABLE 2A–3

Schedule M-1 Ref: S-1 inventory policy	GOWINGPLACES COMPANY Budget for Year Ending 12-31-74 Manufacturing Schedule				
	Quarter 1	*Quarter 2*	*Quarter 3*	*Quarter 4*	*Whole Year*
PART 1–PRODUCT A					
Sales (units)	2,000	2,200	2,600	2,200	9,000
Add: Ending inventory for quarter	660	780	660	600	600
Less: Beginning inventory for quarter	(600)	(660)	(780)	(660)	(600)
Required production	2,060	2,320	2,480	2,140	9,000
PART 2–PRODUCT B					
Sales (units)	3,500	3,200	3,200	3,600	13,500
Add: Ending inventory for quarter	960	960	1,080	960	960
Less: Beginning inventory for quarter	(1,050)	(960)	(960)	(1,080)	(1,050)
Required production	3,410	3,200	3,320	3,480	13,410

Any particular unit of A or B has a "standard composition" in terms of direct inputs. It is necessary to extend these inputs to the scheduled production in order to determine the total input (materials and labor) requirements. Table 2A–4 contains the expected direct inputs to A and B and their expected prices during 1974.

The physical units column is multiplied by the quarterly production requirements for the respective product to obtain the physical units

TABLE 2A–4
Expected Inputs to A and B

Product	Input Identity	Physical Units	Cost per Unit
Product A	Raw material X	6	$5
	Type I direct labor hours	10	3
Product B	Raw material Y	10	3
	Type II direct labor hours	20	4

TABLE 2A–5
Total Direct Production Inputs

Quarter	Quarterly Production Product A (Schedule M–1)	Units Raw Material X Required	Hours Type I Direct Labor Required
1	2,060	12,360	20,600
2	2,320	13,920	23,200
3	2,480	14,880	24,800
4	2,140	12,840	21,400

Quarter	Quarterly Production Product B (Schedule M–1)	Units Raw Material Y Required	Hours Type II Direct Labor Required
1	3,410	34,100	68,200
2	3,200	32,000	64,000
3	3,320	33,200	66,400
4	3,480	34,800	69,600

of S, Y, and the two types of direct labor which are required as inputs each quarter. The results are shown in Table 2A–5.

These requirements can be used as support for a schedule of materials inventories and purchases and a schedule of labor skills requirements. We first prepare these schedules in terms of physical units just as we did Schedule M–1—except of course that labor cannot be inventoried. Schedule M–2 in Table 2A–6 presents these schedules for materials.

2A–7 presents as Schedule M–3 the quarterly requirements for labor.

To complete the description of manufacturing operations, you need a statement of indirect manufacturing costs other than labor.

Indirect materials and supplies are estimated to be 10.6 percent of

TABLE 2A–6

Schedule M–2
Ref: M–1, inventory
      policy, direct
      inputs tables,
      quarterly pro-
      duction computa-
      tion

GOWINGPLACES COMPANY
Budget for Year Ending 12-31-74
Schedule of Materials Inventories
and Purchases

	Quarter 1	Quarter 2	Quarter 3	Quarter 4	Whole Year
PART 1–MATERIAL X					
Needed for production	12,360	13,920	14,880	12,840	54,000
Add: Ending inventory for quarter.	4,200	4,500	3,900	3,700	3,700
Less: Beginning inventory for quarter.	(3,700)	(4,200)	(4,500)	(3,900)	(3,700)
Required purchases	12,860	14,220	14,280	12,640	54,000
Times purchase price per unit	×5	×5	×5	×5	×5
Purchases material X.	$ 64,300	$71,100	$ 71,400	$ 63,200	$270,000
PART 2–MATERIAL Y					
Needed for production	34,100	32,000	33,200	34,800	134,000
Add: Ending inventory for quarter.	9,600	10,000	10,400	10,200	10,200
Less: Beginning inventory for quarter.	(10,200)	(9,600)	(10,000)	(10,400)	(10,200)
Required purchases	33,500	32,400	33,600	34,600	134,100
Times purchase price per unit	×3	×3	×3	×3	×3
Purchases material Y.	$100,500	$97,200	$100,800	$103,800	$402,300

total direct labor. Fixed costs total $55,000 per quarter. All results are shown as Schedule M–4 in Table 2A–8.

We're now ready to prepare the pro forma cost of goods manufactured and cost of goods sold statements.

As presented, these statements are prepared in *contribution analysis* form; they do not report any allocation of fixed costs to units of product. Such allocation is necessary in actual financial statements but is undesirable in budgets, which are intended to be used within the firm.

TABLE 2A–7

Schedule M–3
Ref: M–1, direct inputs
tables, quarterly
production
computation

GOWINGPLACES COMPANY
Budget for Year Ending 12-31-74
Schedule of Labor Hours and Dollars

	Quarter 1	Quarter 2	Quarter 3	Quarter 4	Whole Year
Direct labor hours:					
Type I	20,600	23,200	24,800	21,400	90,000
Times wage rate.	×3	×3	×3	×3	×3
Type I wages	$ 61,800	$ 69,600	$ 74,400	$ 64,200	$ 270,000
Type II.	68,200	64,000	66,400	69,600	268,200
Times wage rate.	×4	×4	×4	×4	×4
Type II wages	$272,800	$256,000	$265,600	$278,400	$1,072,800
Direct labor wages	$334,600	$325,600	$340,000	$342,600	$1,342,800
Indirect labor hours (.20 × total direct labor hours).	17,760	17,440	18,240	18,200	71,640
Times wage rate for indirect labor	×3	×3	×3	×3	×3
Indirect labor wages	$ 53,280	$ 52,320	$ 55,720	$ 54,600	$ 215,920
Total wages	$387,880	$377,920	$395,720	$397,200	$1,558,720

Indirect variable costs amount to $215,920 (labor) and $142,340 (materials, supplies, etc)—a total of *$358,260.* From Table 2A–7, the total number of direct labor hours worked (of which variable indirect costs are primarily a function) is 90,000 + 268,200 = *358,200* hours. From these two figures, you can compute a reasonable budget allocation rate for indirect variable costs of $358,260/358,200 hours = *$1* per direct labor hour. Since 10 direct labor hours are used to make one unit of product A, $10 of indirect variable costs will be included in the manufacturing cost of each unit product A made. Similarly, the 20 direct labor hours included in each unit of product B require $20 of indirect costs in the manufacturing cost of each unit of that product made.

TABLE 2A–8

Schedule M–4 Ref: M–3	GOWINGPLACES COMPANY Budget for Year Ending 12-31-74 Indirect Manufacturing Costs				
	Quarter 1	Quarter 2	Quarter 3	Quarter 4	Whole Year
Depreciation........	$20,000	$20,000	$20,000	$20,000	$ 80,000
Insurance, etc........	5,000	5,000	5,000	5,000	20,000
Other fixed expenses.........	30,000	30,000	30,000	30,000	120,000
Total fixed costs........	$55,000	$55,000	$55,000	$55,000	$220,000
Indirect labor wages..........	$53,280	$52,320	$55,720	$54,600	$215,920
Indirect materials and supplies	35,470	34,510	36,040	36,320	142,340
Total variable indirect costs........	$88,750	$86,830	$91,760	$90,920	$358,260

The statement of cost of goods manufactured is Schedule CGM–1, shown as Table 2A–9. Remember that quarterly fixed manufacturing costs are given in Table 2A–8.

Schedule CGS–1, shown in Table 2A–10, is the projected cost of goods sold statement. It assumes unit prices of $70 for A and $130 for B.

Another important budget statement will show the performance of sales regions, each of which is a responsibility center. Table 2A–11 presents such a statement as Schedule CGS–2.

As another example of a performance statement, suppose that each product line is a profit center. We may prepare Schedule CGS–3, shown in Table 2A–12, to budget their respective performances. This statement does not suffer from the same defect as Schedule CGS–2—the cost of goods manufactured in Table 2A–12 is separated into fixed and variable components. The "Total net margin" line is the most important in this statement.

Although additional performance statements could be prepared, we will go on now and illustrate the remaining budgets for the Gowingplaces Company. There is a central administrative office. The major

TABLE 2A–9

Schedule CGM–1					
	GOWINGPLACES COMPANY				
	Budget for Year Ending 12-31-74				
	Cost of Goods Manufactured				
	Quarter 1	*Quarter 2*	*Quarter 3*	*Quarter 4*	*Whole Year*
Product A:					
Material X inputs (M–2)	12,360	13,920	14,880	12,840	54,000
Times cost per unit.	×5	×5	×5	×5	×5
Material X value.	$ 61,800	$ 69,600	$ 74,400	$ 64,200	$ 270,000
Labor type I (M–3)	61,800	69,600	74,400	64,200	270,000
Total direct costs A.	$123,600	$139,200	$148,800	$128,400	$ 540,000
Direct labor hours (alloc. basis)(M–3)	20,600	23,200	24,800	21,400	90,000
Indirect costs (rate = $1 per DLH)	$ 20,600	$ 23,200	$ 24,800	$ 21,400	$ 90,000
Total costs product A.	$144,200	$162,400	$173,600	$149,800	$ 630,000
Units manufactured (M–1)	2,060	2,320	2,480	2,140	9,000
Cost per unit (to nearest $)	$ 70	$ 70	$ 70	$ 70	$ 70
Product B:					
Material Y inputs (M–2)	34,100	32,000	33,200	34,800	134,100
Times cost per unit.	×3	×3	×3	×3	×3
Material and value	$102,300	$ 96,000	$ 99,600	$104,400	$ 402,300
Labor Type II (M–3)	272,800	256,000	265,600	278,400	1,072,800
Total direct costs B	$375,100	$352,000	$365,200	$382,800	$1,475,100
Direct labor hours (alloc. basis)(M–3)	68,200	64,000	66,400	69,600	268,200
Indirect costs (rate = $1 per DLH)	$ 68,200	$ 64,000	$ 66,400	$ 69,600	$ 268,200
Total costs product B.	$443,300	$416,000	$431,600	$452,400	$1,743,300
Units manufactured (M–1)	3,410	3,200	3,320	3,480	13,410
Cost per unit (to nearest $)	$ 130	$ 130	$ 130	$ 130	$ 130

TABLE 2A-10
Budgeted Cost of Goods Sold Statement

Schedule CGS-1 Ref. as noted	GOWINGPLACES COMPANY Budget for Year Ending 12-31-74 Cost of Goods Sold—Assuming Oldest Units in Inventory Are Sold First				
	Quarter 1	*Quarter 2*	*Quarter 3*	*Quarter 4*	*Whole Year*
Northern region:					
Product A					
(S-1).........	$ 70,000	$ 84,000	$112,000	$ 84,000	$ 350,000
Product B					
(S-1).........	260,000	260,000	260,000	260,000	1,040,000
Total cost.....	$330,000	$344,000	$372,000	$344,000	$1,390,000
Southern region:					
Product A					
(S-1).........	$ 70,000	$ 70,000	$ 70,000	$ 70,000	$ 280,000
Product B					
(S-1).........	195,000	156,000	156,000	208,000	715,000
Total cost.....	$265,000	$226,000	$226,000	$278,000	$ 995,000
Total cost of A:					
Both regions.....	$140,000	$154,000	$182,000	$154,000	$ 630,000
Total cost of B:					
Both regions.....	$455,000	$416,000	$416,000	$468,000	$1,755,000

Note: Cost of sales was computed by multiplying unit sales times unit price from Schedule CGM-1.

functions of administration are accounting, security, and staff. These are shown as Schedule A–1 in Table 2A–13.

There is no research function at Gowingplaces, so naturally there is no research budget. If there were one, it would look a great deal like the administrative budget. We proceed here to an illustration of the capital budget, shown in Table 2A–14 as Schedule CB.

With all these schedules in hand, the firm is able to prepare pro forma financial statements.

There are also other budget schedules, such as the asset additions and retirement schedule and the cash receipts and disbursements schedule which are beyond the scope of an introductory treatment. To conclude this presentation of typical budget schedules, therefore, we select the pro forma income statement (Table 2A–15). We do not prepare the balance sheet because it would introduce factors into the budget other than activities already described.

TABLE 2A–11
Budgeted Regional Sales Performance

Schedule CGS-2 Ref. as noted	GOWINGPLACES COMPANY Budget for Year Ending 12-31-74				
	Quarter 1	*Quarter 2*	*Quarter 3*	*Quarter 4*	*Whole Year*
Northern region:					
Revenue (S-1).........	$ 500,000	$ 544,000	$ 592,000	$ 550,000	$2,186,000
Cost of sales (CGS-1).......	330,000	344,000	372,000	344,000	1,390,000
Gross margin	$ 170,000	$ 200,000	$ 220,000	$ 206,000	$ 796,000
Less: variable selling expenses (S-2).......	(15,000)	(16,320)	(17,760)	(16,500)	(65,580)
Net margin	$ 155,000	$ 183,680	$ 202,240	$ 189,500	$ 730,420
Less: Fixed selling expenses (S-2).......	(11,250)	(11,250)	(11,250)	(11,250)	$ (45,000)
Net contribution, northern region	$ 143,750	$ 172,430	$ 190,990	$ 178,250	$ 685,420
Southern region:					
Revenue (S-1).........	$ 390,000	$ 330,000	$ 340,000	$ 420,000	$1,480,000
Cost of sales (CGS-1).......	(265,000)	(226,000)	(226,000)	(278,000)	(995,000)
Gross margin	$ 125,000	$ 104,000	$ 114,000	$ 142,000	$ 485,000
Less: Variable selling expenses (S-2)........	(7,800)	(6,600)	(6,800)	(8,400)	(29,600)
	$ 117,200	$ 97,400	$ 107,200	$ 133,600	$ 455,400
Less: Fixed selling expenses (S-2)........	(15,000)	(15,000)	(15,000)	(15,000)	(60,000)
Net contribution, southern region	$ 102,200	$ 82,400	$ 92,200	$ 118,600	$ 395,400
Total net contribution	$ 245,950	$ 254,830	$ 283,190	$ 296,850	$1,080,820

TABLE 2A–12

Schedule CGS-3 Ref. as noted	GOWINGPLACES COMPANY Budget for Year Ending 12-31-74 Product Line Performance Budgets				
	Quarter 1	*Quarter 2*	*Quarter 3*	*Quarter 4*	*Whole Year*
Product A:					
Sales (S-1).	$ 190,000	$ 234,000	$ 292,000	$ 250,000	$ 966,000
Variable cost of sales (CGS-1)	(140,000)	(154,000)	(182,000)	(154,000)	(630,000)
Gross margin— A	$ 50,000	$ 80,000	$ 110,000	$ 96,000	$ 336,000
Product B:					
Sales (S-1).	$ 700,000	$ 640,000	$ 640,000	$ 720,000	$ 2,700,000
Cost of sales (CGS-1)	(455,000)	(416,000)	(416,000)	(468,000)	(1,755,000)
Gross margin— B	$ 245,000	$ 224,000	$ 224,000	$ 252,000	$ 945,000
Total gross margin	$ 295,000	$ 304,000	$ 334,000	$ 348,000	$ 1,281,000
Less: Direct selling expenses (S-2)	(22,800)	(22,920)	(24,560)	(24,900)	(95,180)
Total net margin	$ 272,200	$ 281,080	$ 309,440	$ 323,100	$ 1,185,820
Less:					
(1) Fixed manufacturing expense	(55,000)	(55,000)	(55,000)	(55,000)	(220,000)
(2) Fixed selling expense.	(26,250)	(26,250)	(26,250)	(26,250)	(105,000)
Total net contribution . . .	$ 190,950	$ 199,830	$ 228,190	$ 241,850	$ 860,820

TABLE 2A–13

Schedule A–1					
	GOWINGPLACES COMPANY				
	Budget for Year Ending 12-31-74				
	Administrative Budget				
	Quarter 1	*Quarter 2*	*Quarter 3*	*Quarter 4*	*Whole Year*
Accounting:					
Professional salaries.........	$ 22,000	$ 22,000	$ 22,000	$ 25,000	$ 91,000
Assistants' salaries.........	11,000	11,000	11,000	11,000	44,000
Equipment rental....	9,000	9,000	9,000	9,000	36,000
Supplies	3,000	4,000	5,000	4,000	16,000
	$ 45,000	$ 46,000	$ 47,000	$ 49,000	$187,000
Security:					
Guard salaries......	$ 1,500	$ 1,500	$ 1,500	$ 1,500	$ 6,000
Other expenses	3,000	3,000	3,000	3,000	12,000
	$ 4,500	$ 4,500	$ 4,500	$ 4,500	$ 18,000
Staff:					
Executive salaries.........	$ 25,000	$ 25,000	$ 25,000	$ 25,000	$100,000
Secretarial salaries.........	5,000	5,000	5,000	5,000	20,000
Professional salaries.........	10,000	10,000	10,000	10,000	40,000
Supplies	2,000	2,000	2,000	2,000	8,000
Other expenses	1,000	2,000	4,000	1,000	8,000
	$ 43,000	$ 44,000	$ 46,000	$ 43,000	$176,000
Other expenses:					
Depreciation— offices.........	$ 6,000	$ 6,000	$ 6,000	$ 6,000	$ 24,000
Various amortizations.........	5,000	5,000	5,000	5,000	20,000
	$ 11,000	$ 11,000	$ 11,000	$ 11,000	$ 44,000
Total administrative budgets	$103,500	$105,500	$108,500	$107,500	$425,000

TABLE 2A–14

Schedule CB
Supporting
detail on
indicated
schedules

GOWINGPLACES COMPANY
Budget for Year Ending 12-31-74
Capital Additions Schedule

	Quarter 1	*Quarter 2*	*Quarter 3*	*Quarter 4*	*Whole Year*
Marketing:					
Transport vehicles (CB–1).	$28,000	$ 0	$ 20,000	$10,000	$ 58,000
Warehouse in Cleveland (CB–1).	0	10,000	55,000	0	65,000
Total.	$28,000	$10,000	$ 75,000	$10,000	$123,000
Manufacturing:					
Versing machine in plant	$ 0	$ 0	$150,000	$10,000	$160,000
Total.	$ 0	$ 0	$150,000	$10,000	$160,000
Administration:					
Architectural studies for new offices (CB–3).	$ 0	$ 7,000	$ 0	$ 0	$ 7,000
Total capital	$ 0	$ 7,000	$ 0	$ 0	$ 7,000
Total capital expenditures.	$28,000	$17,000	$225,000	$20,000	$290,000

TABLE 2A–15
Budgeted Income Statement

Schedule FS-1

GOWINGPLACES COMPANY
Budget for Year Ending 12-31-74
Income Statement

	Quarter 1	*Quarter 2*	*Quarter 3*	*Quarter 4*	*Whole Year*
Sales (S-1).	$ 890,000	$ 874,000	$ 932,000	$ 970,000	$ 3,666,000
Less:					
Variable cost of sales	(595,000)	(570,000)	(598,000)	(622,000)	(2,385,000)
Variable selling costs	(22,800)	(22,920)	(24,560)	(24,900)	(95,180)
Net margin.	$ 362,200	$ 281,080	$ 309,440	$ 323,900	$ 1,185,820
Less:					
(1) Fixed manu-facturing ex-pense	(55,000)	(55,000)	(55,000)	(55,000)	(220,000)
(2) Fixed selling expense.	(26,250)	(26,250)	(26,250)	(26,250)	(105,000)
Net contribu-tion.	$ 190,950	$ 199,830	$ 228,190	$ 241,850	$ 860,820
Less: Administrative expenses (A-1)	(103,500)	(105,500)	(108,500)	(107,500)	(425,000)
Profit before taxes and divi-dends.	$ 87,450	$ 94,330	$ 119,690	$ 134,350	$ 435,820
Less:					
Estimated taxes	(30,000)	(30,000)	(30,000)	(30,000)	(120,000)
Estimated divi-dends	(20,000)	(20,000)	(20,000)	(20,000)	(80,000)
Estimated addition to retained earnings	$ 37,450	$ 44,330	$ 69,690	$ 84,350	$ 235,820

BIBLIOGRAPHY

Books

Chamberlain, Neil W.   *The Firm: Micro-economic Planning and Action.* New York: McGraw-Hill Book Co., 1962.

Copulsky, William.   *Practical Sales Forecasting.* New York: American Management Association, 1970.

Heckert, J. Brooks, and Willson, James D.   *Business Budgeting and Control.* 3d ed. New York: The Ronald Press Co., 1967.

N.A.A. Research Report No. 42, *Long Range Planning.* New York: National Association of Accountants, 1964.

Miley, Arthur L.   *Directory of Planning, Budgeting, and Control Information.* Oxford, Ohio: Planning Executives Institute, 1969.

Report of the President's Commission on Budget Concepts.   Washington, D.C.: U.S. Government Printing Office, 1967.

Welsch, Glenn A.   *Budgeting: Profit Planning and Control.* 3rd ed. Englewood Cliffs, N.J.: Prentice-Hall, Inc., 1971.

————, and Sord, Burnard H.   *Business Budgeting.* New York: Controllership Foundation, 1962.

Articles

Ansoff, H. Igor, and Brandenburg, Richard C.   "A Program of Research in Business Planning," *Management Science,* February 1967.

Osler, Paul W.   "Long-range Forecasts: Where Do We Go from Here," *Management Accounting,* January 1971.

Prestbo, John A.   "Budgeting Business," *The Wall Street Journal,* December 20, 1965, p. 1.

Schiff, Michael, and Lewin, Arie Y.   "Where Traditional Budgeting Fails," *Financial Executive,* May 1968.

3

Contribution Analysis of
Planning Decisions

NATURALLY, not all information is of equal value in decision making. Much information is collected as a necessary historical record rather than for use in decision making. In this chapter, you develop the formal structure of decision models and see how changes in activity level affect the accounting measures of business profit. You learn how to identify needed information, extract it from accounting files and reports, and use it to make proper decisions. You begin to learn the difference between needed and unneeded information.

The models of decisions discussed in this chapter are preferred whenever they can be clearly established as appropriate. The structure of real decisions is so complex that often a formal model or analysis cannot be established. Nevertheless, the information you would use with a relevant decision model is probably also useful in any substitute decision process, although we cannot prove this.

All decision models have in common that they depend upon development of the *differences* between decision alternatives. Each alternative is said to make a contribution (measured in dollars) to the operation, and so decision analysis based on economic information has come to be known as contribution analysis. We shall present several examples of contribution analysis: make-or-buy decisions, sunk-cost decisions, joint-production decisions, and decisions on the further processing of products and setting the production level of products.

WHAT A DECISION MODEL IS

The decision model is a way of generating a business policy, or *decision-making rule,* from whatever is known about the environment and the consequences of the decision alternatives.

A decision-making rule is always in this form:

> If A happens, do I
> If B happens, do II, etc.

Such a rule presupposes that we can identify all the things (A, B, etc.) that can happen as well as all our alternatives (I, II, etc.). In order to develop and evaluate decision-making rules, you must assess what will happen to the decision maker if he chooses I and A happens, or B happens; or if he chooses II and A happens, or B happens; and so on. This is not easy but it *is* the way of deciding in advance what to do.

Decision Models Compared to Real Decision Processes

Here you may ask, "How did executives make decisions before they had decision models?" The answer is that a few executives came to be very good at logical and intuitive analysis to produce an acceptable or even outstanding solution to an inventory holding and ordering, resource allocation, or waiting line problem. It is also true that many costly and avoidable decision errors were made. "On the job trial and error" best describes such instinctive decision making.

Significance to Accountants of Decision Model Analysis

Accountants participate in use of decision models even though their primary function is that of information suppliers. As information suppliers, accountants are most interested in the kinds of information persons using the decision models need. If you are an accountant you may not want to be an accomplished authority on, for example, linear programming models (though if you *do* want to be, you will find many rewarding paybacks to you as accountant or manager). An accountant will want to know enough about linear programming to understand what kinds of information to provide persons using linear programming.

ACCOUNTING INFORMATION AND OTHER INFORMATION USED IN ECONOMIC DECISIONS

Information describing past activities is useful in decisions only if you expect that future decisions will be made under the same conditions that governed similar past decisions.

Decisions deal with *changes* from a present or contemplated way of doing things. This rule will help identify useful information for decisions:

Information useful in a decision will describe a benefit or cost for each change the decision would cause if implemented.

Totals and averages are not especially useful in decisions: the effects of changes can be buried in a total. For example, there are any number of combinations of price and volume which might produce $1,000,000 in revenue; the single total figure does not tell us which combination actually produced the $1,000,000.

The accounting information we will emphasize (and which can be used in decision models) helps you distinguish between alternative solutions to a problem, identify out-of-control states, and measure the gain or loss from individual business operations.

CONTRIBUTION ANALYSIS ILLUSTRATED: MAKE OR BUY

A common nonroutine decision that confronts most organizations is whether to make or buy a required input. To make this decision properly, you must compute the cost to the business of making the input, and the cost of buying the input. The alternative with the lowest cost is preferred.

The trick to this decision lies in knowing which costs to associate with the manufacture of the input. These should be the costs *which will not occur* if the input is purchased. Here is an example:

The Answer-U Telephone Answering Device Manufacturing Company has designed a new model automatic telephone answerer which requires a series of etched circuits. These circuits could be produced on existing idle equipment for these costs:

1 hour direct labor	$ 5.50
2 KW electrical power	0.08
1 circuit board	0.50
Allocated fixed overhead	10.00
Total, per unit	$16.08

A commercial manufacturer of these boards has offered to provide them for $12 each.

The proper decision is to manufacture the circuit boards internally. The reason is: the allocated fixed overhead represents resource commitments that are independent of volume of activity; these commitments and their associated costs would continue regardless of whether circuit boards are manufactured internally. The general rule in applying contribution analysis is to disregard costs that are not affected by any alternative under consideration.

The only costs affected by Answer-U's decision are those of labor, power, and the circuit board: $5.50 + $0.08 + $0.50 = $6.08. Since this cost is considerably less than the $12 price quoted by the outside supplier, his offer should be declined. If 10,000 circuit boards are required, the savings or contribution of internal manufacture is $10,000 \times (\$12.00 - \$6.08) = \$59,200$.

In summary,

Alternative I: Make board	$ 6.08 cost per unit—proper choice
Alternative II: Buy board	$12.00 cost per unit

TIME DIMENSION OF CONTRIBUTION ANALYSIS: SUNK COSTS

Imagine your bicycle cost you $100 new and has been a real dog: you have spent $300 in repairs for it. Now one more thing goes wrong which will cost $50 to repair, but that repair will make the bicycle equivalent to a brand new one, with absolutely no more repairs needed. Do you make the repair? Or do you junk your bike and buy a new one for $100?

You should say that you will make the $50 repair. It is an important principle of decision making that "sunk" costs (money which has been irrevocably spent and is unrecoverable) are not considered in decision making. This principle is reasonable enough; we do not allow the "dead past" to influence our activities. Nevertheless, it leads to some strange situations that, superficially at least, do not appear reasonable.

The Kallus Shoe Company has just invested in a large automated shoemaking machine. You were the person who persuaded Corn J. Kallus, president, to buy the machine. The machine cost $800,000 and will make 1,000,000 pairs of shoes over its one-year useful life at $9.50 per pair in direct variable costs.

The week after the machine is delivered, installed, paid for and put to work, you pick up a shoe industry trade publication and see an advertisement for a new automated shoemaking machine costing $800,000 and able to make 1,000,000 pair of shoes over its useful life for *$1.40* per pair in direct variable costs.

You turn pale and begin to shake, because you know that you must now tell Mr. Kallus that the machine you told him to buy is *junk;* that he must dispose of it for a pittance; that he must at once spend *another* $800,000 for the new shoemaking machine; that if he does not do so he will be unable to remain competitive in the shoemaking business.

The direct savings of the new machine will be $9.50 — $1.40 = $8.10 per pair of shoes. These savings will, over the lifetime of either machine, total to $8.10 $\times$ 1,000,000 pair = $8,100,000. Even though this is enough to pay for the second shoemaking machine 10 times over, you are not at all sure Mr. Kallus will understand that.

In fact, the new machine could be priced up to $8,100,000 and the decision would still have to be to acquire it—so long as the purchase price is less than the savings it will produce.

The sunk-cost principle illustrates why large development contracts are often continued even though there have been large-scale cost overruns.

The State of Oklayoming let a contract to the Home Development Corporation to produce a prototype low-cost mass-production home. The contract amount was $500,000. Six months after the contract was let, the company told the State that unexpected difficulties would cause the cost to rise by $200,000, but that it was expected the contract would be fulfilled at that price. Twelve months later, giving the same assurances, the company requested an additional $300,000. Each time the State satisfied itself the difficulties were bonafide and made the commitment to reimburse Home Development for the extra costs. The reason it did so was that the additional costs were still less expensive than starting over with a new contractor.

When you approach a decision which may involve sunk costs, it is important that you identify these costs and determine that they are really unrecoverable. Costs of long-lived assets, past wages and materials, and taxes are examples of sunk costs. However, some costs may be recoverable through sale of the asset to which they attach. If the Kallus Shoe Company's "old" shoemaking machine could be sold for $300,000, then the actual sunk cost would only be $800,000 — $300,000 = $500,000.

DECISIONS INVOLVING JOINT PRODUCTS

One of the important axioms of accounting is that causal relationships link events, and therefore the costs and revenues related to these events. When a causal relationship is identified, accountants take advantage of it to combine specific costs and revenues together if they attach to the related events. The sale of dental services and subsequent receipts of payment are causally related to one another, permitting a dentist to conclude that your payment came as a direct result of filling your cavities. Such direct causal relationships might be represented by the arrows in Figure 3–1, which shows events as caused by other events.

FIGURE 3–1
Network of Direct Causal Relationships

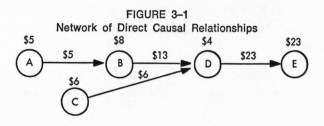

In this diagram, event A causes event B, which together with event C causes event D, which itself causes event E. This network might describe a manufacturing process in which A, B, C, D, and E are individual steps. The number beside each event is the dollar sacrifice in order for that event to take place; the number on each arrow is the sum of these costs for events occurring *before* the event to which the arrow leads. For example, $8 is the sacrifice in order that event B occur. Because this sacrifice causes B to occur, the cost of B is $8. Since A causes B to occur, the cost of A is really part of the cost of B and is transferred to it by the arrow. If E is the final event (the completed product), the cost of all events leading up to E are associated with E ($23) and are referred to as the product cost. In this sense, the $23 figure sums up the chain of events which culminated in the production of E.

Joint Products Illustrated

Not all chains are so easily dealt with as shown in Figure 3-1. Consider the chain in Figure 3-2. Here a single event A has caused two

FIGURE 3-2
Network Showing Joint Causal Relationships

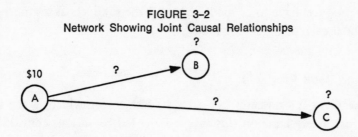

events B and C. The cost of A is $10. What costs are transferred to B? What costs are transferred to C? Perhaps a classic example of this kind of process is the petroleum refinery, which includes a massive reaction chamber called a "catalytic cracking tower" into which crude oil is fed and where, in the presence of catalysts, heat, and pressure, it changes into a variety of hydrocarbon fractions including bunker fuel, kerosene, gasoline, naptha, and cooking gases. What cost should be assigned to each of these products? In the diagram of Figure 3-2, B and C are an illustration of *joint products;* and the bunker fuel, kerosene, and other products of the cracking tower are also joint products. Here are some more examples:

—Peanuts (and other agricultural products such as sorghum, cattle, and hogs) produce a variety of foods, chemicals, and other substances with economic value.
—Coal is the source of many hydrocarbons ranging from ordinary blast furnace coke to dyes.
—Many ores contain more than one valuable metal, most of which are economically recoverable through an integrated process.
—A public expenditure on education has joint benefits: crime reduction, unemployment reduction, earning power enhancement.

You have already studied an example of a process producing joint products—the operation of service centers. Their costs were allocated more or less arbitrarily to those who received the benefits of their services—production centers.

Our concern in studying joint products will be that costs which are truly joint be allocated to the joint products in ways that preserve the actual contribution of all the joint products as a group to business profitability. In other words, decisions to continue, increase, or decrease these products have to be made about all the products as a group—and not about each of them individually.

Costing Joint Products

The Copy-It Company has a large, fast copier which is the firm's principal asset. Time on this copier is rented to various companies in 30-minute increments. The copier is available 24 hours a day and, to encourage off-hours use, the rate after 5 P.M. and before 8 A.M. is 50 percent of the regular rate. The company is open five days per week—5 × 24 = 120 potential hours of use. Many companies rent two or more segments of off-hours time and one segment during regular hours, doing their rush work during daylight hours and the less important copying at night. The Copy-It Company must spend $1,200 per week to keep the copier running and available. This cost is not affected by the actual weekly amount of usage. The company charges $18 per hour for daylight time and $9 per hour for off time.

Recently the Copy-It Company's vice president, Hiram Shortsight, pointed out that the company's costs came to $10 for each and every hour that the firm was open for business, yet the billing rate on two thirds of this time was only $9 per hour. He proposed making the billing rate $18 for all hours, day and night. This was done. Night business fell off by two thirds, from an average 15 hours per night to only 5 hours per night. Daily revenue declined by $45 (why?).[1] The company management was very upset, so they call Frank Debitcredit, your accounting partner, to tell them what they did wrong.

"First of all," Debitcredit says, "your copier time is a joint product. It is made, minute by minute, by all those expenditures which are necessary in order to run the copier 24 hours per day. You cannot say that it costs $10 to run the copier between 2 and 3 A.M.; it costs $1,200 per week to run the copier one hour or 120 hours. Therefore it is foolish to try to price the time so that in some way an allocation of costs is covered and a profit is made. Either you make a profit every week, or you don't. There is no such thing as making a profit on one hour during the week and not on another."

"But," interrupted Shortsight, "how can we know what a good pricing policy is?"

"That isn't easy," Debitcredit replies, "your pricing policy must follow the market factors of supply and demand. When you raised prices on night work, your business fell off very sharply. That is because your customers decided they would rather do without some copying they had been getting, or they took their business to a copying service with lower prices and equivalent services. Prices are set by the market and not by costs. Since you had so much business under your original pricing policy, return to it, and make price changes only after some forethought in the future." After presenting his bill, he left.

Continuing a Joint Product

Now look at the Trash-It Company, which has the contract to collect garbage from a medium-size city. The company brings the garbage to its plant, separates out the recyclable items—cans, bottles, and

---

[1] [8 hrs. $\times$ $18/hr. + 15 hrs. $\times$ $9/hr.] − [8 hrs. $\times$ $18/hr. + 5 hr. $\times$ $18/hr.] = $45
  $279   − $234   = $45

paper—and uses the rest for land fill. Prices for processed waste are set strictly by the markets for the respective items. The present practice of the Trash-It Company is to assign the costs of its separation operation to cans, bottles, and paper by weight. Thus, in a recent month, collections and cost allocations were as shown in Figure 3–3.

FIGURE 3–3
Trash-It Cost Allocations

		Cans	Bottles	Paper
Pounds recovered		45,000 lbs.	75,000 lbs.	60,000 lbs.
Total costs	$ 36,000	(No Direct *product* costs at all)		
Allocation	(9,000)	$9,000		
	(15,000)		$15,000	
	(12,000)			$12,000
	$ 0			
Cost per pound		$0.20	$0.20	$0.20

Trash-It prepares product-line statements, and for that same month, the figures appeared as in Figure 3–4 (inventories are negligible).

FIGURE 3–4

TRASH-IT COMPANY
Product Line Profit Statement

	Total	Cans	Bottles	Paper
Sales	$ 42,000	$20,000	$ 8,000	$ 14,000
Less: Cost of sales	(36,000)	(9,000)	(15,000)	(12,000)
Profit (loss)	$ 6,000	$11,000	$ (7,000)	$ 2,000

After being fired by the Copy-It Company, Mr. Shortsight was employed by Trash-It. His review of the statement in Figure 3–4 caused him to propose that the company stop separating and selling bottles; that instead the bottles be buried in the land fill and no longer sold on the open market. "I am positive," he stated, "that this will save $7,000 per month, increasing our profit to $13,000 per month." There was not much discussion; the idea was approved and the men in the separation process were instructed to no longer take bottles out of the trash. The first month under this new system was similar to the month described above except that the $36,000 in costs were allocated only to cans and paper. The allocation was:

Cans—45,000 lbs.; costs of $15,429 assigned
Paper—60,000 lbs.; costs of $20,571 assigned

This allocation produced the condensed monthly profit and loss statement of Figure 3–5.

FIGURE 3–5

TRASH-IT COMPANY
Condensed Product Line Profit Statement

	Total	*Cans*	*Paper*
Sales	$ 34,000	$ 20,000	$ 14,000
Less: Cost of sales.	(36,000)	(15,429)	(20,571)
Profit (loss)	$ (2,000)	$ 4,571	$ (6,571)

Mr. Shortsight, upon being asked for an explanation of the $2,000 loss, points out that somehow now there is a loss on the paper operation which he attributes to "unforeseen factors." He proposes that the company stop separating paper and concentrate on cans only. Skeptical, the directors of Trash-It turn to Mr. Debitcredit for advice. His report: "Obviously the only effect of discontinuing bottle separation and sale was the loss of the $8,000 you received as a result. Your costs did not change at all. This leads me to believe that cans, bottles, and paper are all joint products which must be considered together. In the last month in which you separated and sold all three, you had a fine profit of $6,000. My advice is to resume bottle separation and continue paper separation."

"But," said Shortsight, "that doesn't explain the loss on bottles as reported in the financial statement for that month. . . . ?"

"I explain it this way," Debitcredit explains. "You made an arbitrary allocation of costs. Your cost allocation made it appear that bottle separation was unprofitable. I suggest that you allocate your costs in proportion to product contributions. That would assure that each joint product received a cost allocation less than the revenue it produced, which would assure that each joint product appears to be profitable—

which is consistent with my contention that the entire separation process is profitable."

Debitcredit produced, after a few moments, the computations of Figure 3–6 to support his argument.

FIGURE 3–6
TRASH-IT COMPANY
Properly Prepared Product Line Performance Statement

Percent of total sales due to cans: $20,000/$42,000 = 0.476 × 100 = 47.6%
Percent of total sales due to bottles: $8,000/$42,000 = 0.190 × 100 = 19.0%
Percent of total sales due to paper: $14,000/$42,000 = 0.334 × 100 = 33.4%

Costs to be allocated to product lines: $36,000 total.
  Cans . . . . $36,000 × 0.476 = $17,142
  Bottles . . . .   36,000 × 0.190 =   6,858
  Paper . . . .   36,000 × 0.334 = 12,000
      Total. $36,000

Profit margin on each product line:
  Cans:
    Sales $20,000
    Less allocated costs   17,142
                                                                   $ 2,858 $2,858

  Bottles:
    Sales . . . . $ 8,000
    Less allocated costs   6,858
                                                                   $ 1,142   1,142

  Paper:
    Sales $14,000
    Less allocated costs   12,000
                                                                   $ 2,000   2,000
      Total margin $6,000

Debitcredit also pointed out that there was not the slightest value for planning and control purposes to any figure in this calculation except the "total margin" which, he said, applied to the separation process *as a whole* and not to any of its components. "The separation process is a single responsibility center. It must be evaluated to show overall output's effect on Trash-It profits."

FURTHER PROCESSING OF PRODUCTS

Frequently a situation will arise in which there is an opportunity to further process one or more products in order to sell them at higher prices. The question that must be answered before such an opportunity is accepted is: Will the extra revenue or other benefit of the processing exceed the extra cost of such processing?

If the opportunity arises in a process in which there are no joint products, there is seldom any question what to do. The Soft-Sit Chair Company manufactures a metal lawn chair which is purchased unfinished by various retail stores who do the finishing themselves. The typical monthly operating statement of SoftSit looks like this:

Sales: 1,000 chairs @ $10 each.	$10,000
Less: Direct cost of sales @ $5 each.	5,000
Contribution margin	$ 5,000
Less: Monthly fixed manufacturing costs.	1,500
Selling and administrative costs	2,000
Income before taxes	$ 1,500

Soft-Sit is considering finishing the chairs itself. If it did so, there would be additional direct costs of $2 per chair and additional fixed manufacturing costs of $500 per month. The chairs could be sold for an additional $3 each. The proposal may be analyzed as follows:

Extra revenue: 1,000 chairs × $3 =		$3,000
Less: Additional direct costs		
1,000 chairs × $2 =	$2,000	
Additional fixed costs	500	2,500
Additional contribution margin		$ 500

Since the additional contribution margin is positive, the proposal should be adopted.

However, now consider a joint-product situation. The Soft-Sit Company is making two metal chairs. They are stamped out together from one piece of sheet metal by one machine. However, one chair requires about twice as much finishing work as the other. The costs of the whole operation are reported to management as they are shown in Figure 3-7.

The quantity of chair A which produced the costs in Figure 3-7 is sold for $65,000; the corresponding quantity of chair B, for $55,000. There is an overall profit of $65,000 + $55,000 − $75,000 − $35,000 = $10,000. The company is satisfied with this.

FIGURE 3–7
SOFT-SIT COMPANY
Product Profit Statement

	Metal Chair A	Metal Chair B
Total joint costs of stamping operation . . . . $ 50,000		
Allocated according to weight of chairs . . . . (35,000)	$35,000	
(15,000)		$15,000
Cost of finishing chairs (direct costs)	40,000	20,000
Total costs	$75,000	$35,000

However, the Hard-Sit Company comes to Soft-Sit and proposes to buy the unfinished chair A production, finish it, and sell them itself. The price offered is $30,000.

"No," argues the ubiquitous Mr. Shortsight, just breaking in at another management position after being terminated at the Trash-It Company. "The allocated cost at the stamping machine is $35,000. How can we possibly sell $35,000 of production for $30,000?"

By now you scarcely need Mr. Debitcredit as a helper; you recognize that these allocated costs are not necessarily valid as any basis for a decision. You develop the network diagram in Figure 3–8 showing the stamping operations and subsequent finishing operations.

FIGURE 3–8
Cost Analysis of Soft-Sit Company Sell-or-Process-Further Decision

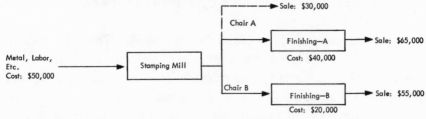

"The purpose of this diagram," you say, "is to make clear the real contribution of this decision's alternatives to Soft-Sit's overall profits. Let us disregard the stamping mill costs entirely, for they are necessary to produce either chair and we all know there is no way to allocate them to chair A and chair B that is useful in a decision. Instead, let us concentrate on the profitability of further processing. Note that at present, the finishing operation contributes to profits as follows:

Sales of chair A	$ 65,000
Cost of further processing	(40,000)
Contribution to profit	$ 25,000

"Now imagine that we accept the Hard-Sit proposal to sell them all our unfinished chair A production for $30,000. We still have the joint stamping mill costs; they are not affected by this decision. However, we fully and completely avoid all the $40,000 of finishing costs for chair A! In other words, the entire $30,000 is a contribution to profit. To me, then, it appears that the proper comparison and choice should be on this basis:

Contribution to profit of finishing chair A	$25,000
Contribution to profit of selling chair A to HardSit	30,000
Excess in favor of selling to HardSit	5,000"

Of course, Soft-Sit fired poor Mr. Shortsight and adopted your proposal as outlined above—to sell unfinished chair A to Hard-Sit. The principle that we employed here is, stated in more formal language, that—

A choice among alternatives is to be made to produce the greatest contribution to profit *regardless* of costs incurred prior to the point in processing at which the choice is to become effective.

We followed this principle by refusing to consider the joint stamping costs in our decision since that operation and its costs had to occur before there would be any unfinished chair A about which to make a decision.

AT WHAT LEVEL SHOULD JOINT PRODUCTION BE SET?

Frequently decisions regarding joint products are made more difficult because they are sold in quite different markets, in which prices move up and down in an unrelated fashion, producing uncertainty as to the best level of operation of the joint process. The analysis outlined here assumes that you know how prices in each market will change with volume changes in the total market, and that you know how your own costs will change as your level of production changes. Furthermore, your total volume is too small to affect any market price by itself.

Let us suppose there are two joint products, A and B, and that during the planning period A is expected to sell for $20 per unit while B is expected to sell for $30 per unit. The nature of the joint process is such that for each one unit of A produced, three units of B are produced. The production level decision will, of course, be so as to equalize marginal cost and marginal revenue at the level chosen (see Chapter 1 to review this rule). The available cost and revenue data are summarized as Figure 3–9. It is clear that *no allocation* of joint

FIGURE 3–9
Joint Production Level Data Summary

Joint Costs	Units A Produced	Units B Produced	Marginal Costs	Revenue from A and B	Marginal Revenue	Marginal Revenue Less Than Marginal Cost?	Profit
$10,000	100	300		$11,000			$ 1,000
			$ 9,000		$11,000	No	
19,000	200	600		22,000			3,000
			8,000		11,000	No	
27,000	300	900		33,000			6,000
			8,000		11,000	No	
35,000	400	1,200		44,000			9,000
			10,000		11,000	No	
45,000	500	1,500		55,000			10,000
			12,000		11,000	Yes	
57,000	600	1,800		66,000			9,000
			14,000		11,000	Yes	
71,000	700	2,100		77,000			6,000

costs to individual products is necessary in order to decide the proper level of production. In this case the proper level lies between 500A/1,500B and 600A/1,800B. As an exercise you should plot this data and determine the optimum level of production.

If a forecast of market conditions in the A market or the B market indicates a price change coming, the "Revenue from A and B" column can be refigured based on the new price, and a new level of production determined. You should be on notice that if marketing these two products becomes the responsibility of two separate marketing organizations (which is logical considering the unrelated natures of the two markets), these organizations will often disagree with each other as to whether production should be increased or decreased. It is possible that prices in one market would rise, as prices in the other market dropped, and that the net effect would be a production decrease. You can easily imagine the "stab in the back!" cry of the person in charge of marketing the product for which prices were rising.

WHEN COST ALLOCATION CAN'T BE AVOIDED

Occasionally managers will insist on some cost allocation to joint products, and certainly the requirements of financial accounting for an inventory valuation and income measurement will necessitate joint cost allocation. Such allocation is permissible *if the joint costs are allocated in proportion to the individual product total contribution margins.* We'll give you an illustration based on the SoftSit Company and its two chairs. Here, for convenience, is the contribution-margin information on these two chairs:

Chair A: Sales – Costs after stamping = Contribution margin
     $65,000 – $40,000 = $25,000
Chair B: Sales – Costs after stamping = Contribution margin
     $55,000 – $20,000 = $35,000
Total contribution margin = $25,000 + $35,000 = $60,000
Total joint costs = $50,000.
Joint costs allocable to chair A: $50,000 × (25,000/60,000) = $20,800
Joint costs allocable to chair B: $50,000 × (35,000/60,000) =   29,200
    Total allocated $50,000

What is the effect of these allocations? Let us show product-line profitability statements:

	Chair A	Chair B
Sales revenue	$ 65,000	$ 55,000
Less: Costs after stamping	(40,000)	(20,000)
Contribution margin before allocating joint costs.	$ 25,000	$ 35,000
Less: Allocated joint costs	(20,800)	(29,200)
Contribution margin after allocating joint costs.	$ 4,200	$ 5,800

If the decision is whether to process one or more joint products further or to sell them in an unfinished state, the key line in such a performance statement is still "Contribution margin *before* allocating joint costs." If the contribution margin is larger than the revenue which could be gained from sale unfinished, then the company should not sell the product unfinished.

If the decision is with respect to the process as a whole, then the key line is the final line, "Contribution margin *after* allocating joint costs." If the sum of figures in this row is positive, the joint process should be continued. If the sum is negative, the process should be discontinued. The individual column totals are useless in such a decision. These are general guides and do not take into account the possibility of not processing some product with negative contribution margin before allocating joint costs, improving process efficiency, or other options which may have to be considered before a broad decision to discontinue an entire process. Nor do we consider changing technology which may make it possible to replace one joint process with two or more nonjoint processes. If that change is a possibility, the apparent unprofitability of a joint product after fixed-cost allocation may be a signal to management to encourage development of nonjoint process technology.

SUMMARY

A decision model is a way of generating a selection among alternatives using whatever is known and is relevant about the decision and the environment. Decision models are useful for studying decision information requirements even when the model does not strictly conform to an actual decision process. Information useful in decisions will predict a benefit or cost for each change the decision would cause if implemented.

The major sources for information used in contribution analysis are the historical accounting system and its reports, the flexible budget, and external economic measurements and opinions. These sources produce *decision-relevant costs and revenues*.

Contribution analysis is a process of associating costs and revenues or cost savings with relevant alternatives of a decision. Only those costs, revenues, and cost savings which will occur as a direct result of an alternative's adoption should be associated with it. These are the same costs that will be avoided if the alternative is rejected. Normally, the alternative will be selected which has the largest contribution, so calculated, to profit.

Opportunities to apply contribution analysis occur in decisions to make or buy some required input; in decisions involving the foregoing of asset services already bought and paid for (sunk-cost analysis); joint product costing, pricing, and further processing; and setting production level.

When it is necessary to allocate joint costs over several products, it should be done so as to preserve the contribution margin relationships among joint products that exist before the allocation occurs.

BIBLIOGRAPHY

Books

Bower, Joseph L. *Managing the Resource Allocation Process*. Boston: Harvard Business School, 1970.

Horngren, Charles T. *Cost Accounting*. 3d ed. Englewood Cliffs, N.J.: Prentice-Hall, Inc., 1972.

Thomas, Arthur L. *The Allocation Problem in Financial Accounting Theory*, Studies in Accounting Research No. 3. Evanston, Ill.: American Accounting Association, 1969.

Articles

Brady, Daniel W. "The Strategic Forces of Profit," *Management Accounting*, February 1971.

Davidson, H. Justin, and Trueblood, Robert M. "Accounting for Decision-Making," *The Accounting Review*, October 1961.

Harris, Jr., William T. and Chapin, Wayne R. "Joint Product Costing," *Management Accounting*, April 1973.

Hobbs, III, William. "Contribution Reporting for Consumer Products," *Management Accounting*, November 1970.

Rawcliffe, George A. "Accounting Concepts for Managerial Decision Making," *Management Accounting*, April 1972.

Solomons, David. "Flexible Budgets and the Analysis of Overhead Variances," *Management International*, 1961–1. Reprinted in *Contemporary Issues in Cost Accounting*, (eds. Hector Anton and Peter Firmin) 2d ed. New York: Houghton Mifflin Co., 1972.

4

Preparing Information
Reports for Management

ACCOUNTING information measures activity and analyses decisions. A planned activity may be considered from many points of view. Each will be the subject of an appropriate accounting analysis which can be prepared and used, as you saw in the last chapter, to help you judge whether the activity should be pursued. There is also a unique accounting representation which will be most useful in *controlling* an activity once it begins to occur. Accounting is essential to control of activities.

To many executives, "control" has the connotation of restrictions on managerial discretion. To you, "control" should mean *full information*. Restrictions and restraints are necessary in any operation, but they have little to do with control. Control exists when a manager is fully informed about the probable consequences of each alternative he is contemplating.

In this chapter you learn to plan for an operating period by using the budgeting process and standard costs as a study whose purpose is to *remove uncertainty* about the future operating period; to relate in dollar-and-cents terms what will be expected of you if you elect given alternatives.

In particular, we show how flexible budgeting, standard costs, and dynamic analysis give a basis for evaluating performance that is superior to the fixed-budget concept. We show how to establish sensible fixed-cost levels through planning and how to report performance through variances from a flexible budget. Finally, we discuss effects that accounting and budgeting information may have on the attitudes and behavior of individuals and organizations.

FLEXIBLE BUDGETING AND PLANNING

Questions to Ask

The Gowingplaces Company budget of Chapter 2, Appendix 2A showed only the *results* of the budgeting process, based on specific policies for business activity during the coming operating period. Managers ask these questions about budgets:

1. How do policies translate into a budget?
2. What if these policies are changed?

"How do . . . ." You saw how a sales forecast led to manufacturing and purchase budgets. The dollar amounts in these budgets were based on quantities of physical resources, production distribution and sales technology, and prices for each unit of input. The "standard cost" of each unit of product A was built up as in Figure 4–1. Standard

FIGURE 4–1
Standard Cost of Product A

1. Six units material X @ $5 each	$30
2. Ten hours type I direct labor @ $3 each	30
3. Variable overhead $1 per hour X 10 hours	10
Total Variable Standard Cost.	$70

costs per unit were used to prepare manufacturing, purchase, and other budgets. The process then was for tentative operating policies to be translated into costs and revenues per unit activity or per time period, then combined to produce projected operating statements for the budget period.

"What if . . . ." Unsatisfactory projected operating statements imply the need for revision of underlying policies. Imagine that Schedule CGS–2 on page 47 is examined by an executive who says, "I doubt

that we can sell 1,000 units of A each quarter in the southern region. If we sell 500 units of A each quarter there, how does our contribution on A look then?"

The quick way to see the answer is to recall that in the southern region the price of A, by quarters, is scheduled to be: $90, $90, $100, and $100. The contribution margin by quarters will be:

(1)	(2)	(3)	(4)	(quarter)
90	90	100	100	(unit price)
–70	–70	–70	–70	(unit cost ex-cluding fixed overhead)
$ 20	$ 20	$ 30	$ 30	
× 500	× 500	× 500	× 500	(volume per quarter)
$10,000	$10,000	$15,000	$15,000	(contribution margin in southern region from A)

We must add these figures to the contribution margin on A in the northern region:

$30,000	$60,000	$80,000	$66,000	(contribution margin in northern region from A)
$40,000	$70,000	$95,000	$81,000	(Total contri-bution margin from A)

The bottom line of figures compares directly with the "gross margin—A" line from Table 2A–12. Our executive can decide whether the differences are substantive.

FLEXIBLE BUDGETING AND CONTROL

Operations actually occur, and sure enough actual sales of A in the southern region are only 500 units per quarter. Here are the rules you must follow:

1. Revise all pertinent budget schedules (sales forecast, sales budget, cost of goods manufactured, etc.) to reflect the actual level of sales. All parties who participated in making the original budget should accept the changes in their budgets necessitated by the actual sales level.

2. Judge the performance of all responsibility centers strictly on the new budget schedules.

If actual sales were 500 instead of 1,000 units of A in the southern region, it is unrealistic to judge southern region sales performance based on the 1,000-unit forecast. The comparison of actual sales with the 1,000-unit budget will be unfavorable and unfair. If production is cut back, lower production rates will make the total direct cost variances from the original budget favorable. The basis for control, which is comparison of reasonable expectations with actual events, will be destroyed unless all performance variances are computed from the standard inputs or costs for the actual levels of outputs.

Sales Variances

A performance report for the southern region should stress failure of this region to sell as many units of A as it agreed to sell in the operating budget. The contribution per unit of A multiplied by the difference between budgeted and actual sales will give the contribution margin lost to the company because of failure to achieve sales goals. Unless there are obvious justifications for the variance (such as unexpected change in economic conditions, market oversupply, etc.), the budgeting and selling processes should both be examined with an eye to producing future budgets and performance that are more in agreement with each other.

In this case, the sales variance for product A, southern region, would be:

Quarter 1: $(1,000 - 500) \times (\$90 - 70) = \$10,000$ unfavorable
Quarter 2: $(1,000 - 500) \times (\ 90 - 70) = \ \ 10,000$ unfavorable
Quarter 3: $(1,000 - 500) \times (100 - 70) = \ \ 15,000$ unfavorable
Quarter 4: $(1,000 - 500) \times (100 - 70) = \ \ 15,000$ unfavorable

Recomputing an Expense Budget

In the Gowingplaces Company, selling costs are computed by region and include fixed costs and costs which are a function of the number of units sold and selling price of each product. A formula which summarizes the southern region sales budget is:

$$\begin{aligned}
\text{Total selling} \\
\text{costs—southern} \\
\text{region}
\end{aligned} = \begin{aligned}
\text{Fixed selling costs,} \\
\text{southern region}
\end{aligned}$$

$$+ \left[\begin{array}{cc}
\text{Total unit sales} & \text{Unit price} \\
\text{southern region} \times & \text{southern region} \\
\text{product A} & \text{product A}
\end{array}\right.$$

$$\left.\begin{array}{cc}
\text{Total unit sales} & \text{Unit price} \\
+ \text{ southern region} \times & \text{southern region} \\
\text{product B} & \text{product B}
\end{array}\right]$$

$$\times \left[\begin{array}{l}
\text{Southern region} \\
\text{direct selling} \\
\text{costs per sales} \\
\text{dollar}
\end{array}\right] \quad (4\text{–}1)$$

Formulas of this sort are called *formula budgets.* This formula (4–1) can be used to create a new standard of comparison for the southern region sales office based on its actual sales of A and B.

Performance Analysis

Table 2A–2 in Appendix 2A to Chapter 2 includes the sales budget for the southern region. Under the original sales forecasts, this budget would have appeared as in Figure 4–2.

FIGURE 4–2
Sales Budget for Southern Region

	Quarter 1	*Quarter 2*	*Quarter 3*	*Quarter 4*
Unit sales:				
A	1,000	1,000	1,000	1,000
B	1,500	1,200	1,200	1,600
Sales dollars:				
A	$ 90,000	$ 90,000	$100,000	$100,000
B	300,000	240,000	240,000	320,000
Total	$390,000	$330,000	$340,000	$420,000
Direct selling expenses:				
$0.02 per sales dollar	$ 7,800	$ 6,600	$ 6,800	$ 8,400
Fixed selling expenses	15,000	15,000	15,000	15,000
Total	$ 22,800	$ 21,600	$ 21,800	$ 23,400

As soon as the actual sales were known, this sales budget would be revised, using equation (4–1) and information in Appendix 2A to Chapter 2. The revised sales budget appears as Figure 4–3.

FIGURE 4–3
Revised Sales Budget for Southern Region

	Quarter 1	*Quarter 2*	*Quarter 3*	*Quarter 4*
Unit sales:				
A	500	500	500	500
B	1,500	1,200	1,200	1,600
Sales dollars:				
A	$ 45,000	$ 45,000	$ 50,000	$ 50,000
B	300,000	240,000	240,000	320,000
Total	$345,000	$285,000	$290,000	$370,000
Direct selling expenses:				
$0.02 per sales dollar	$ 6,900	$ 5,700	$ 5,800	$ 7,400
Fixed selling expenses	15,000	15,000	15,000	15,000
Total	$ 21,900	$ 20,700	$ 20,800	$ 22,400

It is Figure 4–3 that would be used for performance evaluation in the southern region. To see how, imagine that the first quarter of operations has occurred. The actual performance was: 500 units of A sold at $90, 1,500 units of B sold at $200, direct selling expenses of $7,200, and fixed selling expenses of $15,500. These facts are compared with the performance standards of Figure 4–3 as Figure 4–4.

Other formulas, such as (4–2) and (4–3) below may be used to calculate expected performance based on actual levels of activity in the firm:

$$\begin{matrix} \text{Total manu-} \\ \text{facturing} \\ \text{costs} \end{matrix} = \begin{matrix} \text{Fixed manu-} \\ \text{facturing} \\ \text{costs} \end{matrix} + \begin{matrix} \text{Direct costs} \\ \text{of making A} \end{matrix}$$

$$\begin{matrix} + \text{ Direct costs} \\ \text{of making B} \\ + \text{ Indirect variable} \\ \text{labor costs} \\ + \text{ Indirect variable} \\ \text{materials costs} \end{matrix} \qquad (4\text{–}2)$$

$$\begin{matrix} \text{Profit} \\ \text{(direct} \\ \text{costing} \\ \text{basis)} \end{matrix} = \text{Sales revenue} - \begin{matrix} \text{Total} \\ \text{variable} \\ \text{costs} \end{matrix} - \begin{matrix} \text{Total} \\ \text{fixed} \\ \text{costs} \end{matrix} \qquad (4\text{–}3)$$

FIGURE 4–4
Southern Region Sales Performance Report

Category	Budget	Actual	Variance	Remarks
Unit sales:				
A	1,000	500	500 units **unfavorable** $10,000 contribution loss	Note 1
B	1,500	1,500	0	
Selling price:				
A	$ 90	$ 90		
B	200	200		
Sales revenue (for computing direct selling expenses)	345,000			
Direct selling expenses	6,900	7,200	$300 **unfavorable**	Note 2
Fixed selling expenses	15,000	15,500	$500 **unfavorable**	Note 3

Note 1: Unexpectedly large imports of Tasmanian A apparently reduced unit sales; this level of sales was maintained without price reductions.
Note 2: Extra costs represent expense of revising sales presentations to stress advantages of our A over Tasmanian A.
Note 3: Cold weather and higher utilities expenses for first quarter.

The detail of these formulas prevents their illustration here, but be assured that in a practical administrative setting they would be regularly used (computers would accelerate calculations) for appraising the profit and cost effects of changes involving markets, technology, and activity levels; and to compute standards of comparison for operations control.

PRESENTING AND EXPLAINING BUDGET VARIANCES

Budget variances should be part of regular performance reports. Let us take an example of simple variances. Figure 4–5 is the second quarter administrative performance report with budget figures in the first column, actual performance figures in the second column, and the variances in the third column. These administrative costs, although all "fixed" in the sense that they don't vary with production, do vary with administrative events such as unexpected salary changes, equipment rental changes, or addition of new continuing operations.

FIGURE 4–5

GOWINGPLACES COMPANY
Administrative Performance Report
April, May, June, 1974

Expense Category	Budget	Actual	Variance Favorable (Unfavorable)	Remarks
Accounting:				
Professional salaries.	$ 22,000	$ 22,000	$ 0	. . .
Assistants' salaries	11,000	11,800	(800)	Note 1
Equipment rental.	9,000	8,800	200	Note 2
Supplies	4,000	4,100	(100)	Note 0
Total.	$ 46,000	$ 46,700	$(700)	
Security:				
Guard salaries	$ 1,500	$ 1,000	$ 500	Note 3
Other expenses	3,000	2,800	200	Note 0
Total.	$ 4,500	$ 3,800	$ 700	
Staff:				
Executive salaries.	$ 25,000	$ 25,000		
Secretarial salaries	5,000	5,250	$(250)	Note 4
Professional salaries.	10,000	10,000		
Supplies	2,000	2,500	(500)	Note 5
Other expenses	2,000	1,700	300	Note 0
Total.	$ 44,000	$ 44,450	$(450)	
Other expenses:				
Depreciation—offices.	$ 6,000	$ 6,000	0	
Various amortizations	5,000	5,000	0	
Total.	$ 11,000	$ 11,000	$ 0	
Total administrative	$105,500	$105,950	$(450)	

Note 0: Variance is insignificant.

Note 1: New assistant authorized for controller to serve as deputy budget coordinator. Hired 5-1-74 effective 6-1-74 @ monthly salary of $800 per month.

Note 2: Rental on tape drive units lowered by lessor to reflect competitive conditions in this market. Effective 5-1-74 rental will be lower by $100 per month on all units leased from this company. Lessor will give 30 days' notice before posting higher rates.

Note 3: Guard quit at end of May and has not yet been replaced.

Note 4: All staff secretaries given 5 percent salary increase in first quarter; budget figure has not yet been changed to reflect the increase.

Note 5: No reason known why supplies expense should increase.

No doubt there will be an investigation to determine why supplies expense for the staff have increased. You may have already thought that the budget figure for staff secretarial salaries should have been revised so as not to show this variance.

This performance report would in practice be a summary of reports going to each of the four responsibility centers shown in the report. Each responsibility center would learn in detail from its report how

its operations compared with the current budget standards for its operations. The administrative supervisor—perhaps a vice president for administration—would receive the overall report of Figure 4–5.

PLANNING FIXED COSTS

Let us imagine that Gowingplaces Company is currently operating
at nearly its full total capacity, and accordingly is planning to expand
its plant (increasing its fixed costs). At the present time plant profitability and capacity are both related to total direct labor hours which can
be worked per period. For the year 1974, budgeted direct labor hours
add up to 90,000 + 268,200 = *358,200*. The contribution to fixed costs
and profits resulting from this many labor hours is $1,192,500. Thus
the profit per direct labor hour is

$$\frac{\$1,192,500}{358,200} = \$3.33$$

The expansion contemplated will add capacity to work an additional
1,000,000 direct labor hours. Administrative costs remain at the present
level, but fixed manufacturing and selling costs will increase approximately in proportion to the capacity increase itself—from $325,000
to $1,200,000; an increment of $875,000. However, sales *volume* will
not at first require the total capacity. In fact, in the first year after
the plant is expanded, only 200,000 direct labor hours above present
capacity will be worked—only 20 percent of the new capacity will be
used. In the second year of use, 30 percent will be used; and in the
third year, 40 percent. A profitability analysis will appear thus:

Year	New Capacity Used	Contribution Generated	− Additional Fixed Costs	= New Plant Addition to Profits
1975	200,000	$ 666,000	$(875,000)	$(209,000)
1976	300,000	999,000	(875,000)	124,000
1977	400,000	1,332,000	(875,000)	457,000

The expansion will not contribute to profits until its second year of
operation. Further, the first year loss is big enough to knock 50 percent
off the current level of profits.

This is a phenomenon known as *semifixed costs* which you can anticipate using contribution analysis. A cost-volume-profit chart for the company as shown in Figure 4–6 indicates that semifixed costs are those

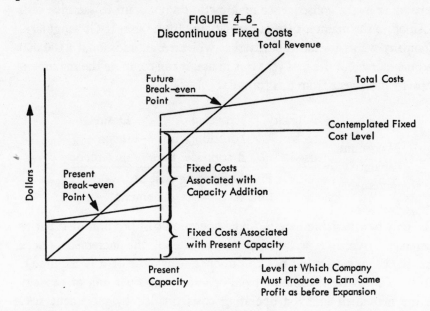

FIGURE 4–6
Discontinuous Fixed Costs

related to a change in capacity. Since capacity changes in relatively
large increments, corresponding fixed (capacity) costs will rise in corresponding large jumps.

The Gowingplaces Company will have to use about 26 percent of
its new capacity if it is to be profitable from the beginning, which
is computed using (4–4) and (4–5).

$$\frac{\text{Break-even}}{\text{capacity}} = \frac{\text{Fixed costs associ-}}{\text{Profit contribution per}} = \frac{\$875,000}{\$3.33}$$
$$\text{increment} \qquad \text{unit of capacity used}$$
$$= 263,000 \ hours \ (break\text{-}even \ point) \quad (4\text{-}4)$$

$$\frac{\text{Break-even percentage}}{\text{of new capacity}} = \frac{\text{Break-even capacity}}{\text{Size of planned}}$$
$$\text{addition}$$

$$= \frac{263,000}{1,000,000} = 26 \ percent \quad (4\text{-}5)$$

A Business Pitfall

The capacity increment decision is a critical one to businesses which, expanding as the consequence of growth, do not want to sacrifice cash position to the maintenance of capacity for future use. If Gowingplaces Company wants to add capacity that will earn an additional $100,000 income increment the first year it is in use, it can compute the maximum capacity increment from this formula:

$$
\text{Maximum capacity increment} = \frac{\begin{matrix}\text{Capacity} & \text{Expected} & \text{Desired} \\ \text{to be} & \times\ \text{contribution} & -\ \text{income} \\ \text{used} & \text{margin per unit} & \text{increment}\end{matrix}}{\begin{matrix}\text{Fixed operating cost per} \\ \text{unit of capacity increment}\end{matrix}} \quad (4\text{--}6)
$$

The only new variable here is "fixed operating cost per unit of capacity increment" which is a function of the size of the increment (since capacity usually costs less per unit to operate as more of it is acquired). To simplify matters, compute fixed operating costs per unit of capacity as the increment in fixed operating costs divided by increment size.

$$
\frac{\$875,000}{1,000,000\ \text{hours}} = \$0.875\ per\ hour
$$

Computation with $(4\text{--}6)$ now gives

$$
\text{Maximum capacity increment} = \frac{\begin{matrix}200,000\ \text{hours to be} \\ \text{used in first year}\end{matrix} \times \$3.33 \begin{matrix}\text{Expected} \\ \text{margin}\end{matrix} - \$100,000}{\$0.875\ \text{per hour operating costs per year}}
$$

$= 646,857\ hours.$ No more capacity than this should be added at once if 200,000 hours will be used the first year and Gowingplaces Company insists on a $100,000 income increment from the addition.

Reduce Capacity, Increase Income

The same phenomenon—semifixed costs—also works in reverse. Suppose a firm is operating below or slightly above its break-even point.

If operating costs are semifixed, it may be possible to reduce them by reducing capacity and earn considerably more profit. That is why one of the first things a new management may do after taking over a troubled firm is try to reduce fixed costs.

BEHAVIORAL DIMENSION OF ACCOUNTING REPORTS

Many persons believe that accounting derives its real significance *not* from the accuracy of its descriptions of historical events but from the influence that accounting reports can have on the behavior of individuals. Here are examples of such influence:

—Ben Howe, noting that the Soft-Sit Chair Company has increased its earnings in each of the last three years, invests his life savings in the common stock of this company.

—Ronald Bennett, foreman of the day shift in the stamping division of Soft-Sit Chair Company, is staying up late tonight working on a new equipment layout he believes will increase the stamping rate and enable him to comfortably exceed the "standard" stamping rate for the first time this month.

—Gloria Smith, secretary for Howard H. Soft-Sit, president of the chair company bearing his name, is doing a slow burn at her typewriter because the monthly performance report shows poor performance on the part of the three billing clerks under her supervision. As a result, she has made mistakes in each of the four letters she has managed to type since the report came out.

—Edward Slansky, TV repairman, has just run his repair truck up a telephone pole. He was exceeding the speed limit and had to swerve to avoid a child on a bicycle. At the time he was thinking of the lecture the shop boss gave him about completing too few service calls per day. The shop boss was referring during the lecture to an accounting performance report.

In each case an accounting report refers to historical events in such a way as to connote approval or disapproval of them to the readers. These persons feel that their satisfaction is affected by their reaction (or the reaction of other persons) to the report. You should be able to identify these elements in each example above. Figure 4–7 gives a diagram to help you do this.

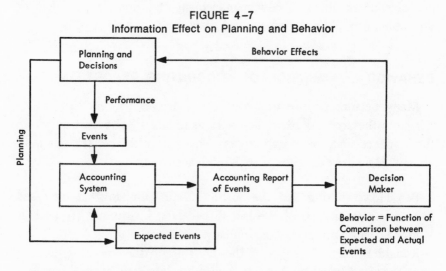

FIGURE 4–7
Information Effect on Planning and Behavior

Most modern organizations utilize collective decision processes. Figure 4–7 also applies when the "decision maker" is more than one person. Study of the response of decision makers, individual and collective, to reports of their performance which imply or permit an evaluation of that performance by comparing it with a previously stated standard, is called the "behavioral dimension" of accounting. Anyone dealing with accounting information should be aware of this behavioral dimension.

The Pressure Model

There are many models describing individual and collective behavior. All of them possess some validity. Here we select one which is suitable for explaining responses to control efforts applied through performance reports. It assumes that individual behavior is motivated by a desire to keep "pressure" below a long-term bearable level. If you want to know what "pressure" is, you can regard it as the strain and anxiety you feel as you prepare for a difficult examination on which you must do very well in order to obtain a grade you want in a course. No one likes that feeling. While you will accept high levels of pressure for a short time, if the pressure is maintained you will find a way to reduce it.

Individuals become members of various organizations in order to reduce pressure. You join a business organization to reduce the pressure of finding food, clothing, and shelter. You join social organizations to reduce the pressure of needing human association and companionship. Once a member of an organization, additional pressures may arise through the organization. Specifically, standards of performance may be set with the implication that nonconformance with such standards may result in ostracism, punishment, or even severance from the organization. These standards may be the result of economic necessity—pressure for those most responsible for the organization's survival and continued ability to satisfy the needs of its members.

Natty Bumppo[1] is an executive in the middle ranks of the Midwest Resources Company, which he joined after pathfinding his way across the country from the East Coast (no charge for this kind of pun). He is pleased with his position. One of his sources of security is that his function in Midwest Resources is defined as bargaining for 1,000 animal hides per month from the dozens of trappers who range the midcontinent countryside. These hides must be secured for an average price of $1 each. Mr. Bumppo takes pride in knowledge that he secures these hides for, on the average, only $0.90 each. This $0.10 per hide saving makes Mr. Bumppo feel that he is contributing significantly to Midwest Resources, Inc., and enables him to deal with the challenges of his job without experiencing unbearable pressure.

One day, however, a new president arrives at Midwest; and after studying the situation, announces, "Our agents must deliver hides to us at lower prices. The trappers are getting rich from our generosity and this must stop. Hereafter the standard price for hides is $0.70."

Mr. Bumppo is dismayed. He has never offered a trapper such a low price. If this is indeed the price Midwest Resources expects him to pay, it leaves him no room at all for the comfortable, pressure-reducing favorable variance to which he is accustomed.

Sure enough, after two months of operation under the new standard, Mr. Bumppo's average price per hide paid is $0.85, all the trappers

---

[1] American literature buffs will recognize the protagonist of J. F. Cooper's *Leatherstocking Tales.*

are angry at him, and he is reporting a $0.15 per hide unfavorable variance. He is angry and frustrated. At first he did try very hard to obtain the new price. He felt as if he had failed the company when his best efforts did not get it. He has visited the company headquarters in Pittsburg, talked with other agents, and discovered that none of them are getting the new standard price. This made him feel better, for if he has failed, he at least is not alone.

After two more months with the new standard, the average price per hide is still $0.85 and the company management is threatening him with punishment if he does not come closer to the standard. Mr. Bumppo hates his job and hates Midwest Resources, Inc.

On his next visit to headquarters, he finds the other agents share his feelings, and over beverages in a Pittsburg tavern, they reach an agreement: among themselves they will honor the old $1 standard. They know Midwest cannot fire them all. They feel that joint action might prevent the company from moving against any of them. They agree to write each other periodically and tell each other how the hide market is in their territories.

Over the next few months, Mr. Bumppo actually pays as much as $1.10 for hides. He no longer feels that the company merits his effort or contribution; instead, he feels his loyalty is to his fellow agents, and he wants to make sure that he does not pay a lower price than they are paying. When the new president, an ex-writer named J. F. Cooper, personally inquires why the prices paid for hides cannot be reduced, Mr. Bumppo replies, "Market conditions. There are not enough deerslayers in the territory and the scarcity of hides has driven up the price." And feeling like the last of the Mohicans, but no longer under the unbearable pressure of the lower price standard, Mr. Bumppo continues to serve as Midwest's agent.

The Example Interpreted. This example illustrates some important responses of individuals to pressure. The pressure was kept to a manageable level when performance was in a controllable relationship to the standard. In the example, this was the comfortable and maintainable margin of the 90-cent price paid to the $1 standard.

Pressure rose to a level unbearable in the long run when the standard was changed. When unbearable pressure is present, something will be done to reduce it. In the example, two things happened:

1. Bumppo and the other agents turned to an *informal organization.* The purpose of this informal organization was to provide substitute goals for those of the formal organization (Midwest Resources) which were causing the pressure. These substitute goals actually were the nonachievement of the formal goals. The substitute goals had to be achieved since the goal of the very low price was impossible to reach anyway.
2. The informal organization set up its own *informal information system.* This information system reported on progress toward the goals of the information organization. The information system of the formal organization, which reported on achievement of the formal organizations goal of the unreasonably low price paid per hide, was increasingly disregarded.

When the informal organization was successful in achieving its initial goals, it developed additional, noneconomic, self-serving goals—its own survival, for one; and protection of all the agents even if Midwest Resources was damaged by the high prices paid for hides. We add this dimension to the illustration to make sure you understand that informal organizations need not be virtuous, altruistic, or even particularly wise—any more than are the formal organizations they counter.

Of course, informal organizations nearly always exist in a business entity. When pressure is generally at tolerable levels, an informal organization will be weak because there is no need for it. It is only when pressure rises that the informal organization becomes strong.

Informal information systems will also exist. They carry rumor, speculation, and much of value that cannot be included in the accounting reports, personnel records, and other components of an organization's formal information system. Informal information systems are dangerous to a business entity primarily when they serve the purposes of strong informal organizations formed to resist pressure.

A General Model

The reader may ask, "Can we change goals and performance standards without arousing the informal organization?" Much can be done if those whose performance will be judged participate in the standard-setting process. This point was made in Chapter 2 and bears repeating here. However, there is a point beyond which such participation will not produce agreement on a proposed standard, and that is the point at which one expects that the proposed standard will not allow one to receive a pressure-reducing evaluation of performance. In other words, if Mr. Bumppo must have at least a $0.05 favorable price paid per hide variance in order to maintain a tolerable level of pressure, and if he can produce such a variance when the standard is lowered to $0.90 per hide, then he will (or should) cooperate with such a change. But since he cannot obtain such a variance when the standard is lower, no amount of participation will cause him to agree to further reductions of the standard below $0.90.

Additionally, persons can withstand more pressure for short periods of time than is possible over the long run. Mr. Bumppo might have agreed to a standard of $0.70 for, say, three months, and would have conscientiously tried to achieve it. But such a prospect becomes unacceptable when proposed on an indefinite basis.

Finally, as the informal organization relieves pressure, one's productivity in the formal organization decreases. Figure 4–8 summarizes this model.

Point 1 on Figure 4–8 shows where pressure begins to rise as productivity is increased by raising the standard of performance—the point at which productivity is no longer increasable without a rise in pressure. At point 2, pressure becomes unbearable and the informal organization appears, followed by a reduction of pressure. (Such a reduction may not always occur; there may be such active conflict between formal and informal organizations that pressure is increased. It is really the *expectation* that pressure will be reduced that leads to the formation of the informal organization and its survival.)

The effects described here may be conditionally reversible if a business takes steps to reduce pressure through the formal organization. This may occur by incorporating all or part of the informal organization into the formal organization. An example would be recognition of a union and deduction of union dues from paychecks. The union actually becomes part of the company; it has been "institutionalized." If a business removes whatever caused the pressure initially, the informal organization may no longer be powerful. This will occur if

FIGURE 4–8
Productivity and Pressure as Functions of Performance Standard

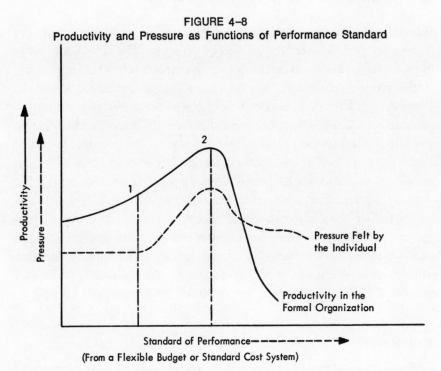

Standard of Performance————————➤
(From a Flexible Budget or Standard Cost System)

employees believe there is no further need to seek the informal organization's protection. On the other hand, the informal organization
may, in order to survive, provoke pressure against its members to stimulate their loyalty and support.

In some organizations the threshold of hostile response to attempts
to increase productivity by increasing standards is very low. No one
is quite sure why this is true. Sometimes, the point of resistance to
such moves can be changed significantly through incentives offered by
a skillful management. Motivation of salesmen is intended to increase
their efforts and result in higher sales, which may be accompanied by
an increased standard. Retraining employees may increase their productivity. Increasing fringe benefits or wages may make employees willing
to perform consistently at levels which they otherwise would resist
vigorously.

When to Change Expectations. Organizations should seek ways
to increase productivity and therefore strengthen their right to exist

economically. In some instances, manipulation of standards may prove to be a temporarily effective method of doing so. The accountant, however, regards standards as objective descriptors of what is possible under given conditions. While he agrees that accounting is important because it influences behavior, he objects to the literal destruction of standards to achieve temporary productivity or behavior changes, especially when distortion of standards holds peril and potential for harm to the organization. The accountant argues that accounting should influence behavior through its comparisons of what is *possible* with what actually *occurs*. The accountant protects the standards from change motivated by the desire to provide cheap incentives for increased productive activity. Only when productivity increases are possible through positive motivation, retraining, upgrading capital equipment, learning effects, wage incentives, working condition changes, and the like may standards reflecting expected performance be legitimately revised.

SUMMARY

Flexible budgeting permits quick recomputation of the operating budget to fit the most valid assumptions or recently adopted business policies, even when these are different from the ones existing when the budget was first computed. Flexible budgeting requires knowledge of fixed and variable costs, as well as semifixed costs—costs which are fixed over some range of activity, then rise or fall to a new level abruptly when activity leaves this range. Use of flexible budgeting permits managers to anticipate the consequences for profits of adding or reducing capacity to produce and sell.

Performance reporting requires comparison of budget with actual operating figures. The resulting variances, if any, must be classified as "not significant" or "significant;" and if the latter, they must be explained. If the variance will tend to be a repeating one, either the budget for future periods should be modified to reflect it (uncontrollable variance or favorable controllable variance) or the cause of the variance removed (unfavorable controllable variance).

Operating control depends on management knowledge of what is happening in the business, why it is happening, and how to secure cooperation to change unsatisfactory situations. Performance reporting provides this management knowledge, and can influence responsible persons to work for the benefit of the organization.

BIBLIOGRAPHY

Books

Caplan, Edwin H. *Management Accounting and the Behavioral Sciences.* Reading, Mass.: Addison-Wesley Publishing Co., Inc., 1971.

Joplin, Bruce, and Pattillo, James W. *Effective Accounting Reports.* Englewood Cliffs, N.J.: Prentice-Hall, Inc., 1969.

Lev, Baruch. *Accounting and Information Theory,* Studies in Accounting Research No. 2. Evanston, Ill.: American Accounting Association, 1969.

Articles

Chambers, R. J. "The Role of Information Systems in Decision Making," *Management Technology,* June 1964.

Dyckman, T. R. "The Investigation of Cost Variances," *The Journal of Accounting Research,* Autumn 1969.

Figler, Homer R. "Goal-Setting Techniques," *Management Accounting,* November 1971.

Fremgen, James M. "Transfer Pricing and Management Goals," *Management Accounting,* December 1970.

Horngren, Charles T. "Motivation and Coordination in Management Control Systems," *Management Accounting,* May 1967.

Kirby, Fred M. "Variance Analysis—the 'Step-Through' Method," *Management Services,* March–April 1970.

Krueger, Donald A., and Kohlmeier, John M. "Financial Modeling and 'What if' Budgeting," *Management Accounting,* May 1972.

Malcom, Robert E. "Sales Variances—A Further Look," *Management Adviser,* March –April 1971.

Ridgway, V. F. "Dysfunctional Consequences of Performance Measurements," *Administrative Science Quarterly,* September 1956.

5

Planning Capital
Investments

In Chapter 2, we showed the form of the "capital" budget (Table 2A–14, page 50)   and indicated that decisions to acquire long-lived assets are handled in a unique way. In this chapter you look closely at the process of selecting long-lived assets for acquisition. You identify important variables affecting such decisions, and learn simple procedures for capital asset decision making.

Capital asset acquisition decisions must be considered apart from other purchasing decisions because a business keeps and uses capital assets over an extended period of time—5, 10, or even more years. Capital assets cost a great deal of money, which often is borrowed and repaid out of future revenues. Capital assets are intended to help produce revenues to cover their own cost and operating expenses, plus an excess which shows up as accounting profit. If the wrong assets are acquired, a firm's earning power is crippled for many operating periods. If the proper assets are acquired, the firm is in an advantageous operating and profit-making position.

Typical capital expenditures might include:

Efficiency improvements in a manufacturing plant or distribution network.
An extended research program.
Entirely new manufacturing or distribution facilities.

Some persons argue that all expenditures are capital expenditures since they contribute to shaping the firm's future ability to compete. Thus, manpower training programs, customer service programs, advertising programs, and environmental control programs are all capital expenditures. You may decide for yourself how far to extend the capital expenditure designation; we shall consider a method of analysis which applies to *any* acquisition you wish to regard as "capital" in nature.

The basis of this method, called the "present value" method, is a comparison of *net cash inflows* resulting from operating a long-lived asset with the *current cash outlay* to acquire the asset.

THE TIME VALUE OF MONEY

The principle behind the time value of money is: *A dollar received now is more desirable than a dollar received at any future date.* As an obvious illustration, consider your savings account, which is an agreement with a financial institution under which you pay the institution $X now, and the institution will pay you $X+ at a future date— the amount of the "+" depending on the interest rate and the precise future date. The "+" is called *interest* and is intended to be your compensation for foregoing use and enjoyment of your money.

Similarly, if you have the opportunity to receive a $10 payment today or a $10 payment one year hence, you will surely choose the immediate payment. But if your choice is between $10 today and $12 one year hence, you will have to stop and decide if the additional $2 compensates you for not having the use of $10 for one year. (You would *not* have hesitated if your choice were between $10 now and $8 a year from now!)

Determination of Investor's Target Rate of Return

When you consider capital investments, you expect to receive more cash receipts in the future than the present cash cost of the investment. This excess may be attributed to the *investor's target rate of return* (abbreviated ITRR). The ITRR is critical to successful evaluation of proposed capital expenditures. Four factors determine ITRR:

1. Basic profit obtainable.
2. Adjustment for inflation.
3. Rate of growth or expansion desired.
4. Compensation for risk desired.

Basic Profit. There is a basic minimum return which anyone can obtain as a compensation for letting others use and benefit from his money or capital. It is not high; probably 2 or 3 percent per year and possibly less.

Adjustment for Inflation. Inflation is an increase in the number of currency units equivalent to a representative collection of marketplace commodities—in other words, a general increase in the price level.[1] It is caused by a money supply which increases faster than the number of things available on which to spend money. The annual inflation rate in the United States has fluctuated since World War II from almost nothing in the 1950s and early 1960s to 6 and 7 percent in the late 1960s and early 1970s. Economists disagree over how much inflation our economy can tolerate. Some economists feel that modest amounts of inflation are harmless; in fact, essential to stimulate growth and investment. Others feel that even slight inflation distorts resource allocation processes and is damaging to investor confidence and consumer psychology. Anticipated inflation is discounted by current interest rates covering loans due in the future. If inflation is expected, interest rates will be higher than if inflation is not expected. If the rate of inflation is expected to rise, interest rates should also rise.

This was observed to happen during a recent inflation, 1967–73. In 1967 and in 1968, most interest rates rose approximately 2 percent. Further increases were experienced in 1969 and 1970. The interest rate increases were determined in money markets and reflect an unwillingness by capital suppliers to forego the use of their money without added compensation for the effect of inflation on monetary value in exchange.

To understand how inflation reduces the return to a lender, consider your situation if you have $100 today. A 5 percent inflation exists. One year from today $105 will only have the purchasing power of about $100 today. You are strongly tempted to spend your money today,

---

[1] A discussion of price changes and the ways accountants measure and report them is contained in Chapter 10.

when its value in exchange is highest. Instead, a borrower offers to take your money and pay you 8 percent interest—pay you $108 one year from today. But if you accept, you will not make $8 profit. Of the eight extra dollars, five will be accounted for as necessary to make up the $105 year-from-now equivalent to the purchasing power of $100 today. The real compensation to you for lending is only $3.

Rate of Growth. Most investors aren't satisfied to receive only inflation compensation plus the barest basic return on their investments. For reasons rooted in sound business practice or deriving from personal motivations, they want a return that is higher. Two reasons for wanting a higher-than-minimum rate of return on investments are:

The industry in which the investor participates is growing faster than the economy as a whole.

The investor has a growth rate goal which requires that new investments earn at a higher rate.

Compensation for Risk. If it is impossible to know exactly all the relevant details about a proposed capital investment, the investment is said to involve *risk*. The *more* risk an investment entails, the higher additional profit or return the investor expects.

The problem of risk anticipation in capital investment planning is one of the most interesting and formidable in all of business administration. Yet risk must be successfully identified if the investor is to decide whether an investment's expected return justifies his accepting the associated investment risk. It derives from the hidden nature of the future, which no one can know with certainty. You can make estimates about the future, but these estimates may be wrong.

Error may occur in estimates of investment useful lifetime, investment cost, investment operating costs, investment cost savings or revenue, or even the tax rate. Such errors are caused by misreading economic conditions, making biased estimates, or simple ignorance of what makes the world tick. Errors are to some extent unavoidable, unpredictable, and in capital budgeting decisions expose a firm to loss and possible termination.

Managers have ways of measuring or estimating error and the associated risk in capital budgeting decisions. One of the simplest is to classify investment proposals into three categories: (1) low risk, (2) medium risk, and (3) high risk.

A *low* risk investment is one for which you believe all the estimates will prove to be accurate in the future. A *medium* risk investment is one in which many of the estimates may prove not to be accurate. A *high* risk investment is one in which many of the estimates may prove to be extremely inaccurate. Of course, these characterizations are approximate and subjective.

A practical procedure for evaluating risk would require risk categories and conditions for accepting or rejecting proposals falling in each category.

Let R_1 = the minimum expected compensation for investing in a project of *low risk*.

Let R_2 = the minimum expected compensation for investing in a project of *medium risk*.

Let R_3 = the minimum expected compensation for investing in a project of *high risk*.

Compensation Must Be Proportional to Risk. By common sense, you want more compensation to attract investment in a proposal of higher risk; less compensation will attract investment in a proposal of lower risk. The financial world bears out this prediction: savings accounts, which are low risk, return less interest than church bonds, which are high risk. Consequently R_1 is less than R_2, and R_2 is less than R_3.

Here is how you would use the risk categories:

1. Designate proposal as high, medium, or low risk (*after* collecting all essential data describing it).
2. Select appropriate value of R (R has been previously determined for high, medium, and low risk proposals). This value represents compensation for risk.

Investor's Target Rate of Return Illustrated

Suppose that the investor's target rate of return is 10 percent. Then any sum of money set aside now as a capital investment would have to earn a return equal to 10 percent annually to satisfy the investor.

A capital investment returns sums of money in the future. It is these *future sums* that a business purchases when it makes a capital investment. The investment now must be small enough that the future sums will produce at least a 10 percent return.

For example, let a capital investment be one which will pay a future sum of $100 at the end of two years. What sum would, if set aside to earn 10 percent interest compounded annually, be equal to $100 in two years?

The amount is:

$$\frac{\$100}{(1.00 + 0.10)^2} = \$82.64 \text{ (See footnote 2.)}$$

You can verify this by letting $82.64 earn 10 percent interest for two years:

Principal at present time	$ 82.64
Interest first year	8.26+
Principal + interest at end of one year	$ 90.90+
Interest second year	9.09+
Principal + interest at end of two years	$100.00

You would not pay more than $82.64 for this future payment if your ITRR is 10 percent. The less than $82.64 you pay, the better you will like your investment.

INFORMATION TO CONSIDER IN PLANNING CAPITAL INVESTMENT DECISIONS

In planning capital investment decisions you will need certain information. By means of an example, let us illustrate this information and how it is used in decision making.

You are executive vice president of Mildew Mining Corporation, a firm operating several open-pit limestone quarries. Stone is cut from

---

[2] The formula used is

$$\frac{\text{Present}}{\text{equivalent}} = \frac{(\text{Future receipt in Period } N)}{(1 + \text{ITRR})^N}$$

or

$$\frac{\text{Present}}{\text{equivalent}} = \frac{\text{Future}}{\text{receipt}} \times \frac{\text{Factor in Figure}}{5\text{--}1 \text{ for period } N}$$
$$\text{in period } N \quad \text{and ITRR}$$

FIGURE 5–1
Factors for Converting Future Receipts to Present Equivalents

$$\frac{\text{Present}}{\text{equivalent}} = \frac{\text{Future receipt}}{\text{in period } N} \times \frac{\text{Table factor}}{\text{for period } N}$$

Investor's Target Rate of Return

Period N	2	4	6	8	10	12
1	0.9804	0.9615	0.9434	0.9259	0.9091	0.8929
2	0.9612	0.9246	0.8900	0.8573	0.8264	0.7972
3	0.9423	0.8890	0.8396	0.7938	0.7513	0.7118
4	0.9238	0.8548	0.7921	0.7350	0.6830	0.6355
5	0.9057	0.8219	0.7473	0.6806	0.6209	0.5674
6	0.8880	0.7903	0.7050	0.6301	0.5648	0.5066
7	0.8706	0.7599	0.6651	0.5835	0.5136	0.4523
8	0.8535	0.7307	0.6274	0.5403	0.4665	0.4039
9	0.8368	0.7026	0.5919	0.5002	0.4241	0.3606
10	0.8203	0.6756	0.5584	0.4632	0.3855	0.3220

Investor's Target Rate of Return

Period N	14	16	18	20	22	24
1	0.8772	0.8621	0.8475	0.8333	0.8197	0.8065
2	0.7695	0.7432	0.7182	0.6944	0.6719	0.6504
3	0.6750	0.6407	0.6087	0.5787	0.5507	0.5245
4	0.5921	0.5523	0.5158	0.4823	0.4514	0.4230
5	0.5194	0.4761	0.4371	0.4019	0.3700	0.3411
6	0.4556	0.4104	0.3704	0.3349	0.3033	0.2751
7	0.3996	0.3538	0.3139	0.2791	0.2486	0.2218
8	0.3506	0.3050	0.2660	0.2326	0.2038	0.1789
9	0.3075	0.2630	0.2255	0.1938	0.1670	0.1443
10	0.2697	0.2267	0.1911	0.1615	0.1369	0.1164

The table factor is the amount that, if invested now at the ITRR interest rate at the head of its column, would increase to $1 in N periods.

these quarries and pulverized, then heated to make "calcined lime," used in cement making and other industrial applications. It is heavy, chemically active, and presents important handling problems. Recently a large machine has been developed which creeps along a limestone pit, ingesting limestone at one end and ejecting bagged calcined lime at the other end. A salesman is urging you to purchase one as a *replacement* for the existing facilities. But how do you know this machine, called a "sublimer" would be a desirable investment for Mildew Mining Company? In other words, what information must you have about the proposed equipment acquisition and about your own business—in order to make the decision?

The kinds of information you should want are these:

1. Net cash revenue or cost savings per unit activity and per time period.
2. Number of periods acquisition may be expected to last.
3. Tax effect of the acquisition.
4. Initial cost of acquisition.
5. *Risk* of the acquisition.
6. Target rate of return for your firm.

Let us examine each of these types of information in turn.

Net Cash Revenue or Cost Savings

For the sub-limer, a unit of activity is "one ton of limestone mined, crushed, calcined, and bagged" and the method of computation would be to compare the variable cost per ton of the new process with the variable cost per ton of the existing process. (This suggests a need to know Mildew's present cost structure.) When a proposed capital acquisition would produce revenue, the excess of revenue over variable costs is taken as the measure of benefit. We may imagine that you have analyzed the sub-limer and compared its costs with those of the facilities it would replace as shown in Figure 5–2. Total savings are computed by multiplying the savings per ton by the number of tons

FIGURE 5–2
Operating Cost per Ton Comparison of Sub-limer and Existing Plant

Cost in Dollars per Ton of Bagged Lime	Sub-limer	Existing Plant
Excavation.	\$2.50	\$2.75
Transportation to crusher	0	0.20
Crushing	0.35	0.35
Calcining.	0.40	0.45
Transportation to bagger.	0	0.10
Bagging.	1.20	1.80
Transportation to warehouse	0.20	0.10
Total.	\$4.65	\$5.75
Excess of existing plant costs over sub-limer costs	\$5.75 – \$4.65 = \$1.10 per ton	⌈ savings if⌉ sub-limer ⌊ acquired ⌋

expected to be produced. Since utilization of the sub-limer may vary from year to year, to compute total savings you need to know (*a*) the useful lifetime of the sub-limer, and (*b*) the utilization Mildew Mining plans to make of it. For convenience and simplicity assume that the sub-limer would be used to produce 200,000 tons of bagged lime per year. Then the savings on operating costs per year would be

200,000 tons per year $\times$ \$1.10 per ton = *\$220,000 per year*

In addition to the variable costs, there will be fixed costs that you will have to consider.

Additional Fixed Costs.   Fixed costs are those costs which must be incurred whether or not the equipment is used, including:

Depreciation (not a cash expense in period taken)
Insurance (may be a cash expense in period taken)
Preventive maintenance (cash expense in period taken)
Supervisory salaries (cash expense in period taken)

Figure 5–3 compares the sub-limer's annual fixed costs with the annual fixed costs of the existing technology.[3]

FIGURE 5–3
Fixed Cost Comparison

Fixed Costs in $ per Year for 200,000 Tons Capacity	Sub-limer	Existing Plant
Depreciation (noncash)	$ 90,000	$ 70,000
Insurance (cash)	5,000	4,000
Preventive maintenance (cash)	14,000	8,000
Supervisory salaries	20,000	25,000
Total	$129,000	$107,000

Acquisition Lifetime

Considerable study and consultation with engineers leads to the conclusion that the sub-limer would last 10 years, the same length of time

---

[3] This is an important point. You are comparing the sub-limer to an existing facility which it would *replace*.

the existing plant should last. Knowing the lifetime of the acquisition lets you schedule its incremental savings or costs by periods.

Additionally, the engineers estimate that neither the sub-limer nor the conventional plant would have any appreciable market value at the end of this period of time.

Depreciation and Tax Effects

As you know, depreciation is not a cash expense. It is a systematic transference of historical asset cost to the category of a current expense, symbolizing the using up of asset services as time passes. The significance of depreciation in capital decisions is as a deduction from income for purposes of computing the federal income tax. The income tax must be paid in cash—and the cash tax expense the company must pay is reduced by depreciation. The amount of the reduction depends on the tax rate—and of course, if there is no income, there is no income tax and no depreciation as a deduction.

Depreciation Expense Reduces Tax Payments. If Mildew Mining Company will continue having income, consider the effect of the additional depreciation deduction available on the sub-limer over the existing assets. The annual excess is $90,000 — $70,000 = $20,000. This extra depreciation reduces taxable income by $20,000 and with a 50 percent tax rate reduces the tax which must be paid by $20,000 × 0.50 = *$10,000 per year*. This is a cash saving attributable to the additional depreciation available on the sub-limer.

Why is this important? In capital budgeting, you compare *cash* expenses and *cash* savings. Obviously even though depreciation does not affect cash flows *its tax effect does*. The procedure to compute one period's net cash savings after taxes is:

Step no:

(1) Add together all cash revenues and/or cash savings.
(2) Add together all cash expenses, including fixed cash expenses.
(3) Compute net operating cash savings before taxes by subtracting (2) from (1).
(4) Subtract depreciation and other noncash expenses from (3).
(5) Compute taxes by multiplying (4) times the tax rate.

(6) Compute estimated net cash savings after taxes by subtracting (5) from (3).

Let us use the expected first year of operation of the sub-limer as an example of these steps (the number in the right-hand column refers to the column number of Figure 5–4):

	Proposed Addition (Sub-limer)	Existing Plant	Difference
Step 1:			
Net sub-limer cash operating savings	$220,000	$ 0	(1)→$220,000
Step 2:			
Annual operating expenses (Figure 5-3)	$129,000	$ 107,000	$ 22,000
Less: Noncash expenses (Figure 5-3)	(90,000)	(70,000)	(20,000)
Total annual fixed cash expense	$ 39,000	$ 37,000	(2)→$ 2,000
Step 3:			
Net sub-limer cash operating savings	$220,000	$ 0	$220,000 ←
Less: Total annual fixed cash expense	(39,000)	(37,000)	(2,000)←
Net cash operating savings before taxes	$181,000	$ (37,000)	$ $218,000
Step 4:			
Less: Noncash expenses	(90,000)	(70,000)	(3)→ (20,000)←
Taxable operating savings	$ 91,000	$(107,000)	(4)→$198,000
Step 5:			
Estimated tax effect [50% of (4)]	$ (45,500)	$ 53,500	$ (99,000)
Step 6:			
Net cash operating savings before taxes	$181,000	$ (37,000)	$218,000 ←
Less: Estimated tax effect	(45,500)	53,500	(5)→ (99,000)←
Net cash savings after taxes	$135,500	$ 16,500	(6)→$119,000

The difference in favor of the sub-limer is $135,000 − $16,500 = *$119,000*. If the sub-limer were not replacing existing equipment, the first column above would be all you'd need. You should study the effect of taxes on estimated cash flows until you understand the computation. *The key point is that depreciation and other noncash expenses do reduce taxes (increasing cash flow) but do not count in any other* *way.* Net operating cash savings are increased by the savings from the depreciation deduction, but depreciation itself is not a cash expense. Figure 5–4 is a tabular computation of net savings after taxes for

FIGURE 5–4
Computation by Periods of Net Cash Savings

				Subheading Corresponds to Step No.		
	(1)	*(2)*	*(3)*	*(4)* *Taxable*	*(5)*	*(6)* *Net Cash*
Year	*Gross Savings*	*Cash Expenses*	*Deprecia- tion*	*Savings (1) – (2) – (3)*	*Tax 0.5(4)*	*Savings (1) – (2) – (5)*
1.	$220,000	$2,000	$20,000	$198,000	$99,000	$119,000
2.	220,000	2,000	20,000	198,000	99,000	119,000
3.	220,000	2,000	20,000	198,000	99,000	119,000
4.	220,000	2,000	20,000	198,000	99,000	119,000
5.	220,000	2,000	20,000	198,000	99,000	119,000
6.	220,000	2,000	20,000	198,000	99,000	119,000
7.	220,000	2,000	20,000	198,000	99,000	119,000
8.	220,000	2,000	20,000	198,000	99,000	119,000
9.	220,000	2,000	20,000	198,000	99,000	119,000
10.	220,000	2,000	20,000	198,000	99,000	119,000

each year in the proposed investment's lifetime. Each row follows the calculation above. For simplicity and convenience, assume that each year's net cash saving will all occur at once, on the anniversary of the sub-limer's purchase.

Initial Cost of Acquisition

The acquisition cost of a capital asset includes the following expenditures:
—Cash price of the asset.
—Shipping and freight.
—Setup costs.
—Startup costs.
—Modifications to new asset or old assets to make them compatible with the new asset.
—Any other costs which are incurred once-only and would not be incurred if the new asset were not acquired.

When comparing an existing facility with a proposed replacement, you must use the *net* cost, which is total acquisition cost of the replacement *less* the salvage or resale value of the equipment replaced. The net cost of the sub-limer is computed in Figure 5–5.   The costs in Figure 5–5 include no sums which would be incurred if the sub-limer were

FIGURE 5–5
Net Cost of Sub-limer
Item

Cash price	$ 2,300,000
Shipping and freight	0
Setup costs.	20,000
Startup costs	20,000
Modifications	10,000
Other.	40,000
Total cost	$ 2,390,000
Less resale value of existing plant.	(1,610,000)
Net cost of sub-limer.	$ 780,000

not purchased. Theerfore, the acquisition cost difference of $780,000 truly represents the additional cost of the sub-limer over the alternative of keeping the present plant. If you combine this extra cost with the information about annual net cash savings, you have a schedule consisting of *one* cash payment now (time of purchase) and 10 equal cash receipts, one on each of the next 10 anniversaries of the acquisition date:

Year		Cash Receipt (Payment)	
(now)	(from Figure 5–5)	$(780,000)	← Payment
1		119,000	
2		119,000	
3		119,000	
4		119,000	
5	(from Figure 5–4)	119,000	Future
6		119,000	receipts
7		119,000	
8		119,000	
9		119,000	
10		119,000	

The question you must ask yourself now, as a decision maker for Mildew Mining Company, is, "Is this extra $780,000 in expenditures justified by the additional $119,000 per year we will receive for 10 years?" If yes, you recommend purchase; if not, you recommend against purchase.

Risk of Acquisition

Mildew classifies proposals according to perceived risk: low, medium, and high. The sub-limer proposal meets criteria for the low-risk category. The corresponding compensation for risk is $R_1 = 3$ percent.

Mildew's Target Rate of Return

Mildew Mining Corporation has adopted, as a matter of company policy, the following target rate of return:

Basic return desired.	3%
Adjustment for inflation	5
Rate of expansion	5
Compensation for risk	3
Total.	16%

In other words, any investment made by Mildew Mining will be expected to return at least this rate of interest, or rate of return.

The Present Equivalent of Sub-Limer Future Sums. How can you tell if the proposed sub-limer offers this rate of return? You must compute the amount which would have to be set aside now, to earn at the rate 16 percent, to produce the future sums shown in the schedule above. An equivalent statement is: If you invest $780,000 today at a 16 percent rate of interest and at the end of each of the next 10 years draw off $119,000, would the last withdrawal leave a positive balance? If "yes" then the sub-limer does offer a return equal to or greater than 16 percent. To give a "yes" or "no" answer to this question, you compute the amounts of money you have to set aside NOW *and* which would grow to $119,000 in 1 year, grow to $119,000 in 2 years, and so on for all 10 years. The sum of these amounts is the *present equivalent* of the proposed investment's net future cash flows, if this sum earns at the assumed investor's target rate of return.

In Figure 5–1 are factors to make this calculation easier. Each factor is the dollar amount which will, if allowed to earn at the column target rate of return, grow to $1 in the row number of periods. Thus, $0.4104 invested at 16 percent will grow to $1 after six periods. To find out how many dollars are equivalent *now* to $119,000 in six periods, multi-

ply $119,000 by 0.4104 and get $48,840. Figure 5–6 applies this calculation to all the expected cash flow associated with the sub-limer, then
sums them to find the sub-limer's present equivalent or present value.

FIGURE 5–6
Present Equivalents of Sub-limer Savings

(N) Year	Present Equivalent of $1 in N Years at 16%(F[N, 16])	Present Equivalent of $119,000 in N Years at 16%($119,000 × F[N, 16])
1........	0.8621 × $119,000 =	$102,590
2........	0.7432 × 119,000 =	88,440
3........	0.6407 × 119,000 =	76,240
4........	0.5523 × 119,000 =	65,720
5........	0.4761 × 119,000 =	56,660
6........	0.4104 × 119,000 =	48,840
7........	0.3538 × 119,000 =	42,100
8........	0.3050 × 119,000 =	36,300
9........	0.2630 × 119,000 =	31,290
10........	0.2267 × 119,000 =	26,980
Total present equivalent.........		$575,160

It is common to all present equivalent calculations that a smaller
present equivalent occurs as the number of periods before receiving
the cash flow becomes larger (because there are more periods in which
interest accumulates). Look for this in Figure 5–6. Thus, $65,720 set
aside now at 16 percent interest compounded annually would amount
to $119,000 in four years. The sum of all 10 numbers such as $65,720
is the total amount of cash that would have to be set aside now at
16 percent interest in order to produce 10 annual payments of $119,000
each. The sum of all these present amounts is $575,160. This is the
present equivalent to the 10-year sequence of payments the proposed
sub-limer is expected to produce. It is the "fair price" you should be
willing to pay now in exchange for receiving the $119,000 payments
annually for 10 years, provided you are willing to earn exactly 16 percent return on the $575,160.

The present equivalent will be larger if the ITRR is smaller and
smaller if the ITRR is larger. If the ITRR happens to be selected so
that the present equivalent exactly equals the present cost, it is said
to be the *rate of return* on that proposal. This is another criterion
for investment decisions but we will not discuss it here.

MAKING THE DECISION

If you invest more that $575,153—for example, invest $780,000—your actual return would be less than 16 percent. Therefore, the sub-limer, whose net cost is $780,000, *cannot* be regarded as a desirable investment at this time.

The rule is: If the present equivalent of the future cash flow the investment is expected to produce (computed as described in Figure 5–6) is *less* than the present cost of that future income, *an investment should not be considered further*. If, on the other hand, the present equivalent of future income is *greater* than the expected cost of the investment, *the investment merits further consideration*. You can put this into a diagram such as Figure 5–7.

FIGURE 5–7
Capital Investment Decision Rule

	Present Equivalent of Investment Income GREATER THAN Expected Investment Cost	*Present Equivalent of Investment Income LESS THAN Expected Investment Cost*
Favorable to investment	Yes	No
Unfavorable to investment.	No	Yes

OTHER FACTORS IN INVESTMENT DECISIONS

Often projects do not compete with each other or are not proposed at the same time and cannot be considered in direct comparison with one another. If this is the case, you should consider investments one at a time in sequence as they are proposed, evaluating each using the methods of this chapter. Projects whose present equivalent exceeds their cost should be considered further.

"Further consideration" will be influenced by these important factors:

—A limit on total funds which can be spent on capital projects.
—Compatibility of proposed projects with existing facilities.

—Changes in investor's target rate of return expected in future periods.
—Different lifetimes of proposals which compete with each other for funds.
—Different investor's target rates of return proposed for different responsibility centers in a firm; that is, the problem of allocating scarce capital among competing entities in the firm.

Because of the extreme complexity of these variables' interactions with one another, many researchers and businessmen have suggested use of business-wide computer-based planning models to produce fast, comprehensive answers to capital allocation questions. In addition, linear programming models are occasionally useful in selecting investments. Although sophisticated refinements are helpful, be assured that great improvements in the efficiency of capital deployment can be achieved through the simple methods of this chapter.

SUMMARY

Capital investments are those expenditures to acquire long-lived assets. The benefits from these expenditures extend through more than one accounting period. Capital investment decisions require specific types of information: estimates of investment cost, annual cash investment revenue or cost savings, annual cash investment expense, investment lifetime, and investment risk. In addition, the economic situation, tax structure, and growth goals of a firm will influence the type of investments it chooses.

Because returns from a capital investment are received in the future, they must be converted into present equivalents for comparison with the expected present cost of the investment. This is done by computing the amount of cash to be set aside now which would, if it earned interest at a rate equal to the investor's target rate of return, be sufficient to produce all of the future returns expected of the proposed investment. If this present equivalent is more than the present cost of the investment, the investment may receive further consideration.

Tax structure of a firm influences capital investment decisions because depreciation and other noncash expenses of capital assets produce reductions in cash tax expense. Risky capital investments must promise a higher return in order to be attractive. Inflation tends to discourage long-term investment by requiring a higher return than would otherwise be necessary:

However helpful procedures are in evaluating investment proposals, they do not *originate* proposals. It is still up to management to produce high quality promising investment proposals if a business is to prosper.

BIBLIOGRAPHY

Books

Bierman, Harold, and Smidt, Seymour. *The Capital Budgeting Decision.* 3d ed. New York: The Macmillan Co.: 1971.

Edwards, James W. *Effects of Federal Income Taxes on Capital Budgeting,* NAA Research Monograph No. 5. New York: National Association of Accountants, 1969.

Kempster, John H. *Financial Analysis to Guide Capital Investment Expenditure Decisions,* NAA Research Report No. 43, New York: National Association of Accountants. 1967.

Articles

Coughlin, John W. "Accounting and Capital Budgeting," *The Business Quarterly,* Winter 1962.

Edge, C. G. "Capital Budgeting: Principles and Projection," *Financial Executive,* September 1965.

Edwards, James B. "Adjusted DCF Rate of Return," *Management Accounting,* January 1973.

House, William C. "Use of Sensitivity Analysis in Capital Budgeting," *Management Services,* September–October 1967.

Wellington, Roger. "Capital Budgeting," *The Journal of Accountancy,* May 1963.

6

Inventory Management

MANAGEMENT literature abounds with references to inventory and the need for its economical administration. For example, the annual cost of keeping inventory worth $1 on hand may be as much as 25 cents. A firm with total assets of $1,000,000 and inventories of $200,000 may be spending as much as $50,000 annually on insurance, pilferage, obsolescence, shrinkage, damage, and other costs of maintaining inventory—a considerable sum. It often happens that inventory analysis using accounting information can *cut in half* the amount of inventory the firm has on hand and the costs of inventory maintenance. In this example, the $25,000 thus saved would raise return on total assets by 2.5 percent (somewhat more on owners' equities)—no small boost to any business.

Inventories serve a valuable function by smoothing out short-run disparities between the supply of an item and the demand for it. Although the advantages of inventory management are demonstrable, and superior methods have been available during most of the 20th century, few firms make use of them. Introducing you to such methods early in your professional education may help correct this peculiar situation.

INVENTORY MANAGEMENT AND POLICY

The management of inventory is to provide service and convenience to the company and its customers at reasonable cost. An inventory policy to perform this function is expressed in this form:

When inventory gets down to a predetermined replenishment point of S units (S may be negative, indicating a shortage), replenish inventory with an order of Q additional units.

The inventory policy guides inventory management performance.

Inventory Models Lead to Inventory Policy

Inventory policies are developed by creating a model of the inventory situation, then using the model to create a policy which meets some criterion for being most acceptable. Without inventory models, it is difficult for a firm to relate its inventory policy to its real needs for inventory service and convenience. Using inventory models, a firm can decide what service it does require in each kind of inventory it keeps—raw materials, work in process, finished goods (it isn't unusual to see a firm which has 10,000–100,000 different *types* of items in inventory)—and compute an inventory policy that gives the level of service for each kind of inventory. Figure 6–1 shows the inventory model graphically.

FIGURE 6–1
Model Showing Inventory Level as a Function of Time, Q, S, and Demand

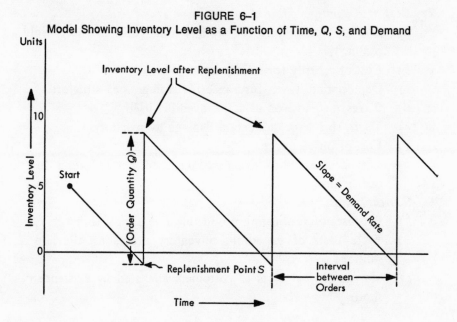

PARAMETERS AFFECTING INVENTORY MANAGEMENT

The inventory environment includes these parameters which affect inventory management:

1. Ordering costs—costs of ordering or replenishing inventory.
2. Carrying costs—costs of keeping or storing inventory on hand.
3. Shortage costs—costs of not being able to satisfy demand from inventory on hand.
4. Demand—future rate of withdrawals from inventory per period.

Let us list costs which could occur in categories 1, 2, and 3.

1. *Costs of Ordering or Replenishing Inventory*
   a) Cost of setting up plant to produce a batch of product for inventory (setup costs).
   b) Cost of preparing and placing an order with a supplier (if item cannot be produced; these are called order costs).
   c) Cost of preparing space for storage of inventory if this must be done each time an order is placed.
2. *Cost of Keeping or Storing Inventory on Hand*
   a) Cost of maintaining the storage area (utilities, heat, light, cooling).
   b) Cost of security for storage area.
   c) Depreciation, taxes, insurance for storage area structure.
   d) Taxes, insurance on value of inventory itself.
   e) Theft, shrinkage, accidental damage to inventory.
   f) Cost of obsolescence.
   g) Lost income due to inventory investment not earning a direct cash return.
3. *Shortage Costs*
   a) Expenses of readjusting production line after a shortage.
   b) Extra costs of expediting inventory orders to alleviate a shortage.
   c) Margin on lost sales to customers alienated by existence of shortage.

The following isn't a cost category, so instead of costs we list sources of information to help you estimate the future demand for withdrawals from inventory.

4. *Future Rate of Withdrawals from Inventory*
   a)   Records of previous withdrawal rates.
   b)   Predictions of future sales, production, etc., prepared during the budgeting process.
   c)   Specialized forecasting models utilizing regression analysis, moving averages, exponential smoothing, etc., and which calculate inventory demand rates as a function of overall business policies and environment.

The accounting system provides a *starting point* for accumulating the cost information you need. A word of caution: you are only interested in the variable costs of ordering, carrying, or being short of inventory. For example, if there is a security patrol of the inventory storage area irregardless whether inventory is stored there, then the security patrol cost is not a relevant cost. If the depreciation and taxes on the storage area don't vary with the inventory quantity stored, they aren't relevant costs either.

The cost of inventory itself didn't enter the inventory model information requirements. The cost of inventory may determine some of the other costs: insurance, for example. But the omission of inventory cost as an information input to inventory decisions is not accidental. You may best understand this by realizing that withdrawals must be paid for whatever the inventory policy is. The demand to be satisfied is not a function of the inventory policy.

Typical Inventory Management Method

Visualize the total quantity of some article as kept in a large container or bin. When this article is requisitioned, the clerk goes to the bin and takes out the quantity requisitioned. One day he goes to the bin and sees a red line emerging on the inside of the bin. This signals him that the article's supply has become so low that it must be re-

ordered. The clerk completes a purchase form and sends it to the purchasing department, retaining a copy that is placed at the article's bin
to show it is reordered. The quantity below the red line should be
sufficient to meet demand until the new order arrives and replenishes
the bin.

This "bin" method is a reasonable system which does not require
management of employee sophistication to work smoothly. But—how
do you know where to draw the red line inside the bin? The average
investment in inventory and inventory costs are determined by the
height of the reorder mark above the bottom of the bin and the size of
the reorder quantity.

The next section explains one way to find a place to "draw the red
line."

SIMPLE ECONOMIC ORDER QUANTITY MODELS

These models were developed generations ago to determine inventory management through reorder points, replenishment points, and
reorder quantities. In the form you study here, they are simple, yet
capable of producing improvements over inventory management already
existing. Sophisticated economic order quantity (EOQ) models accommodate to complex inventory situations. Figure 6–2 contrasts the
assumptions of typical simple and sophisticated models.

FIGURE 6–2
Economic Order Quantity (EOQ) Model Assumptions

Simple *Model Assumptions*	*Sophisticated** *Model Assumptions*
1. Demand is steady during a period, occurring uniformly throughout.	1. Demand is irregular and fluctuates uncertainly.
2. A new order arrives a predictable time after it is placed.	2. Delays in delivery are often and irregular.
3. All inventory-related costs are known and constant.	3. Very few costs are known.
4. Average unit cost is independent of order size or production run length.	4. Discounts are given for large orders; long production runs have learning effects and other economies which lower average unit cost.
* Only simple models are discussed in this text.	

Inventory management will consist of finding the values of Q and
S that minimize costs while satisfying demand.

Influence of Inventory Parameters on Inventory Management

Figure 6–3 shows how order quantity and replenishment point will be influenced by relatively higher or lower values of demand, carrying cost, shortage cost, and order cost in the simple models covered in this chapter.

FIGURE 6–3
Inventory Parameters and Inventory Management

	Effect on—	
Parameter	*Reorder Quantity*	*Replenishment Point*
Order cost:		
1. Higher	Larger	More negative
2. Lower	Smaller	Less negative
Carrying cost:		
1. Higher	Smaller	More negative
2. Lower	Larger	Less negative
Shortage cost:		
1. Higher	Smaller	Less negative
2. Lower	Larger	More negative
Demand		
1. Higher	Larger	More negative
2. Lower	Smaller	Less negative

You can express the relationships in Figure 6–3 more usefully with symbols. Here are symbolic definitions:

S = replenishment point.

Q = reorder quantity.

c_o = the direct cost of placing one order (order cost).

c_h = the cost of holding one unit in inventory for the period with which you are dealing (carrying cost).

c_s = the cost of being unable to fill an order for one unit from inventory for one period (shortage cost).

D = the demand to be filled from inventory during the period with which you are dealing.

Cost of Inventory Policy

With the symbols above you can describe the cost of an inventory policy. The following is not a derivation but an explanation of the parts of an expression for total inventory function costs.

Total   Total   Total   Total
cost   = carrying + ordering + shortage
(*TC*)   costs   costs   costs

$$TC = \text{Average inventory level} \times c_h + \text{Number of orders} \times c_o + \text{Average inventory shortage} \times c_s$$

$$TC = \frac{(Q+S)^2}{2Q} c_h + \frac{D}{Q} c_o + \frac{S^2}{2Q} c_s \qquad (6\text{--}1)$$

Economic Order Quantity Models for Q* and S*

An asterisked symbol denotes the *optimum* (least-cost) value of a decision variable. The use of differential calculus permits (6–1) to yield expressions for the optimal Q and S. These expressions are

$$\text{Order quantity: } Q^* = \sqrt{\frac{2c_oD}{c_h}} \times \sqrt{\frac{c_h + c_s}{c_s}} \qquad \left.\begin{array}{l} Q^* \text{ and } S^* \\ \text{define the} \\ \text{least-cost} \end{array}\right\} \qquad (6\text{--}2)$$

$$\text{Replenishment point: } S^* = -\sqrt{\frac{2c_oD}{c_s}} \times \sqrt{\frac{c_h}{c_h + c_s}} \qquad \left.\begin{array}{l} \text{inventory} \\ \text{policy} \end{array}\right\} \qquad (6\text{--}3)$$

To illustrate the uses of these formulas, assume you are in charge of the resin inventory at the Fiberglass Boat Company. Resin is used continuously and can be replenished by going next door to the resin factory to pick it up—requiring no time at all.

Applying the Models to Compute Inventory Policy

Working with the cost accountant, you have determined that the cost of making an order, going over and picking it up, and sampling it for quality is $8. Similarly, you have determined that the cost of storing 1 unit of resin for one year is $10. This covers insurance, spoilage, interest on investment in resin, and several other minor factors. The Fiberglass Boat Company mass produces standard boats, hence there is a steady and constant demand for the resin. Demand in the coming period is estimated at 3,422.5 units. Finally, you figure that being short of resin costs $100 per year per unit short, in terms of upsetting production schedules and other inconveniences.

You are therefore able to assign the variables in the economic order quantity models the following variables:

c_o = \$8 per order.
D = 3,422.5 units per year.
c_h = \$10 per unit per year.
c_s = \$100 per unit short per year.

You insert these numbers into (6–2) and obtain:

$$Q^* = \sqrt{\frac{2 \times \$8 \times 3{,}422.5}{\$10}} \times \sqrt{\frac{\$10 + \$100}{\$100}}$$

= 74 × 1.054 = *78 units*. This is the amount to be ordered whenever an order is placed.

Now, solving with (6–3) for the replenishment point,

$$S^* = -\sqrt{\frac{2 \times \$8 \times 3{,}422.5}{\$100}} \times \sqrt{\frac{\$10}{\$10 + \$100}}$$

= −23.4 × 0.301 = −7.01 or about −7 *units*.

The replenishment point S^* will never be greater than zero. When it is negative, that means it is cheaper in terms of the overall inventory policy to run slightly short before receiving the next order.

The proper policy is to arrange for delivery of 78 units of resin when you are 7 units short. The cost of this policy will be the lowest possible total cost for this inventory situation, and can be figured from (6–1):

$$\frac{\text{Total}}{\text{cost}} = \frac{(78 - 7)^2}{2 \times 78} \times \$10 + \frac{3{,}422.5}{78} \times \$8 + \frac{7^2}{2 \times 78} \times \$100$$

= \$323.14   + \$351.03   + \$31.41

= *\$705.58*

When the Shortage Cost Is Very High

If you examine (6–3), you will see that a very high shortage cost would cause the expression under the second square root sign to approach zero, implying that the replenishment point also approaches zero. When the shortage cost is very large relative to the carrying cost, a new and simpler set of formulas may be used to find the least-cost inventory policy.

$$\text{Total cost} = \underset{\text{Carrying}}{\underbrace{\frac{Q}{2} c_h}} + \underset{\text{Ordering}}{\underbrace{\frac{D}{Q} c_o}} \qquad (6\text{-}1A)$$

$$Q^* = \sqrt{\frac{2c_o D}{c_h}} \qquad (6\text{-}2A)$$

$$S^* = 0 \qquad (6\text{-}3A)$$

If you apply these formulas to the Fiberglass Boat Company resin inventory situation, you obtain:

$$Q^* = \sqrt{\frac{2 \times \$8 \times 3{,}422.5}{\$10}} = 74 \; units$$

$$S^* = 0$$

$$TC = \frac{74}{2} \times \$10 + \frac{3{,}422.5}{74} \times \$8$$

$$= \$740$$

This cost is not directly comparable with the cost of the previous policy since it assumes an infinitely high cost of being unable to satisfy demand for resin from inventories. However, if you use the policy $(Q = 74, S = 0)$ when shortage cost is actually \$100 per unit short per year [making the policy $(Q = 78, S = -7)$ optimal], you will spend an extra \$740 — \$705.58 = *\$34.42* per year maintaining resin inventories.

Generality of Cost Formulas

Note that the cost formulas (6–1) and (6–1A) may be used to compute the cost of any inventory policy, even if it is not the optimal policy. This makes them useful for calculating the savings that may occur if an optimal policy replaces an existing policy.

Cost Savings

Suppose the Fiberglass Boat Company current resin inventory policy is to order 200 units of resin to arrive when the inventory level is 50 units on hand.

The cost of this policy is

$$TC = \frac{(200 + 50)^2}{2 \times 200} \times \$10 + \frac{3{,}422.5}{200} \times \$8 + \$0 \begin{bmatrix} \text{Since this policy} \\ \text{has no shortages,} \\ \text{there is no short-} \\ \text{age cost!} \end{bmatrix}$$

$$= \$1{,}699.40$$

A change to the optimal policy would save $1,699.40 — $705.58 or $993.82 annually. Such savings are representative of those available when appropriate operating procedures are applied.

Delay in Restocking after Ordering

Now suppose that delivery of resin occurs exactly one working day after Fiberglass Boat Company's order is received. You must place your order for resin well before the replenishment point is reached in order to implement the optimal inventory policy. The inventory level at which an order is *placed* is called the *order point*.

The period during which 3,422.5 units of resin are consumed is one year, which includes 244.5 working days at Fiberglass Boat. Thus, $3{,}422.5/244.5 = 14.00$ units of resin are consumed each working day. If the replenishment point is —7 units of resin, you should dial the resin company and order 78 more units at the exact time that $14 - 7 = 7$ units of resin remain in inventory. The order should arrive the following day just as you are 7 units of resin short. This shortage is immediately filled and remaining part of the order—71 units—is placed in inventory to satisfy future demand.

If the replenishment point is 0 units of resin, your order should be placed one day before the current inventory is exhausted, or when 14 units remain in inventory.

Safety Stock

You may not trust the resin factory to deliver exactly on schedule. No matter. It will cost you a little more, but you can still be reasonably assured of having enough resin on hand by determining a safety stock and *adding* it to the demand during the time lag between ordering and replenishment to get the proper order point. Here is how that would work.

You have noticed that about one time in five the resin factory gets its dates fouled up and delivers after two working days rather than one. This means that 20 percent of the time your shortage before replenishment is 21 units rather than 7—and this shortage also exists over a longer period of time than the smaller shortage. These extra shortage costs are slightly offset by the lower levels of inventory and associated lower carrying costs, but the overall effect is higher costs which you'd like to avoid.

If you are not permitting any shortages at all, the safety stock problem is easy. Simply order when inventory level reaches 28 units. Then, about 20 percent of the time the new order will arrive at an inventory level of zero, and 80 percent of the time, at a level of 14. The extra cost will be approximately the same as the cost of carrying 14 extra units in stock at all times (they are not in stock only about nine days per year—try to figure out why!),[1] or $10 \times 14 = \$140$ per year. Note that preventing stockouts cost you ($140/$706) $\times$ 100 or about 20 percent of the total optimal cost of the inventory function. You may interpret this as the extra cost of assuring uninterrupted supply. If it seems excessive, you could look for a more reliable source of resin supply.

Safety Stock when Shortages Are Permitted. Shortages are permitted only when they are controlled. You are thus willing to be 7 resin units short when you are seeking a least-cost inventory operation—but may not be willing to be 21 units short when that is not your plan and is caused by an unreliable supplier. This section explains how you might adjust inventory policy to minimize the effects of an uncontrollably irregular supply of resin.

---

[1] There are $3,422.5/74 \approx 46$ orders per year, of which 20 percent or 9.2 are delivered late—causing the safety stock to be exhausted.

Irregular deliveries create uncertainty for the inventory policy maker. The simplest approach to analyzing this uncertainty is to recognize that there are really two situations: delivery when the shortage is 7 units, which occurs 80 percent of the time; and delivery when the shortage is 21 units, which occurs 20 percent of the time. Your assignment is to find an inventory policy that covers both situations at the lowest total cost.

You already know the cost of the policy $(S = -7, Q = 78)$ when deliveries are normal; it is $705.58. When deliveries are a day late this policy's cost rises to $841.98 (calculated using $[6–1]$ and $S = -21, Q = 78$). The total cost is a weighted average of these amounts: $TC = (0.20 \times \$841.98) + (0.80 \times \$705.58) = \$732.86$.

Further use of calculus on a modified $(6–1)$ reveals that if Q remains at 78, the single best replenishment point is $S = -4.29$ units of resin. Let S be rounded off to -4 units of resin. The cost of this policy when deliveries are regular is $712.31; when deliveries are a day late, $789.50. The total cost of this policy under all conditions is $(0.2 \times \$789.50) \times (0.8 \times \$712.31) = \$727.75$. The new policy costs $732.86 - \$727.75 = \$5.11$ less per year than the original one. A summary of these results appears in Figure 6–4.

FIGURE 6–4
Comparison of Least-Cost Inventory Policies for Resin
under Different Conditions

c_o = $8 per order	c_h = $10 per unit per year D = 3,422.5 units per year	c_s = $100 per unit per year

	Delivery of Orders after One Day (80% of Time)	Delivery of Orders after Two Days (20% of Time)
A. CONTROLLED SHORTAGES ALLOWED		
1. Q = 78; order point = 7;	$S = -7$	$S = -21$
average $TC = \$732.86$.	TC = $705.58	TC = $841.98
2. Q = 78; order point = 10;	$S = -4$	$S = -18$
average $TC = \$727.75$.	TC = $712.31	TC = $789.50
B. NO SHORTAGES ALLOWED		
1. Q = 78; order point = 14;	$S = 0$	$S = -14$
average TC = (very large)	TC = $740	TC = (very large)
2. Q = 78; order point = 28;	$S = 14$	$S = 0$
average $TC = \$880$.	TC = $880	TC = $880

The calculations to support this demonstration are happily beyond the scope of an introductory course.[2] The purpose of the demonstration is to establish the importance of costs and other information developed through an accounting system in making inventory policy decisions. Although $5.11 may not seem like much, this saving on each item in a 10,000 item inventory amounts to $51,100 per year. The actual savings may vary as circumstances determine.

SENSITIVITY ANALYSIS

Suppose you fail to measure one or more parameters of the economic order quantity model correctly. How wrong will your inventory policy be? Your errors will increase roughly as the square root of the ratio of correct to incorrect parameter value. For example, in formula (6–2A) for Q^*, if actual carrying cost is 2 times your estimate, the order quantity will be understated by $(\sqrt{2} - 1) \times 100 = 41$ *percent.*

Let us assume that in the Fiberglass Boat Company example, you estimate carrying cost as $10 when it is actually $20. The true order quantity should have been 57.29 units. The true replenishment point should have been —9.56 units. Inserting these values into (6–1) gives a cost of *$955.21.* This is the cost of the optimal policy if c_h is actually $20; to find out the cost of erroneous information, compare it with the cost of your erroneous policy. This cost is not $705.58; that was based on the wrong carrying cost. The cost of the erroneously calculated inventory policy ($Q = 78, S = -7$) is actually *$1,028.74.*

The opportunity cost of using the erroneous policy when ($Q = 57.29, S = 9.36$) is optimal is $1,028.74 - $955.21 = *$73.53* per year. This is a small extra cost compared to the substantial savings the economic order quantity policy ($Q = 78, S = -7$) offers over the hypothetical original policy's cost of (using the correct carrying cost $c_h = 20):

$$TC = \frac{(200 + 50)^2 \times \$20}{2 \times 200} + \frac{3,422.5 \times \$8}{200} = \$3,262!$$

---

[2] But see the Appendix 6A if you want to know anyway.

This relative insensitivity of the economic order quantity model to errors in estimating its independent parameter values makes it useful in practice even if you do not have perfect information or if the assumptions about demand or reorder time are not true. Accounting efforts should be directed toward estimating most accurately those parameters which have the greatest impact on inventory policy cost. With a little care, you can be virtually certain that your policy's cost will be within, say, ±50 percent of the lowest possible cost, and well below the cost of the policies it will replace.

INVENTORY MANAGEMENT SYSTEMS

An inventory management *system* is based on analysis similar to that conducted above. Such systems exhibit vast differences, depending on the needs they serve. In a typical manufacturing firm which has 10,000 different items in inventory, the inventory management system would be expected to monitor the levels of all the fastest-moving items (it has been observed that about 20 percent of all the items will account for 80 percent of the capital investment and activity in inventory), monitor demand for these items, to determine a replenishment point in light of the latest information about expected demand, compare the actual level of inventory with the computed replenishment point, and give the signal for placing an order for items in need of replenishment (reorder point higher than inventory level on hand). Computers are used extensively to implement inventory systems. If items are contracted to be purchased from known suppliers, the computer can even print out an order addressed to the supplier for the appropriate number of additional units. Such systems, when they are economically feasible, remove the clerical burden from management and free persons for concentration on business strategies and responsibilities.

SUMMARY

The economic order formulas are among the most commonly used models for analyzing an inventory situation. They make use of estimates of costs of carrying, ordering, and being short of inventory, and of demand for a commodity from inventory. The economic order quantity formulas allow computation, when the assumptions underlying them are met, of inventory policy cost, amount to be ordered at one time, and the inventory level at which replenishment should occur.

Inventory management systems based on economic order quantity analysis seek to make as small as possible the sum of ordering, holding, and shortage costs, while at the same time providing an acceptable level of service from inventory—provision of items from inventory at the convenience of users—with no more shortages and ensuing delays than are acceptable to customers.

Inventory management is an important function in the business because so much money may be invested in inventories. Typically, inventory management is decentralized to the users of inventory; however, the financial and accounting functions perform important services by defining the financial restraints on inventory and the important measures and forecasts of costs and future demands.

APPENDIX 6A

How the Optimal Economic Order Quantity Policy Was Computed When Controlled Shortages Are Permitted and 20 Percent of Deliveries Are a Day Late

TC (irregular deliveries) $= 0.8TC(Q = 78, S)$

$$+ 0.2TC(Q = 78, S - 14) = 0.8\left[\frac{(Q + S)^2 c_h}{2Q} + \frac{Dc_o}{Q} + \frac{S^2 c_s}{2Q}\right]$$

$$+ 0.2\left[\frac{(Q + S - 14)^2 c_h}{2Q} + \frac{Dc_o}{Q} + \frac{(S - 14)^2 c_s}{2Q}\right]$$

If this expression is differentiated with respect to S, the result set equal to zero and solved for S, the resulting value of S will be that which produces the lowest value of TC when deliveries are irregular.

$$\frac{\partial TC}{\partial S} = 0.8\left[\frac{(Q+S)c_h}{Q} + \frac{Sc_s}{Q}\right] + 0.2\left[\frac{(Q+S-14)c_h}{Q} + \frac{(S-14)c_s}{Q}\right]$$

$$0 = 0.8\left[\frac{(78+S)10}{78} + \frac{100S}{78}\right]$$

$$+ 0.2\left[\frac{(78+S-14)10}{78} + \frac{(S-14)100}{78}\right]$$

$$S = -4.29$$

APPENDIX 6B: SQUARE ROOTS OF NUMBERS 1–100

Instructions: To find the square root of a number in this table, follow these steps:

a) Multiply or divide the number by 10 an *even number of times* until the number is between 1 and 100.
   Example: Let the number be 45,000. When divided 4 times by 10, the result is 4.5, which is between 1 and 100.

b) Find the number N in the table which is closest to the result of (*a*). If the number in (*a*) lies between two table entries, note both entries.
   Example: 4.5 is between 4 and 5.

c) Find the square root of the table entry and record it. If two table entries were noted above in (*b*), record both square roots, then take their average.
   Example: Square root of 4 is 2. Square root of 5 is 2.236. The average is $(2.000 + 2.236)/2 = 2.118$.

d) Number found in (*c*) should be divided by 10 (if the original number was multiplied in [*a*] or multiplied by 10 (if the original number was divided by 10 in [*a*]) *half the number of times* the opposite operation was carried out in (*a*). The result is the desired square root.
   Example: 45,000 was divided 4 times by 10 in (*a*). Therefore, multiply 2.118 by 10 two times: $2.118 \times 10 \times 10 = 211.8$. To check, 211.8 squared is 44,859, very close to 45,000.

This procedure will give sufficiently accurate results to solve all problems in this book, and most practical problems as well. A slide rule also gives good square roots. The true square root of 45,000 is 212.1—the error was 0.14 percent.

N	$\sqrt{N}$	N	$\sqrt{N}$
1	1	51	7.141
2	1.414	52	7.211
3	1.732	53	7.280
4	2.000	54	7.348
5	2.236	55	7.416
6	2.449	56	7.483
7	2.645	57	7.549
8	2.828	58	7.615
9	3.000	59	7.681
10	3.162	60	7.745
11	3.316	61	7.810
12	3.464	62	7.874
13	3.605	63	7.937
14	3.741	64	8.000
15	3.872	65	8.062
16	4.000	66	8.124
17	4.123	67	8.185
18	4.242	68	8.246
19	4.358	69	8.306
20	4.472	70	8.366
21	4.582	71	8.426
22	4.690	72	8.485
23	4.795	73	8.544
24	4.898	74	8.602
25	5.000	75	8.660
26	5.099	76	8.717
27	5.196	77	8.774
28	5.291	78	8.831
29	5.385	79	8.888
30	5.477	80	8.944
31	5.567	81	9.000
32	5.656	82	9.055
33	5.744	83	9.110
34	5.830	84	9.165
35	5.916	85	9.219
36	6.000	86	9.273
37	6.082	87	9.327
38	6.164	88	9.380
39	6.244	89	9.433
40	6.324	90	9.486
41	6.403	91	9.539
42	6.480	92	9.591
43	6.557	93	9.643
44	6.663	94	9.695
45	6.708	95	9.746
46	6.782	96	9.799
47	6.855	97	9.849
48	6.928	98	9.899
49	7.000	99	9.950
50	7.071	100	10.000

BIBLIOGRAPHY

Books

Brown, Robert Goodall. *Statistical Forecasting for Inventory Control.* New York: McGraw-Hill Book Co., 1959.

Green, James H. *Production and Inventory Control Handbook.* New York: McGraw-Hill Book Co., 1970.

Naddor, Eliezer. *Inventory Systems.* New York: John Wiley & Sons, Inc., 1965.

Articles

Brady, Edward, and Babbitt, J. C. "Inventory Control Systems," *Management Accounting,* December 1972.

Bruns, William J. "Inventory Valuation and Management Decisions," *The Accounting Review,* July 1965.

Eden, Donald F. "Computerized Inventory Control in a Small Company," *Management Accounting,* August 1972.

Rinehard, Jack R. "Economic Purchase Quantity Calculations," *Management Accounting,* September 1970.

Toy, James H. "Controlling Sales Goods Inventory," *Management Accounting,* September 1972.

7

Cost Analysis for Project Planning and Control

NOT ALL BUSINESS activity is routine manufacturing work. Construction of a home or building, development of a subdivision site, completion of an audit, closing the books of a large company, changing the machine layout in a large plant, launching a communications satellite, and hundreds of other tasks have nothing routine about them. They are unique. There is much opportunity to capitalize on knowledge of accounting in planning and carrying out unique projects if procedures especially developed for them are used.

These procedures allow you to perform the following planning and control steps:

1. Identify the steps or subactivities which together comprise the overall activity to be planned and controlled.
2. Identify and estimate:
    a) Costs which will be incurred as a direct result of performing a step. These costs may be:
        (1) Independent of step completion time, that is, basic materials in pouring a building foundation; or
        (2) Related to the time taken to perform the step, that is, extra costs of overtime and special equipment if the foundation is to be completely cured by artificial means after it is poured in order to save time. In general, costs related to the planned time to perform a step may be

128

lowered if the planned time is increased and raised if the planned time is decreased.

b) Costs which will be incurred as a result of undertaking the activity as a whole. These costs also consist of:

(1) Costs independent of project completion time; and

(2) Time-related costs. An example of a time-related project cost would be the interest expense on funds borrowed to finance the project. These costs tend to increase as planned project completion time increases.

3. Determine the step and project completion times which will produce the lowest total overall project cost.

4. As the project is underway, monitor rate of activity completion and activity costs; variations from your plans give clues to the need for extra managerial attention.

The accounting function supplies expected values for step and project costs independent of and related to time. These costs serve as building blocks for a budget to control the entire project. The accounting function reports rate of progress and cost accumulation compared with plans to project the step managers.

IDENTIFYING PROJECT COSTS

The key to project planning and control is to identify steps comprising the project and identify time-related and time-independent costs for both individual steps and the project as a whole.

Step Costs

Most unique activities or projects consist of many individual operations or steps. Some of these steps occur simultaneously; others, in a distinct order or sequence. Each step has an identifiable beginning and end. Normally, a step will be assigned to a manager who can identify when the step begins and when it is completed. When a step is identified in this manner, the step-related costs associated with it can also be identified.

Step Costs Independent of Time. Certain costs will be incurred regardless of the step completion time. Imagine a hole to be dug for a pump site foundation. The hole dimensions will have to be surveyed and marked, and the cost of this will not vary with the planned excavation time. Generally, costs of direct materials are time independent, as are administrative costs and some labor costs.

Step Costs Related to Time.   Other step costs do vary with time. For example, if one man with a shovel could dig the foundation in 10 days, it does not follow that 10 men with 10 shovels could dig the hole in 1 day. The 10 men would get in each other's way, efficiency would be reduced, and some time period between 1 and 10 days would be required to dig the hole. Thus, when a step is made shorter, the cost of the step may be expected to increase. The actual relation between completion time and total step costs may be complex, but for simplicity we assume a linear relationship. In Figure 7–1, the dotted line is a typical actual cost-time relation and the solid line is the assumed linear relationship that is used for project planning and control.

FIGURE 7–1
Variation of Step Cost with Time

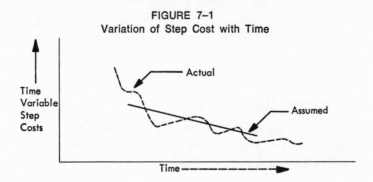

Project-Related Costs

Some portion of the total cost of a project is not directly relatable to component steps. These project-related costs are estimated, controlled, and accounted for without reference to steps. Project-related costs in turn consist of time-related and time-independent costs. Obvious time-related costs are interest charges on money borrowed and penalty or bonus amounts written into a contract and related to a normal completion time. Although such costs don't relate to any particular step, they do relate to the project as a whole and have to be analyzed as such.

The *total* project costs are then determined as

$$
\begin{array}{ccc}
\text{Total} & \text{Project-} & \text{Step-} \\
\text{project} = & \text{related} & + \text{related} \\
\text{costs} & \text{costs} & \text{costs}
\end{array}
\qquad (7\text{--}1)
$$

Or, adding the classification of costs according to their relation to step and project completion time,

$$
\begin{array}{l}
\begin{array}{l}
\text{Total} \\
\text{project} = \\
\text{costs}
\end{array}
\left[
\begin{array}{l}
\text{Time-} \\
\text{independent} \\
\text{project-related} \\
\text{costs}
\end{array}
+
\begin{array}{l}
\text{Time-} \\
\text{related} \\
\text{project} \\
\text{costs}
\end{array}
\right] \\[3em]
+
\left[
\begin{array}{l}
\text{Time-} \\
\text{independent} \\
\text{costs for} \\
\text{step 1}
\end{array}
+
\begin{array}{l}
\text{Time-} \\
\text{related} \\
\text{costs for} \\
\text{step 1}
\end{array}
\right]
\qquad (7\text{--}2) \\[3em]
+
\left[
\begin{array}{l}
\text{Time-} \\
\text{independent} \\
\text{costs for} \\
\text{step 2}
\end{array}
+
\begin{array}{l}
\text{Time-} \\
\text{related} \\
\text{costs for} \\
\text{step 2}
\end{array}
\right]
+
\begin{array}{l}
\text{etc., for all} \\
\text{other steps} \\
\text{in project}
\end{array}
\end{array}
$$

The relations developed in this section are summarized in Figure 7–2.

FIGURE 7–2
Summary of Project Cost Classification and Behavior

	Costs	
	Step Related	*Project Related*
Time Related	Decrease as step completion time extended	Increase as project completion time extended
Time independent.	Should not change	Should not change

ESTIMATING STEP COSTS

Now you have defined the time and cost elements of a project and are ready to use these elements in a project description, as you estimate step costs.

Project Description

After steps are identified and defined, you find the sequence of steps—what steps have to be completed before others can begin, and what step(s) begin the project and what step(s) complete the project. As an example, you might be considering construction of a house. A simplified list of steps and planned or expected completion times t_e is:

Step	t_e (Days)
Foundation	7
Framing	14
Electrical	4
Plumbing	8
Roofing	9
Appliance installation	3
Painting	15
Flooring	5
Cleaning	2

Let us expand on the information in this list by showing what the sequence of steps is:

Step	Step before—	Step after—
Foundation	None	Framing
Framing	Foundation	Electrical, Plumbing, Roofing
Electrical	Framing	Appliance installation
Plumbing	Framing	Appliance installation
Roofing	Framing	Painting
Appliance instal- lation	Electrical, Plumbing	Flooring
Painting	Roofing	Flooring
Flooring	Appliance installation	Cleanup
Cleanup	Flooring	None

This is sufficient information to allow you to make a *network* describing the relationships of steps within the project. The network, which is used extensively in planning the project, is shown in Figure 7–3. Each arrow corresponds to a step. The two dotted arrows do not correspond to real steps; they are only there to show the sequence of steps. "Dummy 1" shows that appliance installation cannot begin until electrical work is finished. "Dummy 2" shows that until painting is completed, flooring cannot begin. All dummy steps have zero completion time; no dummy has any costs associated with it.

It is easier to refer to a step in a network by the numbers at the head and tail of the arrow corresponding to the step. These numbers

FIGURE 7–3
Network Showing Step Relationships

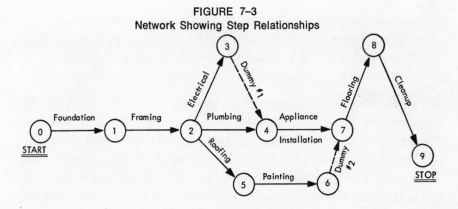

are related to the network structure. Notice that the numbers are arranged so that—

1. The number at the *head* of the arrow is larger than the number at its *tail*.
2. The *lowest* number is at the tail of the *first* step.
3. The *highest* number is at the head of the *last* step.

The numbers corresponding to steps are then

Foundation	01	Appliance	47
Framing	12	Painting	56
Electrical	23	Dummy II	67
Plumbing	24	Flooring	78
Roofing	25	Cleanup	89
Dummy I	34		

Hereafter we shall refer to these steps by the appropriate numbers.

Step Completion Times

Since a substantial part of project costs are related to step completion time, it is important to secure reliable step cost estimates as a function of step completion time. Here is a simple way to work out linear relationships:

1. Secure estimates for the longest reasonable or *u*pper step completion time t_u and the cost of the step if completed in this time.

2. Secure estimates for the shortest reasonable or *lower* step completion time t_l and the cost of the step if completed in this time.
3. Using the two data points thus secured, compute the equation of the straight line joining them.

These estimates should come from persons responsible for carrying out the steps. Their performance will be judged according to how well the step completion time and costs conform to their own estimates.

The interval from t_l to t_u is the interval in which you expect the step completion time eventually chosen to fall. It is the relevant range for the cost estimates. That is, the cost estimates for steps have to be good representations of actual costs within this range of step completion times.

Now let's consider the completion times for the steps of our project. Figure 7–4 below represents step completion time estimates by each

FIGURE 7–4
Completion Times for Steps

Step No.	Step Name	t_l	t_e	t_u
01	Foundation	4	7	9
12	Framing	10	14	21
23	Electrical	2	4	8
24	Plumbing	6	8	9
25	Roofing	4	9	12
34 (dummy)		0	0	0
47	Appliance	1	3	5
56	Painting	10	15	25
67 (dummy)		0	0	0
78	Flooring	4	5	8
89	Cleanup	1	2	4

of the contractors on this particular house. The estimates are for lowest reasonable completion time, expected completion time, and upper reasonable completion time.

Concept of Critical Path. In order to perform the cost-reducing process which will be described shortly, you must understand the idea of a critical path. Consider the short network in Figure 7–5.

The numbers at the midpoints of the arrows represent t_e, the expected time required to complete the step corresponding to the arrow.

FIGURE 7–5
Illustrative Network Showing Critical Path

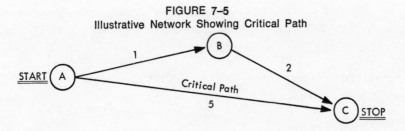

You can see that both steps AB and AC can be started at once. Step AB will be finished in one day and when it is finished, step BC may begin.

Step AC, meanwhile, is still in progress even when both AB and BC are finished. If two crews were working, the ABC crew will sit idle for two days until the AC crew finishes. The project cannot be considered complete until both steps BC and AC are completed. Therefore, it is *critical* that step AC be completed as quickly as possible. *The steps forming the path through the project network which together require the greatest time to complete are the critical path.* The project cannot be completed until all steps on this path are complete. Delay in completing any step on this path will delay the entire project.

That is not true of steps not on the critical path. Here, steps AB and BC are not on the critical path. These steps could be delayed up to two days without lengthening the time required to complete the entire project. If savings result from so doing, these steps' planned completion times should be stretched out by two days. You will find it important to identify the critical path and devote extra planning and control to steps included in it.

Step Completion Costs

We have explained that step costs decline as step completion time is lengthened. Figure 7–5 shows the *variable costs* associated with each step (fixed costs do not change as completion time is varied). The third column is the savings per day if the step is lengthened (this is, of course, the same as the extra cost per day if the project is shortened). In addition, the second column is the *total cost* of each step, if it is completed in its expected time t_e, to serve as a base point.

To illustrate the information content of Figure 7–6, imagine an equation like (7–3) that applies to an individual step:

$$\begin{bmatrix} \text{Step cost} \\ \text{if performed} \\ \text{in time } t \end{bmatrix} = \begin{bmatrix} \text{Step cost} \\ \text{if performed} \\ \text{in time } t_e \end{bmatrix} + (t_e - t)\begin{bmatrix} \text{Incremental change} \\ \text{in step cost per} \\ \text{unit time} \end{bmatrix} \quad (7\text{–}3)$$

where $t_l \leq t \leq t_u$.

FIGURE 7–6
Step Cost as a Function of Completion Time

Step No.	Step Name	Step Cost if Completed in t_e	Incremental Change in Step Cost: $ per Day
01.	Foundation	$ 4,000	$150
12.	Framing	6,000	200
23.	Electrical	1,000	50
24.	Plumbing	1,500	100
25.	Roofing	2,000	200
34 (dummy)		0	0
47.	Appliance	2,200	60
56.	Painting	3,000	120
67 (dummy)		0	0
78.	Flooring	1,500	80
89.	Cleanup	300	30
	Total.	$21,500	

For step 23, numbers would make (7–3) look this way:

$$C_{23,t} = 1,000 + (4 - t)50$$

where $2 \leq t \leq 8$.

Figure 7–7 shows some values of t for step 23 and the corresponding step cost, $C_{23,t}$.

PLANNING COSTS FOR PROJECT AS A WHOLE

You may ask, "If all step costs can be reduced by stretching out step completion times, why cannot we simply require all steps to be done in the longest possible time and thereby minimize project cost?"

The answer is that there are costs for the project as a whole which increase as time passes. In our home construction case, let the construction company incur project-related penalty, interest, and insurance costs

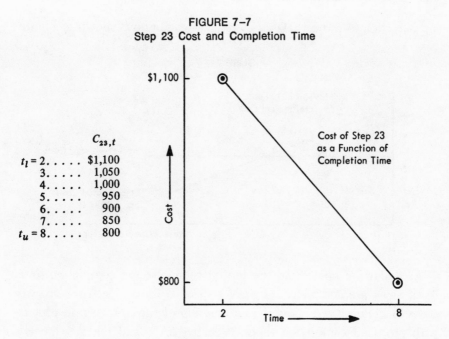

FIGURE 7–7
Step 23 Cost and Completion Time

$C_{23,t}$	
$t_l = 2$.....	$1,100
3.....	1,050
4.....	1,000
5.....	950
6.....	900
7.....	850
$t_u = 8$.....	800

Cost of Step 23
as a Function of
Completion Time

of $300 per day for each day the home remains uncompleted. *Our problem now is to find the completion schedule which has the smallest sum of step-related and project-related costs*, as shown in Figure 7–8.

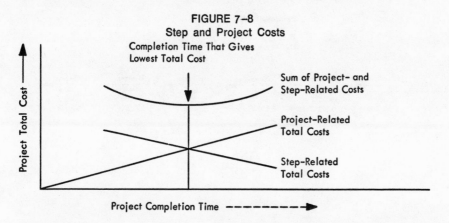

FIGURE 7–8
Step and Project Costs

This lowest total project cost occurs when lengthening the project an additional time unit would incur more project-related costs than would be saved by reducing step-related costs, and shortening the project would incur more additional step-related costs than the corresponding reduction in project-related costs. This condition is shown in Figure 7–9.

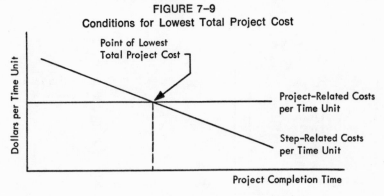

FIGURE 7–9
Conditions for Lowest Total Project Cost

As a starting point, find the project total cost and completion time if all steps are completed in their respective initial t_es. To help, we show in Figure 7 -10 the original diagram of the construction project with projected completion times, expected costs, and the incremental change in dollars per day shown in the middle of each step arrow.

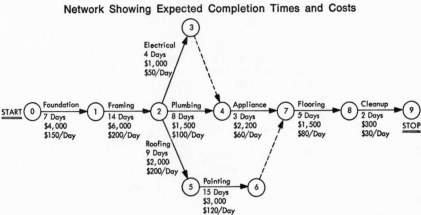

FIGURE 7–10
Network Showing Expected Completion Times and Costs

Total cost = \$37,100; Total time to complete = 52 days.

Here are all three possible paths from *start* to *stop*:

1. 01234789   requires 35 days to complete.
2. 0124789   requires 39 days to complete.
3. 01256789   requires 52 days to complete.

Obviously, path 3 is the critical path since it requires 52 days to complete, which is longer than any other path. The entire construction project will cost $21,500 (the sum of step costs from Figure 7–10) and 52 days times $300 equals $15,600 in project costs—a total of $37,100.

Stretching Out Steps

The first thing that should occur to you is that there is no point in hurrying through the steps which only appear on path 1 or path 2 since these steps do not affect the project completion time. We can save money by stretching out the steps which are unique to these paths.

Rule 1. Look for the steps that will save the *most* money when they are stretched out. Stretch these steps *first.*

The steps unique to path 1 are: 23 and 34. Step 34 is a dummy step and is not considered here. However, step 23 can be stretched out from 4 days to 8 days. The savings will be $4 \times \$50 = \$200$. Then both paths 1 and 2 will arrive at node 4 at the same time.

The step unique to path 2 is 24 (47 is also on path 1). This step may be extended by one day, at a saving of $100.

Step 47 is not unique to any path, but it is not on the critical path. It may be lengthened two days at a saving of $120.

Ideally, you stretch all paths to the same length as the critical path. That is not possible here. We have obtained all the benefits possible from stretching out steps not on the critical path. The revised project cost, step completion times, and overall completion time stand as shown in Figure 7–11.

Shortening the Critical Path

The remaining way to save money is to reduce the length of the critical path. This will run up costs associated with completing steps more rapidly, but also result in a savings of $300 of *project* time-related costs for every day the critical path (and therefore the project) is shortened. This will be desirable so long as the savings exceed the extra expense. The point to stop is where marginal cost $\leq$ marginal savings;

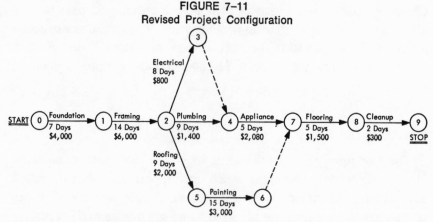

FIGURE 7–11
Revised Project Configuration

Total revised cost = $36,680; Total completion time = 52 days.

that is, any further step shortening would cost more than $300 per day in this illustration. Examine Figure 7–9 again and locate this point.

Rule 2. Look for the steps that cost the *least* money to shorten, and reduce their length first. Shorten *only* steps on the critical path(s).

Step 89 will cost only $30 to shorten by 1 day $(t_e - t_l = 2 - 1 = 1)$.[1] Since this step also shortens the critical path, we go ahead and shorten it. The net saving is $270.

Step 78 may be shortened by one day $(t_e - t_l = 5 - 4 = 1)$ at a cost of $80, so we shorten it next. The net saving is $220.

Step 56 may be shortened by 5 days $(t_e - t_l = 15 - 10 = 5)$, for a cost increment of $600 and a saving of $900 (net).

Step 01 may be shortened 3 days for a net saving of $450.

Step 12 may be shortened 4 days for a net saving of $400.

Step 25 may be shortened 5 days for a net savings of $500.

These changes produce new times to complete the critical and other paths:

Path	Time to Complete (Days)
1. 01234789	32
2. 0124789	33
3. 01256789	33

---

[1] t_e and t_l are shown in Figure 7–4.

You can see that now there are two critical paths: 2 and 3, each requiring 33 days to complete. There are no more steps which may be shortened. Figure 7–12 shows the final version of the project.

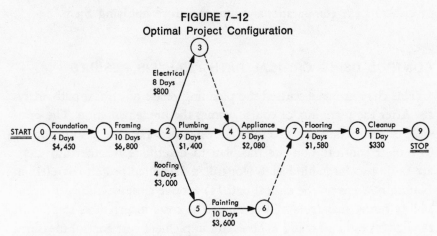

FIGURE 7–12
Optimal Project Configuration

Total optimal cost = $33,940; Total optimal completion time = 33 days.

Compare the optimal completion time of 33 days with the original completion time of 52 days; compare the present lowest completion cost of $33,940 with the original estimated completion cost of $37,100. You expect to build the house faster and save money doing it. This is not the same thing as making water run uphill; you did it by making commonsense judgments, based on accounting information estimates, about which steps in the project to expedite and which to delay and stretch out.

COMPUTER APPLICATIONS

The form of analysis we have demonstrated was developed in the 1950s as a way of expediting completion of military weapons systems. Cost control and analysis features were added when the technique came to be applied to nonmilitary projects.

The calculations quickly become overwhelming if you try to do them by hand on a project of any size. Even special work sheets do not guarantee you will keep track of every path and every step. Luckily, there are computer programs available for commercial computers and through computer centers that perform the calculations for you, turning out tables of step completion times and cost in only a few seconds. Therefore, you need not be an expert about the theory or technique of critical path computational routines before applying them.

CONTROL USING CRITICAL PATH ANALYSIS RESULTS

This chapter has discussed the planning phase of critical path analysis. After the planning, of course, comes the implementation. The principle of comparing actual results with planned expected results applies to project control. You use the plan to determine whether any steps are falling so far behind as to jeopardize scheduled project completion. Naturally, steps on the critical path(s) receive closest scrutiny. Responsibility center managers will compare the costs incurred on steps with the budget estimates, and if necessary implement cost control measures to curb cost overruns. Computer programs are used to make the time and cost comparisons and calculations and print out performance reports in good form which go to responsibility centers supervising the various steps. The computer programs will even indicate which if any future steps in a project should be expedited to keep the project as a whole on schedule.

SUMMARY

Critical path analysis is the most effective means known of organizing, planning, and controlling complex projects when the necessary information input is available. Its calculations are routinized and can be performed by computers, freeing managers to act on the consequences of computer output. To use critical path analysis, you must know the steps in a project, their sequence, their shortest and longest feasible completion times, and the structure of step and project costs as a whole. Critical path analysis assumes (at least in its simplest forms) linear decrease in step costs with increasing step completion time and linear increase in project-related costs as project completion time increases. Solution procedures work to achieve a minimum cost for a project by selectively expediting and stretching out steps. The output of critical path analysis contributes to operational control by providing a realistic project "budget" for comparison with actual project experience.

BIBLIOGRAPHY

Books

Stilian, Gabriel N., *et al.* *PERT: A New Management Planning and Control Technique.* New York: American Management Association, 1962.

Wiest, Jerome, and Levy, F. K. *Management Guide to PERT-CPM.* Englewood Cliffs, N.J.: Prentice-Hall, Inc., 1972.

Articles

Bawly, Dan A., and Dotan, Joseph M. "Using PERT in Accounting Reports," *Management Services,* July–August 1970.

DeCoster, Don T. "Pert-Cost: The Challenge," *Management Services,* May–June 1964.

Schoderbek, Peter P. "Is PERT/Cost Dead?" *Management Services,* November–December 1968.

8

Production Mix and Profit Maximization

CHAPTER 1 presented the dynamic analysis of a business entity. There you learned the basic formulas and concepts that enable businessmen to predict the accounting profit response of companies to new products, selling price changes, capacity changes, direct cost changes, and the economic phenomena which are the cause of such events. That analysis works only when there is just one product or activity. Normally, many activities are carried out together. The activity mix is a major controllable variable in most companies. To assume it is constant is to forego use of a powerful profit-influencing tool, and also unnecessary.

In this chapter you discover linear programming, a simple and useful method of relating accounting profit to degree of participation in different alternative business activities. Here are some of the questions you will see linear programming help answer for a company:

1. What activity mix will produce the largest contribution margin?
2. What is the least expensive way to carry out specific required activities?
3. If the contribution margins on different activities change, should the activity schedule be changed to obtain more profit?
4. Should activities be dropped from or added to a program?
5. How should production capacity be increased or decreased to improve total contribution margin?

Computer programs to solve linear programming problems are widely available; you may never have to solve such a problem of any size yourself, and you will be able to use linear programming in decisions before you understand all the calculations involved. But you must know (and this chapter tells you) how to successfully approach a problem using linear programming and how to identify information describing these problems with corresponding elements of the linear programming model.

Simplifying Assumption—Linearity

The simplifying assumption that makes linear programming models possible is *linearity*. This assumption manifests itself in two ways:

1. The profit or cost associated with one unit of product or activity is the same regardless of when during a period that unit occurs, or whether it is the first, last, or other unit of the period.
2. The resource inputs to a unit of activity are the same regardless of when during a period that unit occurs, or which units of resource inputs are actually included in the activity.

An economist has a way of stating these effects: "Constant returns to scale and no production efficiencies or disefficiencies." Real situations are full of exceptions, but often these can be ignored in order to obtain an easily solved model that gives useful information.

CONSTRAINTS AND CAPACITIES

A linear programming model consists of three sections—

1. A set of constraints describing availabilities, limitations, and relationships of resources to products.
2. Constraints requiring that all variables have values equal to or greater than zero.
3. An objective function—maximized or minimized—which is a weighted linear sum of all the decision variables in the problem.

Constraints are explained in this section; the objective function is explained in the following section.

Illustrative Example

Let us take an illustrative situation involving the Richer Chemical Corporation, which makes commercial organic fertilizers. There are three steps to the manufacturing process: *cooking, drying,* and *packing.* Each process has its own capacity, and each organic fertilizer made has its own slightly different production process. Each fertilizer requires these same three basic steps, however.

Constraints Arising from Productive Capacity

Fertilizer production is planned for one week at a time. Only one 40-hour shift is worked. The cooking and drying processes therefore each have 40 hours per week of operating time. Fertilizer is made by the ton. At the present time, Richer Chemical Corporation is only making two kinds of fertilizer, which we shall refer to as type X and type Y. Both of these fertilizers go through cooking and drying but require different amounts of time. Figure 8–1 gives the times required for cooking and drying per ton of type X and type Y fertilizer made.

FIGURE 8–1
Cooking and Drying Times for Fertilizers X
and Y

	Fertilizer	
	Type X	*Type Y*
Cooking	0.1 hour	0.2 hour
Drying	0.2 hour	0.1 hour
Packing.	0.16 hour	0.16 hour

Each fertilizer process may operate up to 40 hours per week. We can make "time balances" which account for all the time available for cooking, drying, and packing:

Cooking:

Hours spent	Hours spent		
cooking type X +	cooking type Y $\leq$ 40 hours per week	(8–1)
fertilizer	fertilizer	

Drying:

Hours spent   Hours spent
drying type X + drying type Y ≤ 40 hours per week   (8–2)
fertilizer   fertilizer

Packing:

Hours spent   Hours spent
packing type X + packing type Y ≤ 40 hours per week   (8–3)
fertilizer   fertilizer

The actual number of hours spent cooking type X fertilizer is 0.1 × (number of tons of type X fertilizer made). Similarly, the actual hours spent cooking type Y fertilizer is 0.2 × (number of tons of type Y fertilizer made).

Let us choose the symbol X to mean the number of tons of type X fertilizer made per week, and the symbol Y to mean the number of tons of type Y fertilizer made per week. Then the cooking time balance will be:

$$0.1X + 0.2Y \leq 40 \qquad (8–4)$$

You can quickly construct the symbolic representation of the drying and packing time balances using the same principles:

$$0.2\ X + 0.1\ Y \leq 40 \qquad (8–5)$$
$$0.16X + 0.16Y \leq 40 \qquad (8–6)$$

Constraints Describing Nonnegativity

Now, X and Y might either or both be zero, but neither could ever be negative—logic, experience, and the second law of thermodynamics forbid it, but mathematics will not unless we expressly so state. So you also have the statements:

$$X \geq 0 \qquad (8–7)$$
$$Y \geq 0 \qquad (8–8)$$

Equations (8–4), (8–5), (8–6), (8–7), and (8–8) describe the technology and physical characteristics of Richer Chemical's fertilizer production process. Because the relations they describe act to constrain the ways in which that process can operate, we name these equations and others like them, *constraints.*

A *constraint* is a symbolic representation of a restriction on the values which the controllable variables in a linear programming model may assume.

The system of constraints for Richer Chemical can be plotted on rectangular coordinates, such as those in Figure 8–2. Let X be the hori-

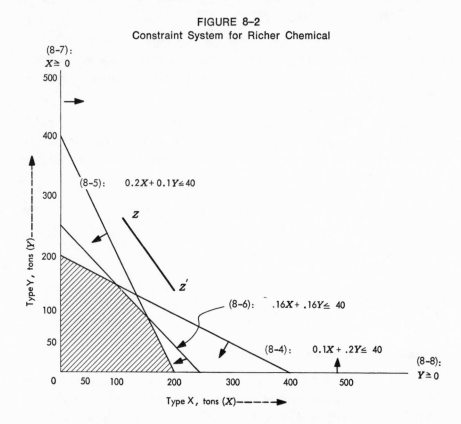

FIGURE 8–2
Constraint System for Richer Chemical

zontal axis and Y be the vertical axis. The graph shows *regions* or areas that correspond to the constraints. For example, all the area *above* the X-axis corresponds to the constraint $Y \geq 0$. All the area to the *right* of the Y-axis corresponds to the constraints $X \geq 0$. Thus, the upper right quadrant is the area that satisfies the two "nonnegativity" constraints, (8–7) and (8–8). Similarly, the area below and to the left of the line labeled (8–4) is the area represented by the inequality $0.1X + 0.2Y \leq 40$. The area below and to the left of the line labeled (8–5) is the area which satisfies the inequality $0.2X + 0.1Y \leq 40$. The area below and to the left of (8–6) satisfies *that* constraint.

All of these areas come together and overlap each other in the cross-hatched area in the lower left-hand corner. The points on the border of and inside this cross-hatched area satisfy all the inequality constraints. Any of them would be a possible plan of operation for Richer Chemical Corporation's fertilizer plant. For example, the point $X = 50$, $Y = 50$ is within this cross-hatched area. You can insert these values for X and Y into the equations and verify that the plant could indeed produce 50 tons of type X and 50 tons of type Y fertilizer:

$$0.1(50) + 0.2 \ (50) = 15 \text{ hours} \leq 40 \text{ hours cooking time}$$
$$0.2(50) + 0.1 \ (50) = 15 \text{ hours} \leq 40 \text{ hours drying time}$$
$$0.16(50) + 0.16(50) = 16 \text{ hours} \leq 40 \text{ hours packing time}$$

Thus under this plan there would be *slack capacity*—25 hours of idle time for the cooker, 25 hours for the dryer, and 24 hours for the packer.

This is not the best plan for operating the fertilizer plant. But in order to know the best plan, we need to know more about the cost and price structure of Richer's fertilizer products.

OBJECTIVE FUNCTION

The selling prices of types X and Y fertilizer are:

Type X . . . . $120 per ton
Type Y . . . . 130 per ton

The variable costs of manufacturing these fertilizers, to the extent they can be identified with a specific fertilizer, are:

Type X . . . . $ 80 per ton
Type Y . . . . 100 per ton

By subtracting the variable costs from the selling prices, we compute the *contribution margin* on each fertilizer:

Type X . . . . $40 per ton = C_x
Type Y . . . . 30 per ton = C_y

The total contribution Z is given by the function:

$$Z = 40X + 30Y \tag{8–9}$$

We are at last ready to make a formal statement of the problem:

Maximize	$Z = 40X + 30Y$	(8–9)
Subject to	$0.1\ X + 0.2\ Y \leq 40$	(8–4)
	$0.2\ X + 0.1\ Y \leq 40$	(8–5)
	$0.16X + 0.16Y \leq 40$	(8–6)
	$X \qquad\quad \geq 0$	(8–7)
	$Y \geq 0$	(8–8)

This statement says that the problem is to find values of X and Y which satisfy the first three constraints (called *technological* constraints since they describe the technology of the fertilizer production process) as well as the last two *nonnegativity* constraints, and also maximize (8–9), the objective function. If Z is made as large as possible, the contribution from fertilizer activities will be maximized by the corresponding values of X and Y. Note that fixed costs, which are a function of time rather than activity mix, are not considered when constructing linear programming models.

GRAPHICAL SOLUTION

Return to the graphical solution of this problem in Figure 8–2. The line ZZ' in the center of the graph has the same slope as the equation $Z = 40X + 30Y$. A line such as ZZ' is plotted by assuming a value for Z, finding any two points corresponding to this equation, plotting those two points on the graph, and drawing the straight line corresponding to them.

Thus, we let $Z = 12,000$. Two points which satisfy $40X + 30Y = 12,000$ are $(X = 0,\ Y = 400)$ and $(X = 300,\ Y = 0)$. Any other two points satisfying the equation would also be satisfactory. When these two points are plotted on Figure 8–2 and connected, the line ZZ' is seen to be part of that line.

The significance for the graphical solution of the line ZZ' and its slope is this: the further to the right or upward a line with the same slope as ZZ' is drawn, the larger is the value of Z, the objective function. *The only limit to how high or how far to the right the objective func-*

*tion line may be pushed is the requirement that it pass through at
least one point in the shaded area or on its boundaries,* which represent
the limitations of the constraints on the solution.

Clearly, the point which produces the largest value of Z must lie
on the boundary of the shaded area, for if it lay inside the shaded
area Z could be pushed higher or further to the right. In short, to
solve the problem *find the Z line which is highest and furthest to
the right and still just touches the boundary of the shaded area. The
point of tangency gives the values of X and Y which are the solution.*

Let us proceed to the graphical solution of the problem before us.
Do this by slowly bringing ZZ' downward and to the left until it *just
touches* the area of acceptable solutions (use a ruler or index card
to get a straight line; move the ruler down until it just touches the
shaded area; keep it parallel to ZZ'). This *tangency* occurs at the corner
caused by the intersection of (8–5) and (8–6) and is the point
($X = 150$, $Y = 100$). Therefore the solution to this linear programming problem is $X = 150$ and $Y = 100$; that is, in the real world,
produce 150 tons per week of type X fertilizer and 100 tons per week
of type Y fertilizer. To show that these values satisfy the technological
constraints, insert them into (8–4) (8–5), and (8–6).

$$0.1(150) + 0.2(100) = 35 \leq 40 \qquad (8\text{–}4)$$
$$0.2(150) + 0.1(100) = 40 \leq 40 \qquad (8\text{–}5)$$
$$0.16(150) + 0.16(100) = 40 \leq 40 \qquad (8\text{–}6)$$

The constraints are all satisfied. Note that (8–4) is satisfied as an
inequality; that is, there are five hours of idle time in the cooking process. This idle time is unavoidable if contribution is to be maximized
by producing type X and type Y fertilizers. A reasonable step for management to take would be to sell or lease this surplus capacity to others
or attempt to eliminate it and its corresponding period-fixed costs.[1]

---

[1] The solution will always be on the boundary of the area containing the
points satisfying the constraint system. In fact, this is critical in solving
complex linear programming problems. We can go even further and say that
the solution will lie at a "corner" of the area satisfying all constraints. Thus, in
complex problems you need only systematically identify all the "corners" of
the area satisfying all constraints, compute the value of Z for each one, and
choose the variable values corresponding to the "corner" which produces the
highest value of Z.

ADDITIONAL PLANNING INFORMATION

What additional information can we gain from the linear programming model of the Richer Chemical Company? All of the questions on page 144 can be answered.

1.   Activity Mix Producing Largest Contribution Margin.
Refer to the preceding section and the solution, $X = 150$ and $Y = 100$.

2.   Least Expensive Way to Carry Out Required Activities.
In the illustration as carried to this point, there is no "required" activity. But suppose Richer Chemical Company was obligated by contract to supply 200 tons of type X fertilizer, and the direct costs of the three input processes were known. Then the objective would be to make the required amount of fertilizer at the lowest total cost. This is called a *minimization problem.* The constraints are usually of the form (left-hand side) $\geq$ (a constant). The line representing the objective function must be moved as close as possible to the point $(0, 0)$ and still pass through one point in the area of points satisfying all constraints. The latter area does *not* include the origin in a minimization problem.

3.   Adjusting Activity Mix to Changes in Activity Contributions.   First of all, you can determine whether a change in the selling price or manufacturing cost of type X or type Y fertilizer would affect the weekly production mix. To illustrate, let us choose two new sets of values for the contribution margins on type X and type Y and recompute the optimum product mix. These sets are:

	Type X	Type Y
Contribution set I	40	53.3
Contribution set II	40	35
(Original contribution set)	(40)	(30)

In Figure 8–3 we have plotted ZZ', the original objective function, II' ($Z_I = 40X + 53.3Y$), and II II' ($Z_{II} = 40X + 35Y$).

We have moved the original objective function line ZZ' down to pass through the solution point in Figure 8–3. The objective function II II', which has a contribution margin per ton of type Y of \$35 instead of \$30, also passes through the same solution point as ZZ'. This means that despite the \$5 increase in margin per ton of type Y, the weekly

FIGURE 8–3
Sensitivity to Activity Unit Contributions

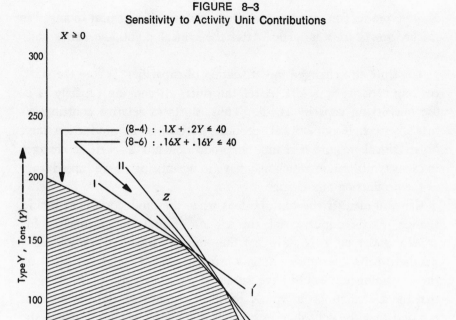

production mix should remain unchanged. The value of Z increases from 9,000 to 9,500 dollars, but the mix itself is unchanged at $X = 150$ and $Y = 100$.

The objective function II′ passes through a different point; however, $X = 100$ and $Y = 150$. This corresponds to changing the production mix from 150 to 100 tons of type X and from 100 to 150 tons of type Y. This change was brought about by a \$23.30 increase in the contribution margin for type Y.

When the contribution margin per ton of type Y increased to a critical point when compared with the contribution margin on type

X, the production mix was shifted. Before this critical point was reached, no shift was made. After the critical point, the *entire* shift was made.

The shift also changed the utilization of capacities. Before the shift, cooking capacity was idle. After the shift, all cooking capacity is in use but drying capacity is idle. Thus, shifts in relative contribution margins may, if not critical, produce no change in production mix; or, if critical, require a change in production mix as well as changes in capacity utilization which may have to be anticipated well in advance of the production mix change.

Can you identify the contributions when the production plan should change? At the critical point, the relation of contribution margins for type X and type Y is such that the objective function line is exactly parallel to the line representing constraint (8–6)—and *any* point on the constraint line would have produced the *same* value of Z. Imagine that the contribution on type X fertilizer remains constant at $40 per ton and that the contribution per ton of type Y increases. When the slopes of ZZ′ and (8–6) are equal, the lines are parallel and coincide. The appropriate proportion that must be solved to find the critical contribution on type Y that makes this happen is

$$
\frac{\text{Type Y critical contribution}}{\underset{\substack{\text{(Coefficient of } Y \\ \text{in } [\,8\text{–}6\,])}}{0.16}} = \frac{\overset{\text{(Old contribution per ton of type X)}}{\$40}}{\underset{\substack{\text{(Coefficient of } X \\ \text{in } [\,8\text{–}6\,])}}{0.16}} \tag{8–10}
$$

Type Y critical contribution = $40

For any type Y contribution over $40, 150 tons of Y would be produced (of course, there is also a value for type Y contribution which would cause NO type X to be produced and 200 tons of type Y to be produced). It is important that the management information system be able to distinguish when this or other critical changes have occurred, to permit adjustments in production mix. It is similarly important not to think the changes have occurred if they haven't—with the attendant unnecessary production mix changes.

To complete this illustration, let us find the *lower* critical limit on the type Y contribution margin. The appropriate proportion this time is:

$$\underset{\substack{\text{(Coefficient of } Y \\ \text{in } [\,8\text{--}5\,])}}{\underset{0.1}{\underbrace{}}} \frac{\text{Type Y critical}}{\text{contribution}} = \frac{\$40}{\underset{\substack{\text{(Coefficient of } X \\ \text{in } [\,8\text{--}5\,])}}{\underset{0.2}{\underbrace{}}}} \overset{\text{(Old contribution}}{\text{per ton of type X)}} \qquad (8\text{--}11)$$

Type Y critical contribution = $20

Recall that (8–5) is the constraint whose boundary is below and to the right of the original solution point. Its slope is more negative than that of the equation for Z. The range of contribution on type Y when type X contribution is constant at $40 is

(Lower) $20 $\leq$ Margin on type Y $\leq$ $40 (upper)

and so long as the margin on type Y remains within these limits, the original optimal production mix will remain at $(X = 150, Y = 100)$.

To show how these limits can be related to decisions, here is the decision rule assuming type X contribution is constant:

	Weekly Production Schedule	
Type Y Contribution	*Tons of X*	*Tons of Y*
0–$20	200	0
$20–$40.	150	100
$40–$80.	100	150
$80+.	0	200

These bounds are valid only if *one* margin is changed (that of Y) and *all* others are held constant. Advanced techniques exist for determining the ranges of validity for margins when two or more change at the same time.

The advantage of knowing these ranges is illustrated by this brief episode from the history of Richer Chemical Company:

Richer Chemical's major competitor was Green Valley Fertilizer Company, which also makes and sells type X and type Y fertilizer.

On March 1, Green Valley announced a major decrease in the price of type Y fertilizer. Since Green Valley sold nearly 90 percent of all the type Y fertilizer sold in the market, Richer Chemical would have to follow the price leader and decrease its price also. The price decrease worked out to a new margin on type Y for Richer of $22 per ton.

"Well," said the president of Richer Chemical, "now that type Y is so much less profitable, perhaps we should attempt to make and sell a great deal less of it than we were when the margin on it was $30. After all, the margin on type X fertilizer remains unchanged—so it seems that a more efficient use of our facilities would be to use them to make more type X fertilizer, and less type Y fertilizer."

You are familiar with linear programming analysis. Quickly you show the president that no change from the present production mix of 150 tons of type X and 100 tons of type Y is necessary; that this production mix still produces the largest possible total contribution margin.

Active businesses are often faced with such decisions, precipitated by changes in market prices for products or product inputs. Linear programming gives decision makers information they can obtain no other way—information concerning the profitability of proposed production mix changes in such circumstances. The accounting responsibility is to define the basic cost and price information required by the linear programming model, then interpret the model output (through decision rules) to management.

4. Adding New or Dropping Old Activities. Often the decision arises: should an old product continue to be made? Should a new product be added to the line currently marketed? Assume that all the products, old and new, are earning revenues in excess of their direct costs and that in one or more respects the company is operating at capacity. Then the decision rule to follow is:

Decision Rule: If an activity change (adding or dropping activities) will *increase* the value of Z, the change should be made.

In a problem of the sort represented by the Richer Chemical Company, scarce resources such as drying and packing time (remember that there is a surplus of cooking capacity) are being employed to produce the maximum total contribution margin. Each scarce resource contributes its share (by imparting value to the products) to the total contribution margin. In a linear programming model this value can be identified for each scarce resource represented by a constraint in the problem formulation.

Example. Let C = value per hour of cooking capacity, D = value per hour of drying capacity, and P = value per hour of packing capacity, all for Richer Chemical when the optimum program as explained earlier is implemented. Further, we know (by a process to be partly explained later) that the values of these variables are:

C = $0 (remember not all cooking capacity is used)
D = $100 per hour
P = $125 per hour

To assure yourself that these are correct values, you might hypothesize that the total contribution margin must be the same as the value it imparts to all the resources used to produce it. The value of Z, the total contribution margin, is:

$40 per ton of type X × 150 tons of type X
 + $30 per ton of type Y × 100 tons of type Y = $9,000   (8–12)

The value of all resources, using C, D, and P as defined above, is:

$0 per hour of cooking capacity × 40 hours
    + $100 per hour of drying capacity × 40 hours
 + $125 per hour of cooking capacity × 40 hours = $9,000   (8–13)

Further, no product may have resources included in it which have a value larger than its contribution margin. For type X,

$0 per hour of cooking capacity × 0.1 hours per ton type X
  + $100 per hour of drying capacity
  × 0.2 hours per ton type X
    + $125 per hour of packing capacity
  × 0.16 hours per ton type X

= *$40 per ton type X* = margin on type X   (8–14)

For type Y,

$0 per hour of cooking capacity × 0.2 hours per ton type Y
  + $100 per hour of drying capacity
  × 0.1 hours per ton type Y
    + $125 per hour of packing capacity
    × 0.16 hours per ton type Y

$$= \$30 \text{ per ton type } Y = \text{margin on type Y} \qquad (8\text{–}15)$$

The values of C, D, and P are sometime called *shadow prices* because they tell the additional contribution of units of scarce resources in a linear programming problem.

Now imagine that Richer chemical is considering a new product: let it be called type Z fertilizer. This material would have to be made with existing capacities, and would require these inputs:

Cooking . . . . 0.2 hours per ton
Drying . . . . 0.3 hours per ton
Packing. . . . . 0.2 hours per ton

Except for cooking, these resources would have to be obtained by *not making* type X and type Y mixes, which would entail a loss of contribution margin. The original decision rule then becomes:

Make a change in the activity mix if the benefit from the change is greater than the loss from the change.

The loss per ton of type Z fertilizer made is:

0.2 cooking hours per ton × $0 per cooking hour
  + 0.3 drying hours per ton × $100 per drying hour
  + 0.2 packing hours per ton × $125 per packing hour

$$= \$55 \text{ per ton of type } Z \qquad (8\text{–}16)$$

Remember, this loss is due to decreased ability to make type X and type Y fertilizers.

The benefit per ton of type Z is its contribution margin. If this benefit is more than $55 per ton, Richer Chemical should make type Z. If this benefit is less than $55 per ton, type Z should not be made. Thus, if the margin per ton of type Z is $50, type Z should not be made; capacities are being more effectively used to make type X and type Y fertilizer.

Re-solving the program would tell you how much type Z to make and what the new X and Y quantities will be if the margin were more than $55.

It should be apparent that accounting systems must distinguish between direct and indirect costs, and provide standard costs of sufficient accuracy to permit decisions such as this one to be made properly. Note that if the unit contribution on the proposed product is quite high or low (say $100, or $20), the accounting measurement does not have to be nearly so discriminating as if the first estimates put it in the neighborhood of $55!

5. *Changing Production Capacities to Improve Contribution Margin.* The "shadow prices" developed above are also useful in determining whether to add capacity. The shadow prices C, D, and P may be regarded as the *contribution* to total contribution margin that would be made if *one* additional unit of a resource is made. (Now you can better understand why $C = \$0$; adding more cooking capacity would not permit more fertilizer of type X or type Y to be made and sold.) *If an additional unit of a resource will cost less than this contribution, it may be acquired.* Thus, if one additional unit of packing capacity will cost $125 or less per week, it should be acquired. If a unit of packing capacity will cost more than $125 per week, it should not be acquired.

SHADOW PRICES IN OPERATIONS CONTROL

Because shadow prices do represent sacrifices of profit if resources are not used optimally, as well as additions to profit if resources are used optimally, they can be used to prepare an unusual operating budget for the Richer Chemical Company. Let a single responsibility center have control of the drying operation. This center's budget is as shown in Figure 8–4.

Now, during the week, the drying department does not quite adhere to this budget, and actual production is 60 tons of type X and 160 tons of type Y. The performance report would appear as shown in Figure 8–5.

This sort of performance report shows the contribution to company performance in terms of scarce capacity utilization. Try to understand

FIGURE 8–4

DRYING DEPARTMENT
Weekly Budget

	Drying Hours per Ton	Total Drying Hours	$ per Hour	Total Contribution
Tons of type X to process:				
150.............	0.20	30	$100	$3,000
Tons of type Y to process:				
100.............	0.10	10	100	1,000
		40		$4,000
				(Planned contribution)

FIGURE 8–5

DRYING DEPARTMENT
Weekly Performance Report

Activity	Planned Contribution	Actual Contribution	Variance
Type X	$3,000	$1,200*	$(1,800) Unfavorable
Type Y	1,000	1,600†	600 Favorable
Total.........	$4,000	$2,800	$(1,200) Unfavorable

* Twelve hours (to dry 60 tons of type X) multiplied by $100 per hour of drying time.
† Sixteen hours (to dry 160 tons of type Y) multiplied by $100 per hour of drying time.

where all the numbers come from in both Figures 8–4 and 8–5. The latter is simplified by considering only production mix variations, and the entire total variation is due to production changes from the original budget which result in idle drying time.

Shadow Prices in Companywide Control

The shadow prices, as the value per unit of optimally used resource, may be used to describe losses of contribution margin due to nonoptimal operations. The linearity of the programming model somewhat restricts this use, but the information is useful if understood. Any nonoptimal use of capacity will produce a total contribution that is *less* than the total value of resources used. The difference represents the loss due to nonoptimal operations—departures from the plan. Because this is a difference of actual from planned contribution rather than actual from planned cost, it is unique. Figure 8–6 shows how a performance statement for the entire company might look.

FIGURE 8–6

RICHER CHEMICAL COMPANY
Weekly Performance Report

Total contribution from operations:

60 tons Type X × $40 per ton	$ 2,400
160 tons Type Y × $30 per ton	4,800
	$ 7,200

Total value of resources used in production:

Cooking time 40 hours × $0 per hour	$ 0
Drying time 40 hours × $100 per hour	4,000
Packing time 40 hours × $125 per hour	5,000
	$ 9,000
Unfavorable variance	$(1,200)

The unfavorable variance in Figure 8–6 is superficially attributable to idle capacity in the drying and packing departments. The real culprit is the improper product mix, which does not allow the departments to use their capacity optimally. Again, efficiency variances have been omitted from Figure 8–6.

Be sure you understand that Figures 8–4, 8–5, and 8–6 do take into account the actual and expected costs of materials, labor, and other inputs as shown on page 149. The control you get through use of contribution figures based on these costs and expected selling prices is significant because it is *direct control of profits.* All activities and variances are reported in terms of their effect on profits. Shadow price analysis is complementary to cost accounting control and control based on budgets and costs directly; it does not replace other types of control or reporting.

SUMMARY

Linear programming offers an extremely powerful analytical and decision model for describing resource allocation problems in terms of accounting and technological information. A linear programming model consists of—

1. A set of constraints which describe resource availabilities, limitations, and relationships to products;
2. Constraints which require all variables to have values equal to or greater than zero; and
3. An objective function which is to be maximized or minimized and is a weighted linear sum of all the decision variables in the problem.

All these relations are linear.

A more efficient method of solving linear programming problems is the *simplex* method; however, when there are only two variables, the graphical method of solution employed in this chapter may be used. In terms of a numerical example, we answered three of the questions posed in the beginning of the chapter. These questions were: best activity mix, changes in activity schedule if relative activity profits change, and adding or dropping activities from the schedule of those performed.

Linear programming models also have an interesting similarity to accounting: although the objective function is expressed in a single type of unit, such as dollars, the decision variables are each in their own dimension—such as units of type A and units of type B fertilizer, and the constraints are each in a different dimension—units of cooking and units of drying capacity. This recalls the many different units (or dimensions) of fundamental accounting processes. The objective function's single dimension recalls the linear aggregation of physical units and prices or costs used to develop a single-dimension measure of entity welfare. Thus, accounting techniques of aggregation and summation to record historical events and evaluate them in terms of a single entity must be used to prepare a linear programming decision model intended to find optimum decisions for a single entity. This similarity may be the reason that so many accountants and managers use linear programming for business planning, operating directly from accounting data and expressing the results in the form of accounting statements.

APPENDIX 8A: WHERE DO SHADOW PRICES COME FROM?

Profit Balance

The key to understanding and computing shadow prices is the notion that the total combined contribution margin produced by products such as type X and type Y fertilizers is equal to the total value *imparted to these products* by the combined cooking, drying, and packing capacities available. Express this equality as

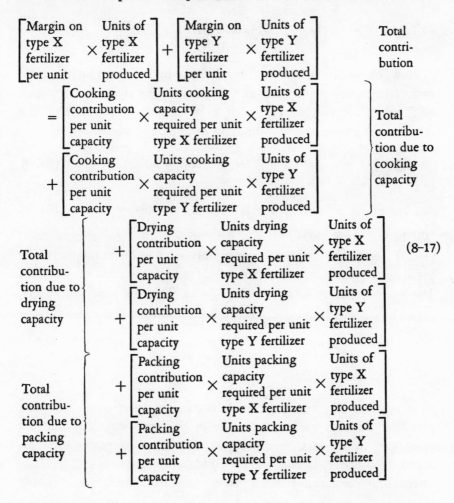

The contribution of a resource per unit capacity *must* be the same regardless of which product it is used in. If this were not so, then resource units would be shifted from the low-contribution products to the high-contribution products, and since you already have an optimum production mix, this cannot happen.

The massive equality above may be expressed much more compactly using the already-introduced symbolic notation of the chapter:

$$40X + 30Y = 0.1CX + 0.2CY + 0.2DX + 0.1DY$$
$$+ 0.16PX + 0.16PY \quad (8\text{-}18)$$

You may rearrange the right-hand side of this equation to produce:

$$40X + 30Y = (0.1C + 0.2D + 0.16P)X$$
$$+ (0.2C + 0.1D + 0.16P)Y \quad (8\text{-}19)$$

Now, make two equations from this one by noticing that the same two variables appear on each side—X and Y, and that the coefficients of X and Y on the left side of (8-18) should be the same as the corresponding coefficients on the right-hand side.

$$0.1C + 0.2D + 0.16P = 40 \quad (8\text{-}20)$$

and

$$0.2C + 0.1D + 0.16P = 30 \quad (8\text{-}21)$$

We have greatly simplified the development of these relationships. (8-20) and (8-21) become constraints in a new linear programming problem, a *minimization* (because C, D, and P are costs of resources and you want to minimize costs) problem. This new *dual* problem is:

$$
\begin{aligned}
\textit{Minimize} \quad & 40C + 40D + 40P \\
\textit{Subject to} \quad & 0.1C + 0.2D + 0.16P \geq 40 \\
& 0.2C + 0.1D + 0.16P \geq 30 \\
& C, \quad D, \text{ and } P \geq 0
\end{aligned}
$$

This problem may be solved in 3-dimensional space using the same graphical concepts used to solve the original problem. You plot the constraints as volumes, then note the volume of acceptable solutions *above* the boundary lines and to the *right* (since these are "greater-than-or-equal-to" constraints). Since you are minimizing, you would choose the point on the boundary plane which was lowest and furthest to the left. In this particular case, that point is:

$$C = \$0 \qquad D = \$100 \qquad P = \$125$$

as assumed in the body of the chapter.

BIBLIOGRAPHY

Books

Driebeek, Norman J. *Applied Linear Programming*. Reading, Mass.: Addison-Wesley Publishing Co., Inc., 1969.

Gass, Saul I. *An Illustrated Guide to Linear Programming*. New York: McGraw-Hill Book Co., 1970.

Levin, Richard I. and Lamone, Rudolph P. *Linear Programming for Management Decisions*. Homewood, Ill.: Richard D. Irwin, Inc., 1969.

Loomba, N. Paul. *Linear Programming, An Introductory Analysis*. New York: McGraw-Hill Book Co., 1964.

Articles

Demski, Joel S. "An Accounting System Structured on a Linear Programming Model," *The Accounting Review*, October 1967.

Ijiri, Yuji; Levy, F. K.; and Lyon, R. C. "A Linear Programming Model for Budgeting and Financial Planning," *Journal of Accounting Research*, Autumn 1963.

Moore, Joe F. "What Operations Research Means to the Accountant," *Management Advisor*, November–December 1966.

Palmer, B. Thomas. "Management Reports for Multiproduct Plants," *Management Accounting*, August 1970.

Samuels, J. M. "Opportunity Costing: An Application of Mathematical Programming," *Journal of Accounting Research*, Autumn 1965.

Summers, E. L. "The Audit Staff Assignment Problem," *The Accounting Review*, July 1972.

Wilson, J. R. M. "Profitability as a Tool in Product Planning," *The Arthur Young Journal*, Winter 1966.

9

Decision Making and Information System Performance

THUS FAR you have studied four important recurring managerial decisions—capital budgeting, inventory planning and management, large-scale project planning and control, and production mix analysis. Each decision has its information requirements, which accounting analysis and accounting systems help to satisfy. In this chapter, you learn the conceptual relationships between decisions and information systems.

Some Basic Terminology

Let us suppose you are a "Popcorn King" and have the football game popcorn franchise. You must decide how much popcorn to buy for sale at football games. Figure 9–1 gives the matrix of payoffs occurring for each combination of number of bags of popcorn bought and number of bags demanded at the Big Game.

The range of bags of popcorn you can buy before the game is called your *set of alternatives*. Your alternatives consists of all the values of all the variables you control. For example, you may have any number of popcorn suppliers arrive up to one hour before game time and charge any price per bag you wish. Here we are assuming that you already have determined the price per bag (10 cents), have selected

FIGURE 9–1
Popcorn King Payoffs
(in cents per bag)

Bags of Popcorn Bought	Number of Bags Demanded at Game					
	0	1	2	3	4	5
0	0	0	0	0	0	0
1	(5)	5	5	5	5	5
2	(10)	0	10	10	10	10
3	(15)	(5)	5	15	15	15
4	(20)	(10)	0	10	20	20
5	(25)	(15)	(5)	5	15	25

a supplier of popcorn who charges you 5 cents per bag, and begin to sell popcorn exactly as the game begins. Thus the only remaining variable whose value must be set is the number of popcorn bags you will buy.

The range of the number of bags that may be demanded at a game is called the *set of states* (those who appreciate a touch of the metaphysical will say "the set of states of nature"). Your states of nature contain variables you cannot control. For example, the number of bags demanded at a game may depend on the weather or how many season ticket holders come to the game. The state of nature that actually occurs—how many bags of popcorn you sell—is composed of all the variables and factors you as a decision maker must accept as "given" and uncontrollable.

Your objective in deciding how many bags of popcorn to buy is to obtain the largest *payoff* possible. The payoffs are the figures you have worked out in the body of the matrix table, Figure 9–1.

As a decision maker you will find there are two types of decisions depending on the availability of the information you have to work with—decisions under certainty and decisions under uncertainty. These decisions together with their information systems are discussed in the sections that follow.

WHEN ONLY ONE STATE IS POSSIBLE

A decision under certainty is characterized by the unique circumstances of there being possible only *one* state, which is fully and completely known in advance. All of the decisions studied so far are decisions under certainty. Here is an elaboration:

Decision	Variables Defining State
Capital allocation	Proposed investment's lifetime, cost, net cash flows, and appropriate investor's target rate of return (ITRR) explained in Chapter 5. Your alternatives were possible capital investments. You found it easy to compute each one's current equivalent, then to select those whose current equivalents were highest.
Inventory management	Demand, order cost, carrying cost, shortage cost. When certain assumptions are valid, you just "plug" these figures into formulas and compute the least-cost inventory policy, which was the preferred alternative.
Project planning and control	Project and step completion times, time dependent and time independent costs. By use of special algorithms you selected the schedule which completed a project at lowest total cost.
Product mix analysis	Resource availabilities and capacities, technological coefficients, and product contribution margins. Graphical and numerical methods allow you to calculate a maximum-profit or least-cost product mix.

With decisions under certainty, the decision steps are to develop all the information needed, compute the payoff associated with each alternative, and choose the alternative with the highest payoff. As an example, if you know that demand for popcorn at the game will be precisely four bags, you would see from Figure 9–1 that the highest profit of 20 cents would then be earned if four bags were purchased. In other words,

If this many bags are bought:	0	1	2	3	4	5
The payoff is:	0¢	5¢	10¢	15¢	20¢	15¢

By inspection you quickly decide to buy four bags to sell.

Expectations and Reality

Of course, when you are planning, the numbers 0, 5, 10, 15, 20, 15 are only your best **expectations** about the payoffs of the respective alternatives. Until you actually buy popcorn and try to sell it you won't know the *true* payoff.

Your information about expected payoffs was derived from your decision information system. If this information is not completely accurate, you may or *may not* be led into a wrong decision. So long as the information leads you to select the alternative "buy four bags of popcorn," the information system for decision making is operating satisfactorily. If you are led to choose some other alternative, the information system is not operating satisfactorily and it *may* be in your interest to improve it.

Effect of Information System Error on Decisions

Due to price fluctuations, weather, etc. which are known to you but which your information system improperly evaluates, your decision is based on the predicted payoffs in the second column below. The actual payoffs observed later appear in the third column.

Number of Bags Bought	Information System Predicts This Payoff	Actual Payoff Would Be This
0	0	0
1	5	8
2	10	16
3	15	24
4	20	32
5	15	24

Using the predicted payoffs, you would come to the same decision as you would if you knew the actual payoffs. There would be no point in attempting to improve this information system, for it leads to optimal decisions. But below is the output of a system which would mislead you:

Number of Bags Bought	Information System Predicts This Payoff	Actual Payoff Would Be This
0	0	0
1	6	8
2	10	16
3	16	24
4	20	32
5	24	24

Your information system leads you to buy five bags rather than four, causing you to forego 8 cents (not 4 cents) of profit a better information system might have brought you. Worse still, you compare the predicted 24 cents of profit with the actual 24 cents of profit and conclude that your decision worked well. Thus, you were not only deprived of additional profit, but also of the feedback that would have helped you discover something was wrong with your decision and decision information.

Cost of Information

The cost of information has a critical bearing on whether you attempt to improve a malfunctioning information system. In the data immediately above, you would be willing to spend up to 8 cents to discover the proper number of popcorn bags to buy (equal, of course, to the gain in contribution that would result from the improved information).

In repeating decisions, the problem whether to improve the information basis is itself an important resource allocation decision that should be regarded as a capital budgeting decision. To illustrate, let your firm have an ITRR = 20 percent and let the popcorn decision be made 10,000 times per year for five years. An information systems consultant has offered to provide completely accurate data describing the payoff of all such decisions, given only the demand for popcorn at each game. You expect this would produce the average 8 cents per game improvement, or $0.08 × 10,000 = $800 per year. There would be no direct costs of the additional improved information, only a one-time charge of $2,000. Should you pay this charge and shift to completely accurate data?

The current equivalent of five annual payments of $800 each with a 20 percent ITRR is $2,392. This is greater than $2,000 and therefore should receive favorable consideration. Had the current equivalent of the improved information been less than $2,000, the information would not produce enough improvement in decisions to justify its cost. A similar evaluation would apply if the improved information produced a direct cost, say $0.01, that had to be deducted from the contribution increment of $0.08. Your annual payment due to improved information would then be ($0.08 − $0.01 = $0.07) × 10,000 = $700.

Decision Models' Sensitivity to Information

All of the decision models you have studied in this section are sensitive to changes in the information used to describe the existing state of nature. Here are brief examples, taken from the numerical illustrations already presented.

Capital Allocation. Suppose that your information system misestimates annual cash operating savings on the sub-limer investment decision discussed in Chapter 5. The true figure turns out to be $180,000 (rather than the expected $119,000) annually. The current equivalent of this sum is $870,000, making the sub-limer more attractive in operation than it was in contemplation.

If the sub-limer was rejected on the basis of available information, Mildew Mining Company would in effect have foregone the benefit of having the sub-limer: $870,000 — $780,000 = *$90,000.*

The decision is also sensitive to changes in ITRR. Given the cash flows in Chapter 5, their current equivalent varies with ITRR as indicated:

ITRR	Cash Flow Current Equivalent
8	$798,000
16	575,153
18	534,810

However, if the information error involves just a few of the cash payments, the significance of the error is greater if it occurs early in the proposed investment's lifetime. A $10,000 overestimate of net cash flow, using a 20 percent ITRR, will overstate current equivalent by $8,333 if it occurs in the first year, but only by $1,615 if it occurs in the 10th year.

Inventory Management. In Chapter 6 we indicated that the inventory model is relatively insensitive to measurement errors of its major variables. The stress there was on the value of the model even when information to support it did not appear of especially high quality. Now, we show the benefit that could be achieved by "cleaning up" this information.

Recall that in the Chapter 6 discussion of sensitivity analysis, the information system was assumed to estimate carrying cost as $10 when it was actually $20. The result was an inventory policy which cost $1,028.74 per period rather than $958.38, the optimal policy cost. The loss due to imperfect information was $1,028.74 — $958.38 = *$70.36* per period. You should be willing to pay up to this amount per period in order to obtain perfect information about the carrying cost. This $70.36 should not be confused with the savings realized by going from the original non-EOQ policy to an EOQ policy based on imperfect information, which was much larger.

Project Planning and Control. The steps in the critical path(s) of a project are those for which information errors can produce the most spectacular delays and costs. A cost estimation error cannot be exaggerated or minimized regardless of the step in which it occurs, but an error in fixing the completion time of a critical path step may produce scheduling errors and attendant correction costs in many other steps. These errors arise because you plan to complete a step in, say, 40 days, then discover that the rate of work you thought would yield this completion time actually produces a 45-day completion time.

To try to anticipate this sort of information error, planners may, after the ideal schedule has been established, seek estimates of the longest and shortest completion times. The former will occur under pessimistic assumptions about the activity; the latter, under optimistic assumptions. If a probability distribution is assumed to govern the distribution of step completion times, you can compute estimates of *expected* (in the probabilistic rather than the planned sense) step completion time and the *variance* of this expected completion time. You can add together the expected completion times of all steps along a path and obtain an expected completion time for that path, and by adding variances obtain a variance for the completion time of the path. Some illustrative results of such analysis appear in Figure 9–2. The thing to notice is that any of the paths in this project *could* be critical paths and lack of perfect information prevents you from identifying one as unquestionably the critical path.

FIGURE 9–2
Illustrative Results of Analysis of Variation
in Step and Path Completion Times

Path	Expected Path Completion Time (Days)	Standard Deviation of Path Completion Time (Days)
1	100	20
2	90	30
3	115	25

If path 1 is delayed, for example, due to information system error in relating rate of completion to resource input, it may easily extend beyond the 115 days path 3 is expected to last, and replace the latter as the critical path. Or if paths 1 and 3 proceed unexpectedly rapidly, path 2 may be the critical path. Path 3 itself may be delayed and extend the entire project.

The costs of the imperfect information would be those costs incurred to avoid the worst of its effects. You may decide to expedite *all* paths by 10 days to assure that the entire project may be completed in 115 days. Such expediting would not be necessary if your information was known to perfectly anticipate the project's dynamics; and so its cost would be avoidable if you had perfect information. If the cost of expediting is estimated at $1,000 per day, you would spend up to $10,000 to obtain improved information.

Of course, expediting in the absence of pinpoint estimates doesn't guarantee project completion in *any* chosen time frame—just makes it more likely.

Product Mix Analysis. In Chapter 8, you saw how sensitivity analysis could show you the proper solution to a product mix problem when the contribution per unit of the different products changed. The same methods may be used to show how information errors lead to additional costs in such decisions.

The original contributions in the Chapter 8 illustrative problem were $40 per unit of X and $30 per unit of Y. Let these be the actual contributions. Now, let the information system erroneously estimate C_y as $35 per unit. Despite the error, the Z-line in Figure 8–3 still passes through the same solution point as the actual Z-line, and the solution that is optimal with the estimation error turns out to be optimal when the decision is implemented.

If C_y is estimated at $53.30 per unit, the estimation error is large enough to cause a nonoptimal solution to be selected. In Figure 9–3 we give the two solutions and the loss of contribution (measured by using the actual C_y rather than the erroneous estimate) from choosing the nonoptimal solution.

Let us examine the problems arising from the information error and nonoptimal product mix chosen as a result.

The first problem arises when actual results are compared with ex-

FIGURE 9–3
Cost of Information Error in Product Mix Analysis

True Values	Information System Values	Optimal Total Contribution	Total Contribution Realized
$C_x = 40$ . . . . $C_x = 40$ $C_y = 30$ . . . . $C_y = \$53.30$		$9,000	$8,500

pectations. The plan called for 100 units of X and 150 units of Y to be produced. Assume this occurred; the total contribution *expected* would be $100 \times \$40 + 150 \times \$53.30 = \$11,995$. The actual contribution observed will be $8,500, and the $3,495 difference would be regarded as a most puzzling unfavorable variance. This variance might be attributed to production, sales, uncontrollable factors, or to imperfect information.

The second problem arises when deciding what to do about the information system error. The computed variance of $3,495 is not the amount that can be spent to improve information, for the $11,995 contribution was never (and never will be) achievable. Better information will be worth up to $9,000 - $8,500 = *$500*—the difference between the optimal and nonoptimal decision payoffs, computed using the error-free contribution rates.

WHEN MORE THAN ONE STATE IS POSSIBLE

Only one state may occur at the time your decision is effective. In *decisions under uncertainty* you don't know what that state will be. You know it will be one of a set of such states, and you also have (for purposes of this discussion) the *relative frequencies* with which states occur. These relative frequencies are expressed as a set of numbers between 0 and 1.0, which together add up to 1.0, and each of which relates to one state. These numbers are called the *state probability distribution*. If you allow a friend to flip a coin which cannot stand on edge, two states are possible: heads and tails. Each state is equally likely—has the same relative frequency—and so the state probability distribution is $[p(\text{heads}) = 0.50; p(\text{tails}) = 0.50]$.

Decision Rules and Policies

A decision rule is a policy which tells you which alternative to choose to give the highest payoff when you believe a particular state is going to occur. In terms of the Popcorn King example, here are a few of the many decision rules which could have been adopted to guide you in making that decision when you do not know exactly which state might occur (Figure 9–4).

FIGURE 9–4
Popcorn King Decision Rules

If You Expect to Sell This Many Bags	Then Order This Many Bags			
	Rule 1	*Rule 2*	*Rule 3*	*Rule 4*
0.	0	0	5	2
1.	1	0	5	2
2.	2	0	5	2
3.	3	0	5	2
4.	4	0	5	2
5.	5	0	5	2

Rule 1 is the rule to use if you can tell in advance how many bags will be demanded, for it always produces the largest payoff if that demand occurs. Rule 2 is a conservative rule that will never get you into trouble, for it requires no investment and stands no chance of loss—or of profit. Rule 3 is the riskiest rule unless you are able to sell five bags. If five bags aren't sold, you suffer declining profits. You might choose rule 3 if you did not mind having leftover bags as much as you minded losing sales due to inadequate inventory. Rule 4 requires that you buy two bags of popcorn regardless of the state. Rule 4 produces the highest *average* payoff possible if the same number of bags must be bought before *every* game.

Identifying the Highest Average Payoff Alternative. To explain development of decision rule 4, you must distinguish between two kinds of decisions under uncertainty:

a) Decisions in which no information is available about the future state of nature that will occur when the decision becomes effective beyond that describing the relative frequencies of states.

b) Decisions in which, in addition to the relative frequencies of states, you know or can find out more about which state of nature will occur when the decision is effective.

Identifying the Highest Average Payoff Alternative when No Information Is Available. To predict demand, you could rely totally on records of past popcorn demand at previous games. Assuming all football games are alike, the same sort of popcorn demand should occur in the future, and thus a *prior distribution* as shown in Figure 9–5 applies to possible popcorn demand levels.

When no additional information is available, you must identify the number of bags to order that will give the highest total payoff over a large number of games whose popcorn demands are distributed as in Figure 9–5. Return to the payoff table in Figure 9–1 and note

FIGURE 9–5
Prior Distribution over Popcorn Demand Levels

Number of Bags to Be Demanded	*Probability of This Demand*
0.	0/6
1.	1/6
2.	3/6
3.	1/6
4.	1/6
5.	0/6
	6/6 Total (always = 1.0)

that if you order one bag, in 0 games you will not sell this bag, in 1/6 of the games you will sell this bag exactly, and in $3/6 + 1/6 + 1/6 = 5/6$ of all games you could sell more than one bag. Your expected payoff for ordering *one* bag is then:

$$(5\cent) \times (0/6) + 5\cent \times (1/6) + 5\cent \times (5/6) = 5\cent$$

Your expected payoff for ordering *two* bags is:

$$(10\cent)(0/6) + (0\cent)(1/6) + 10\cent(5/6) = 50/6\cent$$

Your expected payoff for ordering *three* bags is:

$$(15\cent)(0/6) + (5\cent)(1/6) + 5\cent(3/6) + 15\cent(1/6) + 15\cent(1/6) = 40/6\cent$$

You should try the computation for 0, 4, and 5 bags and confirm that the expected payoffs are 0, 20/6 cents, and (10) cents respectively.

These are the average payoffs per game if the indicated number of bags is bought constantly. In no one game will the payoff be exactly that much—only the average over a large number of games will approach the expected payoff.

Since buying two bags has the highest expected payoff for the given prior distribution, you should buy two bags before every game.

Identifying the Highest Average Payoff Alternatives when More Information Is Available. When more information is available to identify the state of nature that will occur when a decision becomes effective, it is usually possible for the decision maker to choose a different alternative for each state if he thinks that state will occur. The additional information affects the state probability distribution, making one or more states appear much more likely to occur than before. To fully realize the impact of additional information, suppose you go to the game and sell your two bags, and also have opportunities to sell two more bags. Although you bought and sold two bags for a profit of 10 cents, you wish you had known that you could have sold four bags. Ideally, you wish you had known that you could have sold *exactly* four bags so you could have realized a profit of 20 cents, just as you would have done in a decision under certainty. This is rarely possible, but progress toward this goal can often be made.

For example, when you approach a busy traffic intersection, you don't know if the intersection is clear until you are in it. As a *data-gathering process* before you reach the intersection, you glance at a traffic light, which is green. You interpret this as an indication that the intersection will remain clear until you finish crossing it. Traffic accident statistics attest to the occasional fallibility of such reasoning, but the system does work with a substantial degree of reliability.

Suppose you discover a close relationship between advance ticket sales (announced Friday before the game) and popcorn sales at the game. The data-gathering process consists of calling the ticket office and asking the quantity of tickets already sold. Figure 9–6 shows what you found out.

You can calculate the potential value of this information. Decision rule 1 in Figure 9–4 advised you to always buy the number of bags you expected to be demanded and now, through advance tickets sales,

FIGURE 9–6
Results of a Data-Gathering Process

Advance Ticket Sales	Bags of Popcorn Demanded at Game
20.	0
30.	1
40.	2
50.	3
60.	4
70.	5

you have knowledge in advance—perfect, unequivocal knowledge—what demand will be. In Figure 9–7 we use decision rule 1 with this

FIGURE 9–7
Calculation of Expected Value of Decision

0/6 of demand will be for 0 bags. Buy 0 bags
and make 0¢. Multiply this by 0/6 and get 0/6
1/6 of demand will be for 1 bag. Buy 1 bag
and make 5¢. Multiply this by 1/6 and get 5/6
3/6 of demand will be for 2 bags. Buy 2 bags
and make 10¢. Multiply this by 3/6 and get 30/6
1/6 of demand will be for 3 bags. Buy 3 bags
and make 15¢. Multiply this by 1/6 and get 15/6
1/6 of demand will be for 4 bags. Buy 4 bags
and make 20¢. Multiply this by 1/6 and get 20/6
0/6 of demand will be for 5 bags. Buy 5 bags
and make 25¢. Multiply this by 0/6 and get 0/6

6/6 = *sum of weights* *Expected value of decision* . . . . .   70/6¢

perfect knowledge of the future state to compute the expected value of the decision with perfect knowledge.

The value at bottom right in Figure 9–7 is the expected contribution of the decision when you are perfectly informed about the state of the environment that will exist when the decision is effective. To compute it, you simply took the largest payoff for each state and multiplied it by the probability of that state's occurring.

Value of Information. Without the data-gathering process, the best you could expect from this decision was 50/6 cents. Having perfect information is worth an additional $(70 - 50)/6 = 20/6$ *cents.* For perfect information you would pay up to 20/6 cents per game.

Less than Perfect Information. Most data-gathering processes, such as those operated as accounting information systems, deliver less-than-perfect information. Imperfect information's benefits have to be reckoned against its cost so you know whether to acquire it. The marginal return on resources employed to obtain information should be the same as the marginal returns on resources employed otherwise. Assume decreasing marginal returns to scale; then if the marginal return from information is *less* than the marginal return from other resource uses, the resources dedicated to information gathering should be *reduced;* if the marginal return is greater, the resources dedicated to information gathering should be *increased.*

Imperfect information will change the prior probability distribution so that fewer states are favored. As an example of imperfect information, let popcorn demand be determined by advance ticket sales *plus* other factors about which you have no knowledge. The relations in Figure 9–8 are observed.

Here is an explanation of Figure 9–8. You are interested in the significance of advance sales = 40. Out of the last 18 games, advance

FIGURE 9–8
Example of Imperfect Information

Game	Advance Ticket Sales	Popcorn Demand	Total Times Advance Ticket Sales = 40	Total Times Advance Ticket Sales = 40 Followed by Popcorn Demand =		
				2	or	3
1.	30	1				
2	40	3	1			3(1)
3	40	2	2	2(1)		
4	40	2	3	2(2)		
5	50	2				
6	60	4				
7	40	3	4			3(2)
8	30	1				
9	40	2	5	2(3)		
10	50	2				
11	60	4				
12	50	2				
13	30	1				
14	40	2	6	2(4)		
15	60	4				
16	40	2	7	2(5)		
17	40	3	8			3(3)
18	40	2	9	2(6)		

ticket sales were 40 nine times. Six of those times, popcorn demand was two bags; three times, three bags. Thus it appears that when advance ticket sales are 40, the probability of two bags being demanded is 6/9; the probability of three bags being demanded, 3/9. Figure 9–9 states the new state probability distribution.

FIGURE 9–9
Change of State Probabilities Resulting from
Imperfect Information

Before Data Gathering	*After Data Gathering*	
$p(0 = \text{demand}) = 0/6$	0/6	
$p(1 = \text{demand}) = 1/6$	0/6	
$p(2 = \text{demand}) = 3/6$	4/6	Unique to advance
$p(3 = \text{demand}) = 1/6$	2/6	ticket sales = 40
$p(4 = \text{demand}) = 1/6$	0/6	
$p(5 = \text{demand}) = 0/6$	0/6	

What is the value of the information in Figure 9–9? The analytical process is too detailed to recount in an introductory chapter, but the essence of it is this: Each particular output of the data-gathering process (in this case, values of advance ticket sales) implies a different state probability distribution (the distribution for sales = 40 is contained in Figure 9–9). Using each probability distribution, some particular alternative has the highest expected payoff (computed just as was the expected payoff of each alternative using the probability distribution in Figure 9–5). These alternatives with the highest expected payoffs may be linked to corresponding data-gathering process outputs and form the highest payoff decision rule to use with that data-gathering process.

The best decision rule (that produces the highest payoff when used with advance ticket sales as a predictor of demand) is:

If advance sales are 30	buy 1 bag
If advance sales are 40	buy 2 bags (you can verify this one)
If advance sales are 50	buy 2 bags
If advance sales are 60	buy 4 bags

The expected value of this decision rule is *65/6 cents*. Thus, the rule based on imperfect information cannot perform as well as the rule based on perfect information (expected value = 70/6 cents), but it does much better than the rule based on lack of any additional information whatever, which had an expected value, you recall, of 50/6 cents.

Investing in Information. If you had to pay 9/6 cents in direct costs for the imperfect information in Figure 9–8 each time you decided how much to order, your additional profit would be $(15 - 9)/6 = 1$ cent.

As with other investments, the fact that marginal gain exceeds marginal cost doesn't necessarily mean that you should incur the cost. The return must be equal to or greater than any return you receive from alternative investments. If your 9/6 cents would return you 20/6 cents in a comparable alternative investment, and you have only the 9/6 cents to spend, you should keep your ignorance, use decision rule 4 from Figure 9–4 for the popcorn ordering decision and put your money into the alternative investment.

Competing information systems should be judged not so much on how closely their output approaches perfect information but on how much net return they can produce for you. Figure 9–10 shows three

FIGURE 9–10
Criteria for Evaluating Data-Gathering Processes

	Process 1	Process 2	Process 3
Expected value per decision	68/6	65/6	60/6
Less:			
Expected value of decision *without* more information.	(50/6)	(50/6)	(50/6)
Expected cost of more information	(10/6)	(9/6)	(1/6)
Expected contribution of information	(8/6)	(6/6)	(9/6)

data-gathering processes for the popcorn decision; it happens that the best of these is also the one which gives the least-perfect information. The reason is that its extreme economy enables it to show the highest net contribution.

DECISION MODELS FOR UNCERTAINTY

All of the decision models you have studied in this section have adaptations intended for use when environmental uncertainty exists.

These adaptations are more complex than the models intended for decisions under certainty.

Capital Allocation

Uncertainty is introduced into capital budgeting models in several ways. Perhaps the easiest to visualize is that several different economic conditions are possible, each implying a different set of net cash flows. The fact that alternative cash flows are possible does not alone make an investment proposal *"risky"* in the sense of Chapter 5; for if all economic conditions led to essentially equal cash flows, there would be little risk in the proposal. Thus, risk stems from alternative cash flows which differ in magnitude—and the greater the differences, the greater the investment risk. A decision model format which takes this approach is shown in Figure 9–11.

FIGURE 9–11
Capital Allocation Decision Model under Uncertainty

States.	State 1	State 2	etc.
State probabilities.	p(state 1)	p(state 2)	etc.
Alternatives:			
Proposal A.	Current equivalent of proposal A if state 1 occurs	Current equivalent of proposal A if state 2 occurs	
Proposal B.	Current equivalent of proposal B if state 1 occurs	Current equivalent of proposal B if state 2 occurs	
etc., for all alternative investments			

To use this model, you need to know all alternative investment proposals (or investment programs) and the effect on net cash flow of all such proposals by each possible state.

Inventory Management

To simulate uncertainty in an inventory situation, one usually assumes that all costs are known, but that demand may occur at any one of several possible rates. Optimal policies (or, several alternative policies which are each *nearly* optimal) are known for each demand pattern, and the cost of implementing each one may be computed for all possible demand rates. The decision model for uncertainty for inventory management appears as Figure 9–12.

FIGURE 9–12
Inventory Management Decision Model under Uncertainty

States.	State 1 (demand level 1)	State 2 (demand level 2)	etc.
State probabilities.	p(state 1)	p(state 2)	etc.
Alternatives:			
Policy A	Cost of policy A for state 1	Cost of policy A for state 2	
Policy B	Cost of policy B for state 1	Cost of policy B for state 2	
etc., for all inventory policies			

In the inventory management decision, the choice of policy is on the basis of lowest expected cost rather than highest expected contribution. Additional methods, not based on economic order quantity analysis, exist to provide least-cost inventory policies where the EOQ assumptions are not valid.

Product Mix Analysis

Use of project planning and control and linear programming are both immensely complicated by introducing uncertainty into these decision models. A variety of approaches exist, none of them "intuitively obvious" and most of them requiring considerably analytical skill to set up and computing power to solve.

However, let us illustrate using a simple product mix analysis under uncertainty decision. Uncertainty may occur with respect to any part of the problem; let us assume that different economic conditions may occur and that to each possible economic decision there corresponds a different set of unit contribution margins. Then, assuming these margins differed significantly, you would have a different optimal solution to the problem for each set of economic conditions. Figure 9–13 shows this illustrative model.

FIGURE 9–13
Product Mix Decision Model under Uncertainty

States.	State 1 (contribution margin set 1)	State 2 (contribution margin set 2)	etc.
State probabilities.	p(state 1)	p(state 2)	etc.
Alternatives:			
Production mix A. . . .	Value of objective function for product mix A in state 1	Value of objective function for product mix A in state 2	
Production mix B. . . .	Value of objective function for product mix B in state 1	Value of objective function for product mix B in state 2	
etc.			

The expected value of each optimal solution is determined and, subject to the results of a selected data gathering process, used as the basis for selecting a production mix.

SOME PROBLEMS IN PROVIDING INFORMATION FOR DECISIONS UNDER UNCERTAINTY

When Information Isn't Information

This problem should occur to you almost immediately. Something may be presented as a fact which isn't. Information may change your mind about which state will occur, whether it is true or false. You may receive an experimental result that indicates the sale of five bags of popcorn, yet sell only one.

Information is not information in another case—when it has no *surprise value*. If a data-gathering process leaves the prior distribution unchanged, it provides no information. This might mean the process was worthless, or it might mean you were well informed before the experiment. As a general rule, a data-gathering process should tend to indicate that a specific state will actually occur. A good information system will occasionally surprise you with an unexpected prediction. This is better than having the real world surprise you with an unexpected state of nature.

Understanding Uncertainty

Few persons share a common understanding of a single decision. What appears to be certainty to one person is uncertainty to another; a decision with two alternatives to one has six to another. When an information system serves many decision makers, it is impossible for it to satisfy all their information needs in a single, simple reporting format. An information system can do this for a single decision maker whose decision rules and values are known; great economies and compression of information can be achieved then. But for a crowd of decision makers, the best rule is for the information system to supply uncondensed, unsummarized information, in order that everyone can find therein what they require in their decisions.

Specifically, accounting systems present information as if the world and all its decisions were devoid of uncertainty, or even errors in information processing. Yet such information is used (not without complaints as to its inadequacies) to make decisions which are replete with uncertainty. Various attempts to remove the appearance of certainty from accounting information have so far not been conclusively successful; they fail against the formidable barrier of the heterogeneity of decision-making styles.

Perhaps the best attitude for the accountant is that the world would be a fully deterministic place, ideal for making decisions under certainty, if only we knew *enough* about how it works. Meanwhile, it is necessary to learn as much as possible about decisions under uncertainty.

SUMMARY

There are two basic decision types with respect to information availability—those in which only one state of nature may occur, and about which all factors and variables are determined; and those in which any one of a set of states of nature may occur when the decision is effective. The former are called decisions under certainty; the latter, decisions under uncertainty. In the former, the major recognized problem is the possibility of measurement error, which may mislead a decision maker even when the underlying events occurring are known. In decisions under uncertainty, the major problem is anticipating the unknown future state.

Quantitative decision models exist for many situations. To make these models operate at fullest efficiency, information system managers (most of whom are accountants) need to know their information requirements. Decision models do not differentiate between valid and invalid information; it is the accountant who does that.

BIBLIOGRAPHY

Books

Aigner, Dennis J.   *Principles of Statistical Decision Making*. New York: The Macmillan Co., 1968.

Bower, James B.; Schlosser, Robert E.; and Zlatkovich, Charles T.   *Financial Information Systems*. Boston: Allyn & Bacon, Inc., 1969.

Chernoff, Herman, and Moses, Lincoln E.   *Elementary Decision Theory*. New York: John Wiley & Sons, Inc., 1959.

Cohen, Burton J.   *Cost-Effective Information Systems*. New York: American Management Association, 1971.

Hare, Van Court.   *Systems Analysis: A Diagnostic Approach*. New York: Harcourt, Brace & World, Inc., 1967.

Luce, R. Duncan, and Raiffa, Howard.   *Games and Decisions*. New York: John Wiley & Sons, Inc., 1957.

Raiffa, Howard.   *Decision Analysis: Introductory Lectures on Choices under Uncertainty*. Reading, Mass.: Addison-Wesley Publishing Co., Inc., 1968.

Savage, Leonard J.   *The Foundations of Statistics*. New York: John Wiley & Sons, Inc., 1954.

Articles

Dearden, John.   "How to Organize Information Systems," *Harvard Business Review*, March–April 1965.

Feltham, Gerald.   "The Value of Information," *The Accounting Review,* October 1968.

Mason, Richard.   "Management Information Systems: What They Are, What They Ought to Be," *Innovation,* No. 13, 1970.

Mastromano, Frank M.   "A Data Base Concept," *Management Accounting,* October 1970.

Rothery, Brian.   "The World of Systems," *Data Processing,* April 1967.

Strassman, Paul A.   "Forecasting Considerations in Design of Management Information Systems," *Management Accounting,* February 1965.

10

Managerial Decisions and Price Changes

IT'S HARD to find anyone today who has not heard of or been affected by price changes. A "price change" is, in precise terms, any movement (between two points in time) in the ratio of exchange (price) between any two resources. Because most exchange ratios are expressed in terms of currency, an increase in the number of dollars that must be given in order to obtain a pound of meat is an increase in the price of meat. Less obviously, it is also a *decrease* in the price of money, measured in terms of meat. If meat decreases in price, it is the same thing as money increasing in price (since you have to give more meat to get the same amount of money, or give the same amount of meat for less money).

Relative supply and demand for a scarce resource such as meat is summarized and reflected in its exchange ratio, which is usually expressed in terms of money. One would not expect all prices to increase or decrease together, since normally some commodities are becoming relatively more abundant, causing their prices to decline; others are becoming relatively less abundant, causing their prices to increase. Ideally from the standpoint of judging trends in the relative scarceness of resources, money should always be neither more nor less scarce at different points in time—money's average price should be constant.

In this chapter you learn what happens when money is relatively more or less valuable at some points in time than others—from the managerial decision-making point of view. In particular, you learn how accountants inform decision makers that money's relative scarceness is changing and should be taken into account in decision making.

THE MONEY SUPPLY

Long ago most money was in the form of some durable and useful commodity—so that if money could not be spent it could be worn, eaten, drunk, lived in, etc. As populations increased, skill specialization arose, commerce became more necessary and sophisticated, and the need developed to use a nonperishable, scarce, essentially *useless* substance for money. Gradually the civilized world turned to metals—iron, bronze, silver, and gold. The use of metals as money persists into the present time, although many nations have all but abandoned it. In the United States, the principal money is Federal Reserve Notes, which are in theory IOUs issued by the federal government (get one out and read what is written on it). The government issues or retires these in order to adjust the quantity of money in circulation (the amount of money in circulation is called the "money supply"). The proper concept of money is as something moving from one party to another, enabling each to participate in economic activity by exchanging it for goods and services at appropriate times.

Now think in aggregate terms. Imagine a country with 100,000 units of a multiuse scarce resource in circulation in its economy. This is such a versatile resource that it can be eaten, worn, made into autos, homes, planes—everything that any society or person could desire. When the resource is "used up" it is easily recycled and thus replenished. This country also has a money supply consisting of 1,000,000 "dollars." Thus on the average, each resource unit is matched by 10 dollars in circulation.

Suddenly all the citizens want as many units of the resource as they can obtain. They crowd into the resource stores, buying anything made of the resource or containing it in any form. Storekeepers, finding so much demand, raise the price of the resource and the products it appears in. These price increases serve to balance the increasing demand against the resource supply. The same amount of money is still present in the economy, but the sudden desire of everyone to have more resource when this is not possible makes the resource price go up.

Here are some other causes of such price increases:

1. An increase in the money supply, giving everyone more money with which to pursue the same number of units of the resource.
2. A decrease in the *per capita* number of units of resource available, so that each person will have to settle eventually for fewer units of resource, but has the same money as before with which to buy them.

Cause 1 is known as *inflation*. More money is available but the quantity of goods to buy is the same. Even though inflation is a specific *decrease* in the price of money, its effect is referred to as a "general price level increase." Cause 2 is more complex and usually does not affect all prices at once. In the simple economy above, suppose that autos made from the single resource are suddenly in great demand. Then everyone wants a car. Until car production can be increased, there will be a scarcity of cars, and the imbalance between supply and demand will be reflected in a high price for autos. At the same time, people will have less money to spend on the radios, houses, and the like, and will demand fewer of these items. As a result, the prices of items in less demand may decline to correct the imbalance between supply and demand. No. 2 above is most often responsible for *specific* price changes, which are different from inflation.

We mention but do not elaborate on the principal cause of increases in the money supply—increases in government borrowing. Government borrowing results in issuance of new currency. This is because the government borrows in order to pay for goods and services it receives, in effect printing the additional money it needs to pay for the goods and services. *Welfare economics* and *public finance* are two important branches of economics which deal with the problems of an adequate money supply; if you study them you will find that there are many reasons why a "constant" supply of money cannot be maintained, and why the central government debt is by no means all a bad thing.

SPECIFIC AND GENERAL PRICE LEVEL INCREASES

Let us extend our analysis of inflation. (The other side of inflation is *deflation*, a general decline in resource prices; it is unlikely to be encountered over any but the shortest time intervals.)

Specific Price Increases

First you should think for a moment about what a specific price increase is *telling* a decision maker when the money supply is constant. A price increase would be a signal that the supply of that item was decreasing relative to demand for it. There is a possibility for additional profit if your business can provide additional supply to help meet the additional demand. A price decrease would be telling you that the supply of an item is increasing relative to the demand for it. This situation may be a signal to withdraw from a market in which supply overbalances demand. Thus, specific prices changes are signals for the *reallocation* of resources, including currency, in a properly functioning market economy.

For example, suppose you make water purifiers which sell for about $100 each. Your plant has a capacity of 10,000 filters annually, and actually makes about 7,000 filters. Your profit per unit is about $20.

This year, your sales and production rise to 7,500 units. You raise your price to $110 per unit. Unit sales do not level off but climb to 8,000 units the following year. You raise the price to $120 and sales increase to 9,000 units.

You know now that you are faced with a genuine upsurge in demand but can't participate in it much longer. Your plant capacity is only 10,000 units; another year and you will be unable to further increase production. Your competitors will get the additional business. You must expand your plant. It costs $100,000, but the next year you add capacity to make an additional 1,000 units per year. The demand for water purifiers triggered an increase in supply through higher profit you expected from the expansion.

General Price Increases

Inflation Types. If inflation occurs, all prices rise more or less together, destroying the normal meanings of price changes. Businesses which can't maintain broad contact with the economic situation may be deceived into interpreting the price increases they experience as specific price increases and react to them as such. But in fact inflation does not carry the same signal as a specific price increase.

Inflation is sometimes perceived by businessmen as "cost-push" inflation; that is, their costs rise and in order to remain profitable they must raise the selling prices of their outputs. "Demand-pull" inflation is what businessmen call price increases which occur when demand generally for all commodities rises. Both types of inflation are different perceptions of the same animal. Both must be distinguished from specific price increases.

INFLATION AND BUSINESS PLANNING

The company fortunate enough to sell a product which enjoys an increase in price while product costs are constant is not uncommon. A less fortunate company may find itself selling a product at constant price when the cost of the product components is increasing, thus cutting down the profit margin and return on investment. This invites the business to become more productive, stop that particular operation, or raise its price. How can you determine what is happening in order to make correct decisions?

> The essential information will tell you which accounting costs, asset values, prices, and revenues would have occurred if there were no price changes and compare these with corresponding elements under the actual situation (which includes price changes). This information will let you judge the effect of price changes on all operations.

Two concepts of gain and loss from transactions past and future have been developed about which to organize such information. *Realized* gain or loss arises from operations and transactions which have already occurred. *Realizable* gain or loss is expected to arise from operations or transactions which are currently possible (but not necessary). For example, you buy a car for $3,000. You keep the car one year, using up one fourth of the services the car is capable of rendering in the course of its march to the junk heap. At that time you could purchase a used car exactly identical to yours for $2,000. Since the cost basis of the car is $3,000 — 1/4($3,000) = $2,250, you have a realizable loss of $2,250 — $2,000 = $250. (It is a loss because the market now values three fourths of the car's original services as it valued two thirds of them one year ago; your loss is the value in exchange of one twelfth of the original services.) Had you known of this loss in advance, you would have bought a used car one year ago with one fourth of its service potential intact (for $750), used it one year, then purchased a used car for $2,000 with three fourths of its service potential intact. In any event, your loss is not realized unless you sell your car now.

Effect of Inflation on a Business

Inflation may produce a steady, difficult-to-spot decline of a business' ability to conduct operations. This is because sale of commodities takes place after acquisition of factors of production from which to make them. To give an extreme example, assume that there is a 20 percent per period inflation rate in the prices of all goods, that you buy and pay for the inputs to your product two periods before you sell it, and that you start business with $1,000 in period 0, enough to make 10 units in that period.

Figure 10–1 assumes that the firm seeks to maintain constant levels

FIGURE 10–1
Production Declines, Profit Constant when Inflation Occurs

Period	Manufacturing Costs Cash	Units Made	Units Sold	Unit Selling Price of Product	Total Revenue	Accounting Gross Profit
0	$1,000	10	. . .	$120	. . .	. . .
1	1,000	8.3	. . .	144	. . .	. . .
2	1,000	7	10	173	$1,730	$730
3	1,000	5.8	8.3	207	1,730	730
4	1,000	4.8	7	249	1,730	730

of profit as measured in dollars. Production then declines and profit remains constant—a situation not unlike that evident in the United States in 1970 and 1971.

It is an illusion that gross profit in Figure 10–1 remains constant. Your business is using the proceeds of sales to replace its stock in trade. But by period 4, the business would require 208 percent as much currency as it did in period 0 to make the same number of units—or conversely, can only make 4.8 units with the $1,000 which made 10 units in period 0. The price of money in terms of goods is going down.

The business requires more currency to maintain the same physical levels of operation. In terms of ability to sustain these levels of physical operations, the business' real income and economic power is declining.

Maintaining Economic Power

How could such a decline be prevented? Let us imagine that the firm wishes to maintain a constant *physical* (as opposed to dollar) level of operation. Then Figure 10–1 would be revised to look like Figure 10–2.

FIGURE 10–2
Production Level Steady, Profit Rises when Inflation Occurs

Period	Manufacturing Costs Cash	Units Made	Units Sold	Unit Selling Price of Product	Total Revenue	Accounting Gross Profit	Profit Not Required by Production
0	$1,000	10	. . .	$120	. . .	. . .	. . .
1	1,200	10	. . .	144	. . .	. . .	. . .
2	1,440	10	10	173	$1,730	$ 730	$290
3	1,730	10	10	207	2,070	870	340
4	2,070	10	10	249	2,490	1,050	420

It would appear that the business is earning an upward-trending accounting gross profit. However, since increasing amounts of currency must be devoted to maintaining a constant level of production, many accountants and economists would argue that the real profit is NOT current revenue minus the cost of production. The difference between current and historical cost of production (example: period 3, $1,730 − $1,200 = $530) is an unrealized expense, one that normally is not reported on the accounting performance statements until sale of the goods produced this period. If we subtract this unrealized expense from accounting gross profit, we obtain the amount of accounting profit not required to sustain production. This is a smaller figure— $290, $340, $420—but at least it seems to be increasing!

Indices

But profit is really not increasing, and to show why we introduce the concept of a *price index*. A price index is simply the ratio of the price of a single commodity at one point in time to the price of the same commodity at some other "base" point in time. For example, the ratio of commodity "WF" price in 1974 to "WF" price in 1972 would be computed as

$$I_{wf74} = \frac{P_{wf1974}}{P_{wf1972}} = \frac{\$36}{\$30} = 1.2 \text{ (usually expressed as } 120) \quad (10\text{--}1)$$

Rather than a single commodity, we may define a "market basket" of commodities in the economy as a whole and simply add up their prices at different points in time, taking the ratio of these price sums as a measure of the change in the general value of currency.[1] For example, assume an economy with only two commodities, A and B. We define a market basket as one unit of A and one unit of B and we add their prices together at different points in time. To determine an index showing changes in the general value of currency, we take the ratio of each of these sums to the sum in a period called the *base period*. Let 1972 be the base period. Figure 10–3 shows the calculations.

FIGURE 10–3
Computation of a Series of Indices

Year	Price of A	Price of B	Total Price	Ratio	Inflation Index
1971	$16.5	$25	$41.50	41.5/50	0.83
1972 (base)	25	25	50.00	50/50	1.00
1973	31	29	60.00	60/50	1.20
1974	32	40	72.00	72/50.	1.44
1975	30	56.5	86.50	86.5/50	1.73

A further refinement to the indices computed in Figure 10–3 is to multiply the ratios by 100 so that they are expressed as percentages. The index percentage for a particular year is denoted by I_x where "x" is a subscript giving the year for which the index was computed. Different kinds of indices may be denoted by different letters. Notice that at times the prices of both A and B move in a direction opposite to the index. This illustrates that inflation may exist at the same time

[1] This is only one of many ways to construct an index. You may, as one typical alternative, compute a weighted price sum instead of a simple price sum, choosing the weights as you see fit.

as specific price changes—a very confusing situation we shall deal with as simply as possible later in this chapter.

Real Income

We previously defined real income as the difference between current costs and current revenue. Now let us *deflate* this difference by expressing all elements leading to its calculation in dollars which have the same value in exchange as those in the first period—period 0. Of course, such dollars no longer exist after the first period, but dollars of different periods are really not comparable if their value in exchange differs significantly.

We perform the deflation by dividing each figure in the right-most column of Figure 10–2 by the inflation index for that period. We define the necessary inflation indices and perform the calculations in Figure 10–4.

FIGURE 10–4
Deflating Profit Using Inflation Indices

Period	*(From Figure 10–2)* *Profit Not Required by Production*	*Inflation Index*	*Calculation*	*Deflated Profit*
0 (base)	. . .	100		
1	. . .	120		
2	$290	144	290/1.44	$200
3	340	173	340/1.73	200
4	420	207	420/2.07	200

Each of the figures in the right-most column is equal to $200, the number of 1972-value dollars earned and not required to sustain production. Thus what at first appeared to be an income of $1,050 in period 4 turns out to be, after sustaining production and adjusting for inflation, only $200! These two effects were:

1. The increase in the number of dollars required to sustain the current physical volume of activity.
2. The decline in the value in exchange of currency as time progressed.

The $200 is the same profit the company would have expected if there had been no inflation and its volume had remained steady.

To Beat Inflation

You now see why an inflation should be brought at once to the attention of decision makers. The impression created by the original performance reports was that profits could be sustained through decreased levels of operation, or increased through the same level of operation, which might lead to adoption of one of these alternatives as a goal. In fact, the declining level of operations reduced profits, and the constant operations only held profits constant.

A management unaware an inflation was in progress might mistake its "larger" profits for efficiency improvements and increase its dividends, or stop making the expenditures essential for real efficiency improvements. Such a management would be caught short of capital and resources eventually as the inflation continued.

To illustrate the shortage of capital, remember that prices of new long-lived assets are rising during the inflation. An asset that could have been bought for two years' income in period 2 will, if the company holds income constant in unadjusted terms, have to be bought for $2 \times (207/144) = 2.875$ years' income in period 4.

The only real way to contend with inflation is to recognize it as a signal that the supply of money is outrunning the supply of things to spend money on. No one will want to hold money, a commodity whose value is declining. Thus, a business should look for ways to acquire real-profit-producing assets and activities in exchange for money, or debt. In other words the only way to "get ahead" in real, deflated terms is to provide services and commodities for which increased real demand can be expected.

ACCOUNTING STATEMENTS AND PRICE CHANGES

The balance sheet and the statement of income present the historical dollar equivalents of the assets owned by an entity at a point in time, the dollar claims against those assets by various parties, and a summary of activities, again expressed in historical dollars, which have affected assets and equities during a specified period. Because these statements are prepared as if the price levels of all commodities and resources were not changing, they exclude information about price level changes; they do not show the historical effect of price changes on the business' position or income.

Balance Sheet

Accounting methodologies have been developed to provide such indications. They make use of the tools we have presented in the preceding section—specifically, price indices. Let us first imagine the balance sheet of Dollar Company, as shown in Figure 10–5.

FIGURE 10–5
DOLLAR COMPANY
Unadjusted Balance Sheet
At 12-31-73

Assets		*Equities*	
Cash.	$1,000	Accounts payable.	$2,000
Inventory.	2,000	Owners' equity	4,000
Fixed assets	3,000	Total Equities.	$6,000
Total Assets.	$6,000		

We wish to adjust this balance sheet so that it is in terms of dollars at the end of 1973. All the inventory was manufactured on December 31, 1972. All the fixed assets were acquired at the beginning of 1970. The applicable price level indices are:

12-31-69	100
12-31-70	110
12-31-71	120
12-31-72	115
12-31-73	130

Cash and Cash Equivalents. Since cash is currency, no adjustment of end-of-current-period cash balance is ever necessary. The same is true of accounts receivable and accounts payable. These items are always directly convertible into units of the currency of the present moment. However, note that if we were showing (for comparative purposes) a balance sheet of one year ago, the cash balance at that point in time would have to be multipled by $(I_{\text{present moment}}/I_{\text{one year ago}})$ in order to express cash in current dollars for comparison with the current cash balance. Above, 1,000 dollars held at 12-31-72 would be equal to 1,000 (130/115) equals 1,130 dollars (of 12-31-72) held at 12-31-73. However, the 12-31-73 cash balance shown requires no adjustment.

Inventory. Assume that the inventory was made and paid for with the dollars available one year ago. To show how many dollars would presently be equivalent to that original number of dollars (which was 2,000) we must multiply the original number of dollars by the 12-31-73 value of the index and divide it by the 12-31-72 value of the index. The result is $2,000 \times 130 \div 115 = \$2,260$.

Fixed Assets. The fixed assets were acquired with the dollars available at the end of 1969. In order to show how many 12-31-73 dollars these are equivalent to, it is necessary to multiply the original number of dollars by the 12-31-73 value of the index and divide it by the 12-31-69 value of the index. The result is $3,000 \times 130 \div 100 = \$3,900$.

Often we have assets acquired at different points in time. In that case, compute the equivalent number of current dollars for each asset acquisition separately and add together all the equivalents.

The depreciation provision, if one is shown, is more difficult to compute, and we choose to omit it from this elementary presentation. Succinctly, depreciation taken in each past year must be deflated to its current dollar equivalent.

Owners' Equity. Typically, specific amounts within owners' equity can be identified, and there is a residual called "retained earnings" or some similar title. Any amounts which are specifically identifiable as to source and date can be adjusted to their present dollar equivalent. Assume that the Dollar Company was formed on 12-31-69 and that capital stock was sold for $1,000. Then the current dollar equivalent of this original investment in the firm is $1,000 \times 130 \div 100 = \$1,300$.

Since owners' equity as a whole is a residual, determine retained earnings by applying the balance sheet equation: assets minus liabilities equals owners' equity. This equality translated into current dollars is:

$$\$1,000 + \$2,260 + \$3,900 - \$2,000 = \$5,160$$

Of this $5,160 - \$1,300 = \$3,860$ consists of retained earnings. The adjusted balance sheet is shown in Figure 10–6.

FIGURE 10–6
DOLLAR COMPANY
Adjusted Balance Sheet
In Dollars of 12-31-73
At 12-31-73

Assets		Liabilities	
Cash	$1,000	Accounts payable	$2,000
Inventory	2,260	Owners equity:	
Fixed assets	3,900	Capital stock	1,300
		Retained earnings.	3,860
Total Assets	$7,160	Total Liabilities.	$7,160

You should observe that—

1. Under inflation, the number of current dollars required to represent any durable asset increases.
2. Monetary amounts do not change so long as the obligations are satisfiable in cash. In many nations, "inflation factors" are written into debt instruments to keep the amount of the debt constant in terms of the time at which the instrument is dated, rather than constant in terms of the time the instrument is due, thus protecting the creditor.
3. Comparative adjusted balance sheets would show a *dollar loss* from holding cash and cash equivalents such as accounts receivable during an inflation, and a *dollar gain* from owing money during an inflation. For example, suppose that Dollar Company owes money regularly through the year as accounts payable. The 12-31-72 $2,000 balance would be represented at 12-31-73 for comparison with the 12-31-73 statements as $2,000 \times 130 \div 115 = $2,260, a gain through being in debt of $2,260 − $2,000 = $260—for inflation reduced the purchasing power (as measured in 12-31-73 dollars) required to pay off that much of the debt for Dollar Company!
4. It is wrong to think of the increase in owners' equity as hidden profit for the company. It is not. It is an adjustment of earnings of previous years, as stated in the dollars in existence in those years, *restated* into their equivalent amounts of 12-31-73 dollars.

You might also observe how 2 and 3 above reinforce another phenomenon that occurs during inflation: rising interest rates. A firm is best advised, within the limits of good business judgment, to avoid investment in monetary items and to borrow as much money as possible, since the price of money will be lower in the future when the debt is due.

As all businesses attempt to follow this strategy, bank deposits and short-term securities holdings drop. These are the basis for extending credit by lending institutions, and so just as loan demand is rising, the wherewithal to finance lending is disappearing. The demand for credit expands, and its supply shrivels. The result is a rise in interest rates.

The Income Statement

The traditional (unadjusted) income statement of Dollar Company is presented in Figure 10–7. Adjustment of this statement is not as

FIGURE 10–7
DOLLAR COMPANY
Income Statement
Year Ended 12-31-73

Sales revenue	$10,000
Less: Cost of sales	5,000
Gross contribution margin	$ 5,000
Less: Selling and administrative expenses	4,000
Net profit	$ 1,000

easy as balance sheet adjustment; therefore this discussion will only "hit the highlights."

Sales Revenue. Assume that sales occurred at a level rate throughout the year, and further that the change in the price index also occurred at a level rate. Then the average index at which sales were made is $(130 + 115)/2 = 122.5$. We can assume then that the sales made during the year, at times when the index ranged in value from 115 to 130, are equivalent to having all the sales made at one point in time when the price index has the value 122.5. Accordingly, we can compute the current dollar equivalent of these sales as $10,000 \times 130/122.5 = $10,612.24$.

Cost of Sales. Let us assume that inventory one year ago was $3,000, and further that Dollar Company uses the Lifo flow of costs assumption, permitting us to compute that $5,000 - $1,000 = $4,000 are a result of production activities this year.

The part of cost of sales which was made and placed in inventory one year ago must have a current dollar equivalent of $1,000 × 130/115 = $1,130.44. Now, the $4,000 remaining represents work done all year long at a uniform rate; hence it can be assumed equivalent to work done at a time when the price index was 122.5. Therefore the current dollar equivalent of outlays for cost of goods produced and sold is $4,000 × 130/122.5 = $4,244.90. By adding together these amounts we find that the cost of sales is $1,130.44 + $4,244.90 = *$5,375.34.*

Selling and Administrative. These expenses were also incurred uniformly throughout the year, and applying similar reasoning to them produces a dollar equivalent of $4,000 × 130/122.5 = *$4,244.90.*

Monetary Gains and Losses

Earlier we hinted at the existence of gains and losses through holding money or money equivalents and owing money to be paid in the future. Now we explain how these gains and losses are computed—and they must be computed in order to preserve the traditional debit-credit equality of the accounting process and statements.

Assume that one year ago the monetary accounts were:

Cash . . . . $1,000   Accounts Payable. $4,000

Thus the amounts held through the year are the same as shown on the ending balance sheet down in Figure 10–6. Further assume that the $2,000 reduction in Accounts Payable was all paid on 1-2-73, or immediately after the current period began. We shall accordingly not be concerned with it in this analysis.

The loss through holding cash is

$$(\$1,000 \times 130/115) - \$1,000 = \$130.43$$

The gain through holding liabilities is

$$(\$2,000) \times (130/115) - \$2,000 = \$260.86$$

All these figures go together into an adjusted income statement as in Figure 10–8. This income statement informs us that, expressed in current dollar terms, items of income and expense are about as they were in terms of their relative relationships to one another. The origi-

FIGURE 10–8
DOLLAR COMPANY
Adjusted Income Statement
In Dollars of 12-31-73
Year Ended 12-31-73

Sales revenue	$10,612.24
Less: Cost of sales..	5,375.34
Gross contribution margin.	$ 5,236.90
Less: Selling and administrative expense	4,244.90
Profit before monetary items	$ 992.00
Add: Net monetary gains.	130.43
Net profit	$ 1,122.43

nally reported profits of $1,000, if earned uniformly throughout the year, would have an end-of-year dollar equivalent of $1,122.43; the difference is due to the decrease in inventory, and to the monetary gains and losses. The effects of inflation are most evident when a firm uses up the inputs of prior periods to make current product and sales, and/or has substantial assets and liabilities. However, business welfare during times of changing prices is difficult to properly analyze, and adequate discussion of the practical problems of describing the effects on a specific business of changing prices must be deferred to an advanced accounting course; nor for that matter have satisfactory descriptors for these effects been found in accounting practice.

SUMMARY

Price changes are of two types: specific and general. Specific price changes are signals for reallocations to meet emerging needs and demands profitably. General price changes are called *inflation* or *deflation* and in most modern economies may be attributed to conscious or unconscious government policy.

Modern financial reporting does not recognize the effects on reporting entities of price changes, since all transactions are accounted for in unadjusted historical dollars. However, the accounting profession is committed to the principle of reporting price changes and is devoting considerable resources to research and study of the price level reporting problem. Managers in turn are considering ways to be informed of the effects of price changes and their significance in business decisions.

The most likely proposals for adoption are those which call for all costs and revenues in accounting statements to be restated in terms of dollars with a common purchasing power. Such statements would still be historically based, but would no longer report historical transactions in dollars of many different purchasing powers, arising from the different points in time at which the individual transactions occurred.

Managerial information reports include some general information about price changes—but such information has yet to be integrated into managerial accounting performance reports, contribution analysis statements, and other decision-related applications. The need is there; perhaps persons who understand the need will see that price change descriptors receive proper attention.

BIBLIOGRAPHY

Books

Accounting Research Division. *Reporting the Financial Effects of Price-Level Changes.* Accounting Research Study No. 6. New York: American Institute of Certified Public Accountants, 1963.

Dyckman, T. R. *Investment Analysis and General Price Level Adjustments.* Studies in Accounting Research No. 1. Evanston, Ill.: American Accounting Association, 1969.

Edwards, Edgar O., and Bell, Philip W. *The Theory and Measurement of Business Income.* Berkeley, Calif.: University of California Press, 1961.

Rosen, L. S. *Current Value Accounting and Price-Level Restatements.* Toronto, Canada: The Canadian Institute of Chartered Accountants, 1972.

Articles

Furlong, William H., and Robertson, Leon H. "Matching Management Decisions and Results," *Management Accounting,* August 1968.

Garner, Don E. "The Need for Price-Level and Replacement Value Data," *Journal of Accountancy,* September 1972.

Petersen, Russell J. "Price-Level Changes and Company Wealth," *Management Accounting*, February 1973.

Rosenfield, Paul "The Confusion between General Price-Level Restatement and Current Value Accounting," *Journal of Accountancy*, October 1972.

Ross, Dean "Is It Better to Be Precisely Wrong than Vaguely Right?" *Financial Executive*, June 1971.

11

Taxes and Decision Making

THE INCOME tax and other tax laws have not developed systematically or to accomplish coordinated purposes. The result, in most civilized countries, is a jumble of governmental levys upon many of the things we do that have economic or pleasurable significance. Compliance with these levys and the bureaucracies which collect them is good in the United States—not so good in other Western nations. Consider the number of jurisdictions which may tax you:

> Federal
> State
> County
> City
> School district
> Water or other utility district
> Other districts (e.g., flood or mosquito control)

Taxes may have these purposes:

> To raise money
> To selectively encourage or discourage specific activities
>   such as capital investment
> To discourage imports
> To redistribute wealth

Here are some of the activities which give rise to taxes:

Owning property
Earning money
Gambling
Dying
Giving gifts
Smoking, eating, drinking
Driving
Traveling
Sleeping away from home
Sleeping at home
Acquiring goods made in foreign countries

This chapter reviews taxes and their effect on economic activity. If the U.S. economy operated perfectly, taxes would be devised not to interfere with the competitive processes of resource allocation. This ideal is not achievable, so from time to time tax policy is amended to pursue well-stated goals and *otherwise* interfere as little as possible with resource allocation processes.

TAX SPECIALISTS, PROCESSES, AND INSTITUTIONS

Managers are not so much interested in the computation of taxes as in the relationships between the nature and timing of business activities and tax liabilities. A major example of such a relationship that affects capital asset acquisition decisions was given in Chapter 7. Tax specialists who have expert knowledge of such relationships are found primarily in the legal and accounting professions.

Tax processes and institutions are part of the framework of public finance and monetary system management that pays for government services, keeps currency circulating, and prices stable. At the federal level, Congress enacts tax laws. With the help of tax specialists and industries affected by tax policy, the basic income tax law (first passed in 1913 and recodified in 1939 and 1954) undergoes adjustment by each Congress. The Internal Revenue Service, a part of the Treasury Department, is responsible for taxpayer relations and revenue collection. The IRS maintains a nationwide seven-region computer system to keep track of the tax status of all income-producing persons and businesses. To help administer the tax law, the IRS has prepared its own regulations which interpret the law and have official status within the IRS.

To submit a tax return in compliance with law, regulations, and applicable precedents is easy for many taxpayers to do alone, using IRS forms and self-help booklets. Most businesses, however, require tax specialist services to prepare a proper tax return and compute an appropriate tax liability. The tax specialist is an important part of the voluntary tax collection system; his function is to take the facts as given to him by the taxpayer and compute the lowest possible tax liability consistent with these facts and the tax laws and regulations. The taxpayer is responsible for the facts; the tax adviser is responsible for applying his expert knowledge of taxation to these facts.

Naturally, there are disputes about the meaning of the law and the IRS regulations, and the IRS has a process whereby disputes over a taxpayer's liability can be arbitrated. If this internal arbitration does not satisfy either party, the dispute can be taken to a federal court. The U.S. Tax Court and the federal courts give decisions which result in a continuing interpretation of the basic tax law, making it (like other bodies of law) adaptive to changing business phenomena.

TAX POLICIES OF LOCAL GOVERNMENTS

Local governments rely heavily on taxes on property and sales as sources of revenue, and to date the federal government has respected this reliance by not introducing its own property or sales taxes. Local governments also tax income, but not so heavily or successfully as does the federal government.

The extreme differences in taxation between localities has virtually disappeared. Most states now have a sales tax of 5 to 7 percent. Taxes on property are high in all urban areas, ranging from about 2 to 4 percent of market value. Even so, property and sales taxes at these levels don't supply the total revenue needs of local governments, and the federal government is experimenting with "revenue-sharing" of its own tax receipts with the states.

Sales taxes are not favored by authorities because they are regressive;

that is, they tend to fall more heavily on those who have lower incomes. Property taxes are theoretically more acceptable since they tax wealth. In practice, property taxes are deficient for four reasons: (1) They are extremely high, out of all proportion to benefits received in return. (2) They are a tax on the value of one's property rather than on one's *equity* in property, putting those who borrow money to buy property at a tax disadvantage. (3) Property of equivalent value is taxed at different amounts by different taxing entities. (4) Land speculation is encouraged when undeveloped property is taxed at lower amounts than developed property. Speculation withholds property from development in order to drive its price up. Land speculation is further encouraged by taxation of gains from most land sales at low long-term capital gains rates. There is very little risk in land speculation since property values tend to increase as a result of population and economic growth. Theory advocates, and practice is turning to, taxing land at its value in its *most productive use* regardless of the current application. This encourages landowners to put land to its best use in order to pay the taxes—or sell it to someone who will. However, bear in mind that land development, while desirable from the viewpoint of a taxing authority, may be undesirable from an aesthetic, ecological, environmental, or other viewpoint.

IMPROVING THE TAX SYSTEM

Even if no new tax laws are passed, the changing nature of economic activity assures that tax systems' effect on the individual's tax liability will not remain the same. As an example, monetary inflation and rising productivity combine to give most persons higher incomes in successive periods, subjecting them to ever-higher taxation rates. The tax system, if purchasing power before taxes is constant, leaves the individual with steadily less purchasing power *after* taxes during inflation.

The tax systems' effect on business also changes. The IRS, for example, makes rules which determine the amount of depreciation a business may deduct from revenues to determine taxable income. When a business invests in depreciable buildings and equipment, its depreciation deduction rises, protecting income from taxation and saving cash for the business to use internally or distribute as dividends. The IRS has latitude in determining depreciation rules, and can use them to encourage investment during times of economic slack or discourage investment during a time of economic expansion and potential inflation.

There is discussion and argument over changes more far-reaching than these evolutionary or "fine-tuning" changes. Improvements in the tax system are proposed to advance two goals:

1. Reduce interference of taxes with normal allocation of resources, and
2. Broaden the tax base to reduce alleged inequities.

In this section we discuss some of the current changes proposed or taking place in the tax system to further these goals.

Taxing Nonprofit Entities

Foundations, churches, charities, some hospitals, leagues, fraternal orders, and similar groups are given the special status under the tax law of being exempt from some taxes so long as they pursue humanitarian purposes. These organizations may be exempt from taxes on income, property, and/or their sales or purchases. Since these tax-exempt organizations control a large percentage of the wealth in the United States, and account for much of its total commerce, governments forego a considerable sum of revenue by extending tax-exempt status to so many organizations. Considering foundations only, the Ford Foundation, Johnson Foundation, Rockefeller Foundation, Carnegie Foundation, Kresge Foundation, Moody Foundation, Richardson Foundation, Mellon Foundation, and 20,000 others may distribute all their income or about 5 percent of their assets, whichever is greater, for charitable purposes instead of paying taxes. Congressional critics have raised the question whether the provisions of the tax law permitting tax-exempt status and thus excluding such organizations from the tax base are actually in the public interest.

Those who say tax-exempt status may be indefensible point to the growing share of the national wealth and income beyond taxation (for foundations only, presently about $25 billion in total assets at book value) at a time when tax revenues are increasingly harder to come by. They argue that taxation of at least some of the income of these entities would reduce this accumulation, providing necessary tax revenues and a more equitable distribution of the tax "burden." Should, for example, a church be exempt from taxes on the land under its parking lot, or on the income from its business investments?

Those who argue for the tax-exempt status of such entities say that their accumulation of property is a national response to the greater demands being placed on them by an urban society, and that such private-sector entities are much more efficient in providing "risk resources" for meeting social needs than government would be if government got the tax revenues and the responsibilities the foundations now have.

The following restrictions, in addition to the minimum payout requirement already given, have been placed on foundations:[1]

1. No foundation may own more than 20 percent of the stock of any one company.
2. Each foundation must pay a federal tax of 4 percent of its investment income.

Such restrictions have the general effect of limiting foundation growth, diversifying foundation holdings, and broadening the tax base.

Value-Added Tax

This would be a kind of national sales tax, levied against any increase in value given to produced or processed goods. Thus, if a businessman buys materials and labor for $40 and sells them for $60 (in some different form), he would pay taxes on $60 — $40 = $20 of value added—regardless whether he made a profit on the exchange! (The $20 could be eaten up by overhead, selling, and administrative costs.) The value added would not penalize profitable businesses (which pay the taxes now), nor would it penalize very efficient firms with higher than normal profits. Companies with losses would pay tax since the tax is on "value-added" through operations and is not an income tax.

The value-added tax is used in Europe. There, the tax is rebated to exporters on sales abroad. The effect is to make the manufacturer's cost of foreign sales equal to the cost of economic inputs only. Interna-

---

[1] "New Ball Game for the Foundations," *Forbes,* June 15, 1972, pp. 65–66.

tional agreements prevent subsidies for exports; the rebate of the value-added tax is not a subsidy. On the other hand, the profits tax in the United States does not attach directly to foreign or domestic sales and any refund of or exemption from this tax would be interpreted by other nations as a subsidy of export sales.

Those who oppose the value-added tax argue that it is regressive, resembling a national sales tax and paid by individuals to the extent they are consumers rather than to the extent they receive income. The counter argument is that the tax could be rebated to individuals or families with incomes below some arbitrary level.

The value-added tax has been proposed as a source of revenue to fund operation of local governments should the *ad valorem*[2] tax prove inadequate for that purpose (see discussion of tax policies of local governments). The tax would be collected by the federal government and paid to local governments.

Federal-State Revenue Sharing

States and municipalities depend on property and sales taxes for most of their revenues, with lesser amounts deriving from the income tax. The former two sources are being used to the fullest extent possible; the latter source has been essentially preempted by the federal government. While the federal government is not in especially sound financial condition, it does have the advantage over state and local governments that it can print money it needs to spend in excess of its tax revenues. State and local governments almost without exception are badly in need of financial help, which can only come from the federal government.

Revenue sharing is the name coined to apply to proposals under which federal revenues would be channeled to local governments. These revenues, deriving primarily from the federal income tax, would be used by local governments to meet local needs. Those who favor revenue sharing feel that it will restore the vitality of local government, giving it resources to deal with such problems as welfare and unemployment, public health care, public education, law enforcement, and re-

---

[2] A Latin phrase meaning "based on value."

gional public transportation. Those who oppose revenue sharing feel that local governments will lose control of their finances to the central government, that government as a whole will become more centralized and unresponsive, and that federal finances will further deteriorate, with attendant inflation and higher taxes.

The 1972 modest revenue-sharing plan to distribute $5 billion over a five-year period is certain to be changed and expanded. Accountants can be expected to contribute to this process through financial controls development and interpretation of the law to determine the proper disbursement of federal funds to each eligible government entity.

Negative Income Tax

Millions of citizens receive payments from the federal government. These payments are for social security, medicare, various degrees of disability, and other causes. Millions more receive payments from local governments for the causes above as well as payments to mothers with small children, unemployed men and women, and others. These are called "transfer payments" by economists because they transfer income from some segments of the population to others. The money to provide these payments comes from tax collections and deficit financing. Although it is perhaps unfair to do so, most persons lump these payments together in their minds and think of them as "welfare" and regard the total as "too high." The total is very high, high enough to stimulate a lively debate over a national income distribution policy. There are proposals in the Executive and the Congress for reforming the entire system of government payments to persons to make it more efficient, equitable, and economical.

Let us consider one kind of payment—that to unemployed persons. This payment is made largely by states, supplementing their own funds with money received from the federal government. At present, the payment usually stops if an unemployed person secures a job, even though the job pays little more than does the "welfare" program. There is little incentive under this kind of system, from a purely monetary point of view, for the individual to actually seek employment if he is only substituting one kind of payment for another of similar amount, and sacrificing his leisure time to boot. The result is that second and third generations in the same family are becoming adults knowing nothing about job markets or learning a skill, depending entirely on government payments for survival and unable to participate in the economy.

One way to slow down this phenomenon would be to continue all or part of the government payments after a job is obtained. For example, let "welfare" payments be $250 per month. The head of the household secures employment paying $250 per month. Instead of stopping entirely, the government payment drops to $200 per month, making a total income of $450 per month. In a few months the head of the household receives an increase to $350 per month; the government payment drops to $150 per month and total income is $500.

These graduated family subsidies have been called the negative income tax. It is a *negative* tax because it contemplates a payment by the government to taxpayers instead of the conventional arrangement under which taxpayers pay money to the government. As you can see, at some point the head of the household will no longer receive government payments but will start paying a positive income tax to the government. He is never penalized for seeking employment, as he is under the present system.

The cost of a negative income tax would be very large—some put it as high as $100 billion per year. This payment would be partly offset by the $10 billion savings achieved by eliminating the present government-payments bureaucracy which administers the existing system, and by eliminating $30–$60 billion of the payments made by it. In place of many different payments for different purposes and under different conditions (one person may collect under more than one program), there would be only the income test for eligibility and amount of payment.

Many persons object to such a system, arguing that it is immoral to pay money to working Americans. The issue is before Congress as well as before the public. The next few years should tell whether a beginning will be made toward the negative income tax in the United States, or whether the present system will be reviewed, reformed, and retained.

ACCOUNTING FOR TAXES

There are enough differences between the way income is calculated for financial reporting and managerial purposes, and the way it is calculated for tax computation purposes, that often the tax will not bear a logical relationship to financially reported income. An example of this situation is the use of straight-line depreciation for financial reporting (to increase the income figure by deducting as little depreciation as possible) and simultaneous use of accelerated depreciation for determining income subject to tax (to decrease the taxable income figure and therefore the tax). To dramatize the possible difference, imagine a business earning revenues of $150,000 per year and with expenses other than depreciation of $50,000 per year. The company's only asset is a depreciable one costing $200,000 and obtained at the beginning of this year. The asset has a five-year life and no salvage value. Straight-line depreciation is $200,000/5 = $40,000 per year. Accelerated depreciation this year is $200,000(5/5 + 4 + 3 + 2 + 1) = $67,000. The latter is deducted from revenue to calculate taxable income:

Financial income:

$$\$150,000 - \$50,000 - \$40,000 = \$60,000$$

Taxable income:

$$\$150,000 - \$50,000 - \$67,000 = \$33,000$$

Difference = $27,000

The $27,000 difference in income is taxed at the rate of 48 percent, so that income tax payments in that year are $27,000 × 0.48 = $12,960 *less* than if taxable and financial income were the same.

Now, you should see that over a five-year period the *method* of depreciation does not matter; the same amount of depreciation will be taken ($200,000), and therefore income will be the same, and taxes will be the same. This is illustrated in Figure 11–1. Accounting authorities argue that it is misleading to report tax expenses *lower* than what is apparently due on reported income at some times, yet at other times report tax expenses which are *higher* than what is apparently due on reported income (for example, in the fifth year of the asset's life above, accelerated depreciation would only be $13,000, leading to a tax $11,000 higher than that apparently due on reported income).

The accounting solution is to report the difference between actual tax liability (paid to the government) and what the tax liability would be if figured on reported income. This difference is positive early in the life of an asset and negative later when actual tax liability exceeds

FIGURE 11–1
Comparison of Depreciation Methods

Cost of asset: $200,000
Lifetime: 5 years
Salvage value: $0
Income before taxes and depreciation: $100,000 per year

	1. Depreciation		*2. Taxable Income (Income Less Depreciation)*	
Year	*Straight Line*	*Accelerated*	*Straight Line*	*Accelerated*
1	$ 40,000	$ 67,000	$ 60,000	$ 33,000
2	40,000	53,000	60,000	47,000
3	40,000	40,000	60,000	60,000
4	40,000	27,000	60,000	73,000
5	40,000	13,000	60,000	87,000
	$200,000	$200,000	$300,000	$300,000

	3. Tax Liability		*4. After Taxes Cash Flow*	
Year	*Straight Line*	*Accelerated*	*Straight Line*	*Accelerated*
1	$ 22,300	$ 9,340	$ 37,700	$ 23,660
2	22,300	16,060	37,700	30,940
3	22,300	22,300	37,700	37,700
4	22,300	28,540	37,700	44,460
5	22,300	35,260	37,700	51,740
	$111,500	$111,500	$188,500	$188,500

apparent tax liability. The difference is called "Provision for Tax Expense Incurred but Not Paid." For an example of its computation, consider the facts in Figure 11–1. In year 1 the business, using straight-line depreciation to compute financial income, would have taxable income of $60,000 and tax expense of $22,300.[3] In the same year, tax liability computed using accelerated depreciation is $9,340, computed from taxable income of $33,000. Year 1's addition to the provision for tax expense incurred but not paid would be $22,300 — $9,340 = *$12,960.* Here are the entries for all five years:

Year	1	2	3	4	5
Change in provision.	$+12,960	$+6,240	$0	$–6,240	$–12,960

---

[3] Refer to Appendix 11A for an explanation of how to compute business tax liabilities.

Thus, reported income tax expense is kept in proper relation with reported income, recognizing that over the long run reported income and taxable income will total to the same figure and that differences between them are only due to differences in the timing of income and income tax expense recognition.

ACCOUNTANTS AND TAX POLICY

During the early decades of their history accountants limited themselves to tax return preparation and tax planning for individuals and businesses. The former has become highly routinized and is often done using computers. The latter consists essentially of (*a*) putting as much income as possible into the capital gains category, where tax rates are lower, (*b*) spreading taxable income over as many entities as possible (to avoid the progressive tax rates on income concentrated on a single entity), (*c*) selecting transactions and timing them to take maximum advantage of deductions and exemptions in the tax law, and (*d*) minimizing total estate and gift taxes paid by an individual and his estate.

Accountants' long experience in these areas has left them the most informed profession in the United States about the ways tax laws affect economic behavior of individuals and businesses. As such, accountants have acquired a responsibility to participate in the process of developing tax laws and policies. This process is much more than one of closing loopholes and eliminating tax inequities. The problems of stability and efficiency in a tax system as large as ours, in a society as decentralized as ours, are extremely complex; it is unavoidable that accountants will be expected to use their knowledge of taxation and its consequences in the public interest.

SUMMARY

The system whereby government entities raise money to finance their own activities affects virtually all economic activity. The great and the small pay taxes, whose amounts are determined according to laws and regulations so complex that professional specialists are often required to interpret them. Tax effects are not all predictable in advance; tax

effects also change as the nature of economic activity changes. Consequently the tax system is always under scrutiny and subject to revision.
Accountants, because they help individuals conform to the tax laws,
know better than any other professional class what are the effects of
taxes on individuals. Accountants thus should be involved in criticizing
and changing the tax system. Four probable areas of future tax change
where accounting expertise is needed are: (1) taxation of nonprofit
entities, (2) new sources of revenue such as the proposed value-added
tax, (3) revenue sharing between federal and state governments, and
(4) reform of the welfare system.

The rules which determine income tax *liability* don't always agree
with the accounting principles which determine income tax *expense*.
One result has been difficulty, in financial reporting and even in managerial decision making, in describing the effects of taxes on economic
decision making through the accounting system.

APPENDIX 11A: COMPUTING THE CORPORATE INCOME TAX

This tax is levied primarily by the federal government. There are
state income taxes as well, but they follow the form of the federal tax
and are for much smaller amounts. The computation of the federal
corporate income tax liability is:

Liability =   0.22 (corporate taxable income up to $25,000)
            +0.48 (corporate taxable income in excess of $25,000)
            +0.30 (capital gains during year)[4]

Each term in this equation has a special meaning. We are not concerned
with these meanings as would be a professional tax consultant, so our
definitions are somewhat looser and intended to convey conceptual
meaning. "Corporate taxable income" is virtually the same as the accounting income reported in the annual financial statements. The tax
is levied on income *before* deduction of dividends. "Capital gains"
are the profits made through sale of investments in such assets as land
and securities, You can see that the rates in the equation above favor

---

[4] This is the alternate capital gains tax rate; a corporation with taxable income
less than $25,000 would use 0.22.

smaller corporations and favor income earned from capital investments. Since individual income tax rates progress up to 70 percent, the law also favors corporations over individuals.[5]

Effect of Corporate Income Tax

The 48 percent rate on income in excess of $25,000 means that the government is a partner to that extent in a business' activities. Thus, profits may be only 52 percent of their pretax amounts and expenses only 52 percent of their apparent magnitude. You saw this in Chapter 7 when you studied the effect of taxes on capital investment decisions. As another example, suppose interest rates are 8 percent. Interest is deductible from revenue to determine profit and therefore deductible from revenue to determine taxable income. Thus, a dollar spent on interest reduces taxable income but also reduces the tax liability. The net extra cash outflow as a result of the interest payment is not $1 but only 52 cents. The real rate of interest is not 8 percent but $0.52 \times 8 = 4.16$ percent.

This "sharing" by the government of business profits and expenses tends to make the government interested in the efficiency of business management and the profitability of the business establishment. This interest is more than academic. The government does not undertake any major programs, budget reallocations, or even spending reductions until it has evaluated their effect on its major source of operating revenue. On a more positive side, the government has established many agencies (as the Small Business Administration) which seek to develop the profitability of various types of businesses, incidentally strengthening them as sources of tax revenues. The result is an ever-closer mutually dependent relationship between government and business. The eventual equilibrium of this relationship is not yet clear.

Operating Income and Capital Gains

There is a fundamental bias in the federal tax law in favor of income earned from capital investment appreciation. Such income is called

---

[5] However, the maximum tax on wage-earned individual income is 50 percent.

"capital gains" and is taxed at a much lower rate—30 percent for corporations—than operating income. This lower rate causes businessmen to seek out capital appreciation opportunities. The effect may be to cause businesses to forego investments in operations which will not result in capital gains. To see this, consider two alternatives, one a noncapital expenditure and the other a capital expenditure. Assume the company insists on a 10 percent return after taxes. The pretax return on the noncapital investment (an example would be depreciable equipment) would have to be enough to pay the taxes and still leave the 10 percent return, or $10/(1 - 0.48) = 19.25$ percent. Similarly, the pretax return on a capital investment (as in land held for appreciation) would also have to be enough to pay the capital gains tax and leave a 10 percent return. In this case the lower capital gains tax rate would require only a $10/(1 - 0.30) = 14.29$ percent return. It appears reasonable to suggest that all other things equal, the tax laws do create a bias toward investment in capital items.

Capital Losses

Long-term capital losses are first offset against long-term capital gains in the year of recognition.[6] If there is a *net* capital loss, the business may carry this loss back three years and forward five years to reduce the amount of any capital gains which occur in that nine-year period. Any capital loss remaining after five years is "down the tubes." No capital loss may offset any ordinary income for a corporation.

To illustrate, Figure 11–2 is a schedule of capital gains and losses for the Yippee Corporation from 1964 to 1970.

Spreading Gains and Losses over Several Periods

The tax law recognizes that businesses have good and bad years; there are tax law provisions whereby a business can offset the income

---

[6] Long-term capital gains or losses are those occurring as a result of selling a capital asset held for more than six months. This chapter does not discuss short-term capital losses.

FIGURE 11–2
Illustrative Schedule of Capital Gains and Losses

Year	Net Capital Gains (Loss)	Gain Offset by Loss and Year of Loss	Taxable Capital Gain	Loss Carried Forward	Loss Expiring
1964	$(500,000)	$ 0	$ 0	$500,000	$ 0
1965	0	0	0	500,000	0
1966	300,000	300,000 (1964)	0	200,000	0
1967	(100,000)	0	0	300,000	0
1968	0	0	0	300,000	0
1969	0	0	0	100,000	200,000 (1964)
1970	200,000	100,000 (1967)	100,000	0	0

of good years against some or all of the losses of bad years and thereby pay taxes only on the excess of income over losses for a period of years. Such provisions produce what are called "carrybacks" when a loss is carried back to offset income of subsequent periods. A loss may be used to offset income earned up to three years before the loss occurs, and up to five years after. The provisions as to the treatment of capital losses and operating losses provide for the same periods of carryback and carryforward but must be applied to each type of loss independently.

As soon as a net operating loss occurs, the unfortunate business would file refund claims for the preceding three years (assuming it had profits in any of those years!), saying in effect to the Treasury: "Look, we have made less money over the past four years than we thought we would, and we have overpaid our tax. Please refund $xxxx to us." Such tax refunds are important sources of cash to businesses which are losing money. If there is still an excess of loss over the past three years' income, this excess may be used to offset operating income during the five subsequent years.

In 1968 the Yippee Corporations's operating loss was $2,000,000. Income for the previous three years was $1,200,000, on which the company had paid taxes of $306,000. Upon filing amended returns, the Yippee Corporation receives this entire amount as a tax refund. In 1969, there is a loss of $200,000. In 1970, the firm's operating income is $900,000. The remaining $800,000 of the 1968 loss and $100,000 of the 1969 loss offset this profit, and there is no tax liability in 1970.

The company breaks exactly even in 1971, 1972, and 1973; in 1974, there is an operating profit of $50,000; this is offset by $50,000 of the 1969 loss. At the end of 1974, the last $50,000 of the 1969 loss expires and cannot be used as a tax deduction any longer.

The effect of these rules is generally equitable. In business planning, operating losses produce cash because of their deductibility from past income; capital gains produce cash because of the lower tax on them. If a loss has to be suffered, it should be an operating loss; gains should be capital gains.

Tax Deductions

The government accepts as deductions from revenue (to find taxable income) most of the expenditures which accountants allow as expenses. The principal difference is that whereas an expense to an accountant is the dollar amount associated with *any* resource sacrifice related to a period or to income-producing activities occurring during the period, a tax deduction to the government is only ordinary and necessary expenses (plus uncontrollable losses, as to hurricane or earthquake). The government will not allow excessive, extraordinary, unnecessary expense of any kind as a tax deduction—be it entertainment, salary, production, or whatever. Businesses keep extensive records to justify the expenses they incur as ordinary and necessary.

BIBLIOGRAPHY

Books

Bierman, Jr., Harold, and Drebin, Allan R. *Managerial Accounting: An Introduction.* 2d ed. New York: The Macmillan Co.: 1972.

Bittker, Boris I., and Eustice, James S. *Federal Income Taxation of Corporations and Shareholders.* 3d ed. Boston: Warren, Gorham, & Lamont, 1971.

McCarthy, Clarence F. *Federal Income Tax.* Englewood Cliffs, N.J.: Prentice-Hall, Inc., 1972.

Raby, William L. *The Income Tax and Business Decisions*. 2d ed. Englewood Cliffs, N.J.: Prentice-Hall, Inc., 1972.

Sommerfeld, Ray M.; Anderson, Hershel M.; and Brock, Horace R. *An Introduction to Taxation*. 2d ed. New York: Harcourt Brace Jovanovich, Inc., 1972.

Article

Baylis, A. W. "A Concise Statement on Income Tax Allocation," *Accountants' Journal*, April 1971.

12

The Public Interest and Contemporary Accounting

THE MODERN accounting profession is aware of responsibilities beyond its traditional field of private enterprise. Accounting shares this awareness with segments of society which are entitled to an objective description and appraisal of their programs, interests, and claims.

As one indicator of this interest *The Journal of Accountancy,* the publication of the American Institute of Certified Public Accountants, has published an impressive number of articles dealing with the actual or potential contribution of accountants to the management of various social-type problems. Here are a few recent ones, their dates, and authors:

"Socio-Economic Accounting" (November 1968) by David F. Linowes, pp. 37–42.

"The Modern Management Approach to a Program of Social Improvement" (March 1969) by Robert Beyer, pp. 37–46.

"The Role of Accounting in Emerging Nations" (January 1969) by David F. Linowes, p. 18.

"Macroeconomics and Accounting Practice" (June 1969) by Henry R. Jaenicke, pp. 35–39.

"The Black Minority in the CPA Profession" (October 1969) by Bert N. Mitchell, pp. 41–48.

"The Accountant's Social Responsibility" (January 1970) by Ralph W. Estes, pp. 31–39.

"Social Responsibility of the Profession" (January 1971) by David F. Linowes, pp. 66–69.

"Integration in Fact—A Test of the Professional Accountant as a Citizen" (April 1971) by Edwin R. Lang and John Ashworth, pp. 41–46.

"The New Generation and the Accounting Profession" (May 1971) by George S. Odiorne, pp. 39–43.

"Accounting: A Bridge Across the Generation Gap" (May 1971) by John Lawler, pp. 44–48.

"Accounting and Ecology: A Perspective" (October 1971) by James E. Parker, pp. 41–46.

"Pollution Control through Social Cost Conversion" (November 1971) by Floyd A. Beams and Paul E. Fertig, pp. 37–42.

You may observe that these articles are general in nature and conceptual in title; scanning a few of them will confirm that this is also true of the substance. However, the *Journal of Accountancy* does not publish reports of specific applications; it reports trends and philosophies. The trend these articles report is the accountant's increasing involvement in detailed applications of interpretive accounting to pollution, integration, regional development, economic planning, tax reform, and international economic development.

FACTORS TENDING TO INVOLVE ACCOUNTING IN SOCIAL PROBLEMS

First of all, accounting is a major (though young) established and responsible profession. It is natural and proper that when problems arise, people turn to accountants just as they turn to lawyers, doctors, architects, civil engineers, and other professions with a tradition of service. When large groups of people experience the same problem—such as racial or economic discrimination, environmental pollution, or regional stagnation—then these groups turn to both practicing accountants and to accounting as a discipline and institution for help in managing their difficulties.

Aside from this natural exposure to problems, the nature of the accounting discipline itself places accounting squarely on the front line in public interest resource allocation decisions.

Accounting Is a Measurement Discipline

Accounting assigns numbers to objects. Accountants measure costs, income, revenue, and expenses. Anyone who wants to know the money benefits of a program, the money sacrifice of a problem solution, the money equivalent of a resource—must rely on the discipline of accounting and the analytical powers of accountants. And because proposed solutions to problems involve the reallocation of resources, it is unavoidable that questions arise concerning the costs and benefits of resource reallocation. The designation of such costs and benefits again involves accounting skills.

Accounting Is Entity Oriented

All accounting statements are identified with an entity of some sort. The first accounting entities were individual proprietors. With increasing degrees of abstraction, accounting entities came to include partnerships, corporations, foundations, governments, and entire nations. Entity orientation is essential in accounting because it affords the focus of attention. In preparing accounting statements you measure the transactions of an entity, the net effect of a set of transactions on an entity, the assets of an entity, and the equities (claims upon, or interests) of other entities in this particular entity.

Entities and Goals. The 1960s were characterized by recognition of many interest groups as entities, where a decade before such an identification would not have been accepted as reasonable. Consumer groups are entities. Racial minorities are entities. City dwellers are an entity. Those who wish to stabilize the planet's ecology are an entity. Those who favor population control are an entity. Recipients of welfare payments are an entity. We may agree or disagree about the purposes and representations of such *social entities,* but we no longer deny that they exist with respect to the particular set of problems or goals they advocate and which are peculiar to them.

Accounting may be used to describe the assets and equities, revenues and expenses of the programs advocated by social entities. In fact, the entity orientation of accounting makes it inevitable that social entity spokesmen and analysts will use the language and methods of accounting as a medium of expression and persuasion. For example, those favoring medicare in the early 1960s stated that this federally sponsored health-insurance program would, if adopted, save billions of dollars for the children of persons covered by the program. Irregardless of the truth of the statement, note that the speaker was describing two social entities (one is older persons and the other is their children) and the benefits each would receive from an aggregate transaction consisting of the medicare program, and in so doing was using the jargon and structure of accounting.

If social entities can be identified with respect to a set of goals and/or problems, it follows that such entities may overlap each other— that some of us have membership in many entities at once and may change our memberships frequently. This means that in order for a social entity to be heard, it must be represented by a special interest group or organization which acts as a semipermanent "guardian" for that social entity. For example, the AFL–CIO is one organization representing the social entity *labor,* the AAUP represents college professors, the Sierra Club represents environmentalists, Consumers Union represents consumers, and so on. These special interest organizations are, however, *not* the social entity they represent; and one cannot subrogate such an organization for the entity itself in any policy formulation or application, except at considerable risk.

The Attest Function

Whether in public or private accounting, the name and reputation of the individual accountant is regarded by nonaccountants as a guarantee that information the accountant produces is supportable by reasonable evidence. The most dramatic example is the auditor, an accountant in public practice who specializes in the examination of financial statements which a business (usually a corporation) proposes to publish. The auditor's examination is conducted to gather information and evidence which will allow him to express an opinion as to whether the proposed financial statements present fairly the financial position and results of operations for the company they relate to, and on a basis consistent with that of the preceding year's financial statements. A favorable auditor's opinion on published financial statements is accepted by most entities affected by the business' operations as conclusive evidence that the statements are reliable. When an auditor is found to be violating this essential trust (whether accidentally or purposefully), sanctions including lawsuits and expulsion from the auditing and accounting professions may be visited upon him.

Extending the Attest Function. Recent thought has suggested the auditor's attest function might profitably be extended to other forms of information. Thus, independent auditors might gather evidence to support an opinion that an engineering study of a proposed freeway was properly executed and that its conclusions are supportable, reasonable, and stated fully and clearly. It is up to others then to decide if those conclusions are acceptable. Such an opinion would serve to focus attention on the issues raised by the freeway proposal and engineering study and eliminate the "my engineers are better than your engineers" sort of controversy that makes the source of information rather than the direction it points the overriding (and wrong) issue.

One may imagine accountants someday expressing public opinions on proposed bond issues, regional development plans, government budgets and performance reports, and other activities which involve social entities and resource allocation. These opinions would *not* be for or against the proposals. They would cover instead the basic set of facts laid out for the public to use in deciding the issue. The opinion would state whether these facts were complete, fully stated, supported by evidence, and otherwise adequate as a basis for decision, all with respect to a set of generally accepted principles governing the formulation of such opinions. A deterrent to such opinions is the cost of gathering the evidence to support them and the lack of resources by special interest groups to defray these costs. It is possible (but not especially probable) that governments and foundations may compensate accountants for these expenses, should extension of the attest function actually materialize.

ACCOUNTANTS' SPECIAL ANALYTICAL TOOLS

Aside from the logical and institutional structure of accounting which causes social entities to turn to accountants for assistance, accountants possess a number of skills that are useful in defining problems and selecting solutions to problems.

Performance Reports

You have already seen that the accountant in management prepares reports depicting actual versus expected performance—reports which are necessary if managers are to infer causes for unexpected operating results. Such reports may also be prepared for activities in the public sector and for relations between social entities. A performance report may be prepared showing, for example, a timetable for industrial pollution control alongside actual progress in achieving such control, measured in terms such as tons per day of major pollutants released into water bodies and the atmosphere.

Marginal Analysis

Marginal analysis reveals the differences between alternative courses of action. In the private sector, you use marginal analysis to decide whether to make or buy a required input, whether to invest in a capital project, whether to acquire a new product line, and countless other decisions. Your decision is always based on the marginal addition each alternative will make to some particular measure of your welfare (or the welfare of the entity you represent).

Marginal analysis also has its place in the analysis of social goals and policies. A government decision whether to impose a surtax on imports (and whether to discontinue the surtax) is made because of the *differences* such a surtax is expected to make in a whole series of areas in which the national welfare is affected: international balance of payments, foreign relations, domestic inflation, the federal budget deficit. A consumer organization's decision to sue the government to release the results of government consumer appliance testing comes because of the difference such information may make to consumers who must choose between these appliances. Since accountants through experience, practice, and training are skilled in providing information for marginal analysis, their contribution to the soundness and validity of public decisions relative to social goal budgeting should be especially important.

Forecasting

Large-scale computer based forecasting models can be produced for any entity. One particularly useful class of forecasting model used especially in economic development is the "input-output" model. This model's theory is related to linear programming (Chapter 8) and critical path analysis (Chapter 7). It is used to study the effects on all segments of a regional or national economy when an investment or extra demand is applied to any one segment of the economy.

In the state of Oklayoming, to offer a conjectural example, there was a large minority of underemployed skilled workers. Everyone recognized that the problem confronting this state was to create an economic development program which would generate a maximum demand for the skills these workers possessed. Accountants worked on a team to develop an input-output model of the state's economy and used the model to determine where new investment should be encouraged to achieve the greatest demand increase for skilled labor. Once the type of investments needed were identified, the state began a nation-wide campaign to attract industries of that type. The result was a series of selective investments which reduced Oklayoming's structural unemployment problems.

Data Banks

Accountants in business organizations maintain large quantities of up-to-date information, organized and classified so it can be quickly scanned and, if relevant to any particular decision or problem, presented to a decision maker. Such data "banks" prove extremely useful to managers who are pursuing a line of thought and need information to complete their work quickly.

In the public sector, especially when governments are involved, there is a tendency to resist centralized information systems whenever the information is about individuals. Although the technology exists, there is no sensible reason (other than economy) why there should be a file on any individual accessible by all branches of the government—there is too much "Big Brother" about it. The result is that the position of "government information manager" has emerged overnight as one of the most sensitive and important responsibilities in the public sector.

Data banks containing purely economic information pertaining to a region, a nation, or the global economy can be helpful to private sector investors determining whether they should invest in the area and if so in what ways. A regional data bank would provide instant answers to questions businessmen ask when scouting for investment opportunities.

For example, suppose a business is looking in the Ozark region for a place to locate a heavy-equipment overhauling and repair facility. The business wants local financing, so it needs to know what banks are large enough to handle the capital requirements of the facility's construction. Another requirement is a labor force of 200 for the plant, which the company wishes to be drawn from a total local labor force of at least 10,000 persons. Finally, the company has placed an upper limit on the taxes it will pay. All of these requirements can be phrased as questions to a computer programmed to operate a data bank. A list of all locations potentially satisfying these initial screening criteria is prepared and printed out by the computer. After examining the list, the company searchers pinpoint three locations for detailed investigation. This process has required less than half a day and cost practically nothing to collect information which would otherwise have required weeks and cost thousands of dollars, and the Ozarks have 200 jobs and a new plant that otherwise would have passed them by.

In preparation of data banks, you would make use of the accounting double-entry system of classification and its ability to accommodate measurements made in more than one dimension. Unfortunately the design of such data banks is beyond the scope of an introductory text.

Systems Studies

The "systems" approach is a current notion which deserves considerable attention. At its best, a systems approach is a straightforward detailed study of *all* the operations of an economic or other entity. In this context, systems work is widely done, and the principles of systems analysis are a unifying factor within and between such disciplines as medicine, biology, economics, and marketing as well as accounting.

Some persons have held out that a system approach could solve any problem; that problems exist only because problem solvers are too narrow and confined. In practice, responsible systems analysts have learned that any broadening of the definition of a system increases by many orders of magnitude the complexity of the model required to represent that system—in many cases, to the point of making it impossible to develop models and therefore impossible to study and resolve problems. Most systems are too complex for even a team of analysts to full perceive. Responsible systems work at this time is limited in scope but promising and high in potential.

In accounting, application of systems study is limited to analysis, design, and appraisal of information systems. Within this limit, systems analysis has been developed into an important accounting tool, its value proven by the performance of thousands of business information systems. However, information systems have not been developed to serve public sector entities. As a result, social entities and individuals receive unreliable and "managed" information from special interest organization publicists and thus have difficulty seeing their problems and potential solutions as clearly or objectively as private sector managers and investors see theirs.

To illustrate a typical problem here, consider the social entity which is defined by the transportation function in the United States. Transportation is available by airplane, truck, bus, car, pipeline, and other media, each of which is organized as an industry to present and promote its own advantages over competing modes. All depend to some degree on government subsidy, regulation, and protection. To sustain this government support, all transportation industries produce a flow of information directed at the public and intended to generate pressure on the government to support that industry. Airlines and airline support industries want more and "better" airports; highway contractors want bigger, "safer" highway systems; railroads want an end to "excessive" taxation and subsidies to rivals. In that situation it is difficult to generate support for an integrated transportation policy, especially one which might introduce a new service such as public municipal transportation systems for metropolitan areas.

Conceivably accountants, acting on behalf of those affected by transportation services, could develop information systems which would indicate where and when transportation service deficiencies exist and how they should best be treated. The only difficulty with this kind of proposal is identifying an appropriate entity to sponsor such work; accountants have to be paid salaries like everyone else and neither private sector businesses nor public accounting firms have in the past shown inclination to undertake such projects. Perhaps this will change.

On a broader front, accountants could participate in systems studies of nonbusiness functions in society. A state-sponsored program to train men and women in industrial skills to help them find work was revised, based on a systems study, to provide training for service-type jobs such as home appliance repair, tree surgery, and security guard—for the system study showed that service-type jobs were plentiful whereas industry-type jobs were actually declining in the state. Accounting knowledge of business trends contributed to the success of this study. Another state, studying its system of criminal corrections, concluded that a major cause of recidivism among "graduates" of the correctional system was that the job training offered was out of date—experience in the prison laundry, making license plates, and primitive farming—and of little real value to any employer considering such a person for employment. Although the proposals for advanced vocational training would require increased spending on the correctional system, they were at last word receiving serious consideration. Again, the technical knowledge of business possessed by accountants influenced the study's recommendations.

ACCOUNTING AND ECONOMIC POLICY

Accounting is involved now in formulation or evaluation of national and local economic policies. An "economic policy" is some policy of government whose effects are measurable in economic terms. This section is organized to illustrate accounting participation in economic policy formation in several problem areas—taxation, inflation, and public sector economic growth.

Taxation

Approximately 30 percent of the income of Americans and American businesses is paid in taxes. There is every reason to believe taxes will go up not down in the future. Accountants do not control tax policy at any government level. Nevertheless, accountants are a part of the system which is responsible for tax law. Accountants have an intimate knowledge of tax effects on all sectors of society. As taxes increase, accountants will share the responsibility for assuring the equity of new taxes. Although many persons do not believe that tax policy should be subordinated to achievement of national goals, others hold that tax policy can encourage some goals, discourage others, and still raise government revenue equitably. As one example, consider the often-heard statement, "The government ought to put a tax on pollution-producing processes, to raise their cost and make them uneconomical compared with 'cleaner' processes."[1]

Another possibility would be tax credits for activities judged favorable to the public interest. A mining company strip-mining coal in West Virginia would receive tax credits for restoring the landscape to a semblance of its former contours. The extra expense of doing this would be wholly or partially offset by lower taxes.

Although the primary responsibility for working out such tax policies rests with public finance and other economic specialists, the accountant is the only man who is really in a position to estimate their effect on specific individual businesses. Many of the industrial pollution situations in the United States can be controlled through a relatively small number of firms whose responses may, through study, be objectively anticipated for specific tax proposals. Accountants can conduct these studies.

Special tax provisions might offer credits for hiring and training members of minority groups, for maintenance of mechanical antipollution devices on motor vehicles, for urban or industrial development in the older parts of large cities, for managerial compensation to serve with community development corporations, for promoting export sales,

---

[1] Attractive and simple as this sounds, it would not work just that way. It is likely that the polluting processes would be shut down here and relocated in foreign countries with less-restrictive pollution regulations. Even if this didn't happen, the extra costs to U.S. manufacturers would be passed on to consumers and tend to price U.S. goods out of international markets, upsetting international trade and the balance of payments. Thus, control of industrial pollution will require close international cooperation.

and for other programs judged to be in the public interest. In all cases, the effects of proposed tax policies should be worked out and verified by accounting consultants.

Subsidies

Many of the effects discussed above might also be accomplished through simple selective direct subsidies. One proposal at this writing is to replace many welfare programs with a "negative income tax" (see Chapter 11 for a fuller discussion) or direct subsidy to anyone earning less than some minimum salary. Accountants can and do contribute to cost-effectiveness studies comparing this proposal with existing welfare structures.

However, subsidies have important effects on the behavior of those receiving them, as to a lesser extent do tax penalties and credits. The lack of a tax on the "income" of nonprofit organizations has produced an explosive increase in the total assets controlled by such organizations and serious questions about their efficiency of asset utilization. Persons receiving welfare or other payments (such as farmers) sometimes organize into special interest groups which seek extension and perpetuation of subsidies for their own sake and not for whatever contribution may be made to the national welfare. The depletion allowance given to extractive industries is an example of a tax benefit and the protective attitude towards it of those who benefit therefrom. The national highway building program has been criticised as a subsidy to those using highways (and those building them!) and as a penalty to other modes of transportation, and a considerable amount of influence is exercised to continue the federal and state highway construction programs. There are few industries which could anticipate indifferently the withdrawal of their government business patronage.

CERTIFICATION OF FINANCIAL STATEMENTS

Certified Public Accountants have performed the important function of attesting to the fairness and consistency of corporate financial reports since about 1900. The practice may have arisen as a result of the substantial British investments in U.S. business after the Civil War and the desire of British investors for accurate information about the condition of those investments. There is a general feeling among investors that a favorable opinion on financial statements by a CPA lessens the probability that the financial statements do not accurately present financial position and results of operations. Investors are more willing to act on the basis of information they are reasonably certain is true than on the basis of information they doubt is accurate.

The single major issue that complicates financial reporting, for both the reporting entity and the auditing CPA, is this: The business continues throughout several reporting periods, earning its profits as a result of all its operations, yet it must report its income and expenses for arbitrary intervals which have no relation to the profit generation process. Here are two examples of this problem:

1. An expensive plant is purchased. The plant will last 25 years and will be operated throughout that interval. Then, a final determination can be made whether the plant contributed to business profits. However, at annual intervals business financial statements must be prepared, and these statements must declare whether the plant is profitable during the year preceding the financial statement date.
2. A construction company undertakes a three-year construction project. Profit will be earned only on the entire contract, yet annual financial statements will be issued and these statements will include an estimate of profit or loss on the partially completed project.

In order that financial statements be issued, the business must make judgments as to the portion of cost of such assets or projects which has produced a benefit in the current year reported upon. The dollar figure used, whatever it is, is a surrogate for the benefits received or expired in this reporting period. When that figure appears in financial statements, others will use it to make investment decisions. If these decisions turn out to be wrong because the costs or benefits allocated to a particular reporting period are obviously wrong, users of the financial statements in which they appeared will be justifiably looking for some entity to take the blame and responsibility.

Certified Public Accountants have taken the responsibility of examining the evidence underlying financial statements—the paid and canceled checks, the invoices, the approved requisitions, payroll vouchers, minutes of board meetings, tax returns, depreciation calculations, inventories, assets, and all other things which may tend to support the complex representations in a business' financial statements. The result of this examintion is a standard "short form" opinion that the financial statements—

. . . present fairly the financial position of the‑‑‑‑‑‑‑‑‑‑‑‑Company at (balance sheet date) and the results of its operations for the year then ended, in conformity with generally accepted accounting principles applied on a basis consistent with that of the preceding year.

E. L. Summers, CPA

This is a most interesting statement, and the phrases in it deserve attention, laden as they are with legal and traditional significance. However, we will only discuss that phrase, "generally accepted accounting principles" which is unique in that these principles *have never been defined*. Lack of definition is not for lack of trying; the American Institute of Certified Public Accountants, the major organization of professional accountants and the acknowledged spokesman of the profession, has recognized such definition as its major challenge almost since the date of its organization.

The present approach to the problem of defining generally accepted accounting principles is an independent Financial Accounting Standards Board. This board is, roughly speaking, responsible for authoritative definitions of accounting principles which all AICPA members are obliged to generally accept as a basis to which financial statements must conform. The board issues these definitions as a series of Opinions, additional numbers of which appear irregularly. The Opinions are "committee" efforts and usually represent reasoned compromises among alternative positions advocated by various members of the FASB (who are distinguished accountants appointed for three-year terms). As such the Opinions are extremely detailed and carefully spelled out; they do serve as a practical guide to accountants preparing opinion on financial statements.

The FASB's predecessor, the Accounting Principles Board, was criticised because its members were practicing auditors, corporate accountants, or security analysts and were therefore not obviously objective in their deliberations. A 1972 study by the AICPA's "Wheat Committee" (named for its chairman, Francis Wheat) proposed the seven-person FASB, financially independent of the AICPA, unassociated with any business, paid to do full-time work an accounting principles definition. This proposal has been approved by the AICPA. The sponsoring Financial Accounting Foundation has been established and, in 1973, the Financial Accounting Standards Board became operational.

Why is the CPA's opinion on published financial statements important? We have already stated that this opinion seems to satisfy investors that the statements do not contain deliberate major falsehoods or distortions. This is important because it moves financial statements closer to the concept of "perfect information" discussed in Chapter 9. The better informed the investor, the more efficient will be his resource allocation decisions. They will be more efficient because he is not paying part of the cost of uncertainty and ignorance regarding his investments. To illustrate this point, let us imagine two companies exactly alike in all respects and with exactly similar prospects (never mind if the prospects are good, bad, or indifferent—that is unimportant). You must buy the equally priced securities of only one of these two companies. You know about Company A; you know *nothing* about Company B. Chances are, you will prefer the securities of Company A because you know more about the risk you're taking.

Now suppose you must buy the securities of *both* companies. You will pay a higher price for Company A securities than for Company B securities. The lower price on B securities gives you a margin of safety for unforeseen events which may occur and affect the value of B securities. On the other hand, since you know everything about A securities, you know exactly what you are willing to pay for them and there is no need for a margin of safety. You are always ready to act with respect to A securities; you are always reluctant to act on B securities. Information improves your efficiency as an allocator of resources and makes your investment decisions more timely, more productive, safer, and more profitable. To the extent that audit opinions contribute to better information, they are contributing to faster, wiser resource allocation. If the CPA's audit opinion is compromised, published financial information becomes less reliable, investment decisions use it less, and the cost of capital allocation to profitable opportunities becomes higher.

ACCOUNTING AND SOCIAL INDICATORS

The service of accountants to social entities presupposes that indicators of the goals, objectives, and welfare of such entities can be found and measured. The argument is heard that accounting should be defined simply (and very broadly) as "communication of information necessary for the attainment of goals."[2] This definition goes well beyond the communication of purely financial information and the self-assumed role of the AICPA as discussed in the previous section.

The future acceptability of this definition may depend on acceptance of the notion that an economy, in order to see where it is going and plan its activities, must be able to compare past performance with expectations for the same period. This is the basic principle of control in businesses—but businesses are tightly controlled by their managers, and the national economy is, despite some efforts to mitigate its more pronounced excesses, at this writing a glorious and frightening Bedlam.

However, if we accept the notion of social entities, the need for indicators of social achievement and well-being surely exists for these entities whether or not they have the degree of internal organization which characterizes business entities. What sort of indicators might these be?

A paper by Nestor E. Terleckyj[3] suggests 22 possible indicators arranged in six groups:

I. *Freedom, Justice, and Harmony*
   (The author did not in his paper suggest any indicators of these goals)

II. *Health and Safety*
   A. Mean life expectancy at birth

---

[2] Robert K. Elliot, "Accounting in the Technological Age," *World* (Publication of Peat Marwick Mitchell & Co., CPAs), Winter 1972, pp. 23–27.

[3] Nestor E. Terleckyj, "Measuring Progress Towards Social Goals: Some Possibilities at National and Social Levels," *Management Science*, August 1970, pp. B-765 to B-778.

    B.   Number of persons with chronic disability conditions

    C.   Violent crime rate

III. *Education, Skills, and Income*

    A.   Index of average achievement in language

    B.   Percent of age group completing college

    C.   Average earnings

    D.   Number of persons outside mainstream of labor force

    E.   Number of persons below present poverty standard

    F.   Number of persons in near-poverty conditions

    G.   Number of persons with permanent losses in levels of living over 30 percent

IV. *Human Habitat*

    A.   Proportion of persons living in inadequate housing

    B.   Proportion of persons living in satisfactory neighborhoods

    C.   Index of cost of travel and transportation

    D.   Percent of persons exposed to bothersome pollution

    E.   Percent of persons regularly taking part in recreation

V. *Finer Things*

    A.   Number areas for preservation of beauty

    B.   Number of scientists active in basic science

    C.   Number of active artists

    D.   Average time free from work and chores

VI. *Economic Base*

    A.   Gross National Product

Terleckyj did not pretend that this was a complete or final set of indicators; and, indeed, it appears that some of them (such as IV-B) despair of objective measurement. Terleckyj concluded his presentation with these points (pp. 775–77):

1. Articulation of social goals is important for ascertaining whether they are being reached.

2. Existing statistical systems are not geared to articulating and reporting social goals.

3. Development of simple systems to reflect progress toward some of the generally acceptable goals is feasible.

4. If such systems are to serve as vehicles of information to the general public, they have to be simple and clear-cut.

5. Development of larger systems (to measure more complex social

indicators of progress) depends on progress in basic work that is yet to be done.

If indeed public policy is being made in a knowledge vacuum in this country, it is a serious situation that all of us, readers and textbook writers alike, need to correct. As members of accounting or another business profession you should be prepared to participate, both in collecting information for public decision making and in such decision making itself.

SUMMARY

The policy of the accounting profession is to extend its unique analytical skills and institutional structure into the public service as often and as effectively as possible. Those logical aspects of accounting which are most useful in public service are its measurement and entity orientation and its ability to mark progress toward goals. The independence of accountants and their traditional exercise of the attest function are similarly useful. The tools accountants use most effectively in public communication are the same ones that serve them best in the managerial function: performance reports, marginal analysis, forecasting, data banks, and system studies. The major issues which accountants have already engaged are domestic economic policy and financial statement certification. In the future, accountants are expected to extend their attest function to the information presented for public decisions and to participate in the development of social indicators. Because of their involvement with information processing, accountants cannot avoid contributing to the public interest and are determined to do so in the wisest possible ways.

BIBLIOGRAPHY[4]

Books

Fertig, Paul E.; Istvan, Donald F.; and Mottice, Homer J. *Using Accounting Information: An Introduction.* 2d ed. New York: Harcourt Brace Jovanovich, Inc., 1971.

---

[4] Items cited in chapter introduction not repeated.

Vatter, William J. *Accounting Measurements for Financial Reports.* Homewood, Ill.: Richard D. Irwin, Inc., 1971.

Articles

Beams, Floyd A. "Income Reporting: Continuity with Change," *Management Accounting,* August 1972.

Bergwerk, Rudolph J. "Effective Communication of Financial Data," *Journal of Accountancy,* February 1970.

Beyer, Robert. "Pilots of Social Progress," *Management Accounting,* July 1972.

Buckley, John W. "Accounting Principles and the Social Ethic," *Financial Executive,* October 1971.

Caplan, Edwin H. "Behavioral Assumptions of Management Accounting—Report of a Field Study." *The Accounting Review,* April 1968.

Capon, Frank S. "The Totality of Accounting for the Future," *Financial Executive,* July 1972.

Dembowski, Sig. "The Management Accountant," *Management Accounting,* April 1973.

Enthoven, Adolph J. H. "The Changing Role of Accountancy," *Finance and Development,* June 1969.

Gilbert, Lewis D. "What Stockholders Expect from CPA's in Financial Reporting," *The Ohio CPA,* Spring 1971.

Hagerman, Robert L.; Keller, Thomas F.; and Petersen, Russell J. "Accounting Research and Accounting Principles," *Journal of Accountancy,* March 1973.

Kell, Walter G. "The Auditor's Responsibilities in Financial Reporting," *Michigan Business Review,* March 1967.

Linowes, David F. "Accounting for Social Progress," *New York Times,* March 14, 1971, sec. 3, p. 14.

Mosich, A. N., and Hamilton, Robert E. "The Decline or Rise of Accounting," *Journal of Accountancy,* July 1972.

vonBert, William G. "Accounting for Responsibility," *Journal of Accountancy,* November 1972.

Index

A

Accountants
and attest function, 227, 236
and auditing, 227
and decision model analysis, 54
as government information managers, 231
and information validity, 186
and tax policies, 217
as tax specialists, 207
Accounting
analytical tools, 228
applications in activity analysis, 10
approximation to fixed costs, 5
and behavior, 83
and economic policy, 233
entity orientation, 226
information functions, 72
and linear programming, 162
as a measurement discipline, 226
principles, 237
principles board, 237
profit and inflation, 194
and the public interest, 224
and social indicators, 239
and social problem involvement, 225

Accounting—*Cont.*
statements and price changes, 197
for taxes, 214
and uncertainty, 185
Acquisition cost components for capital investment, 103
Activity analysis
and linear programming, 144
and semifixed costs, 81
Activity level
analysis and profit maximization, 16
analysis purposes, 1
effect of change, 13
and inflation, 194
physical, 194
Activity mix and profit, 144
Ad valorem tax, 212
Alternatives, set of, in decisions, 166
American Institute of Certified Public Accountants, 224, 237
Analysis of performance, 76
Attest function, 227
Attest function extensions, 228, 236, 241
Auditing, 227, 236
Average cost
behavior, 9
defined, 5
Average revenue, 6